D1451553

Human Communication: Principles, Contexts, and Skills

Cassandra L. Book   Bradley S. Greenberg
Terrance L. Albrecht   Hal W. Hepler
Charles Atkin   Mark Milkovich
Erwin P. Bettinghaus   Gerald R. Miller
William A. Donohue   David C. Ralph
Richard V. Farace   Ted J. Smith III

*Under the general
editorial supervision of*
Cassandra L. Book

Human Communication: Principles, Contexts, and Skills

St. Martin's Press
NEW YORK

Photograph Credits
Page 7: Joel Gordon; page 14: Joel Gordon; page 22: Ginger Chih/Peter Arnold, Inc.;
page 50: Joel Gordon; page 62: Steve Allen/Peter Arnold, Inc.; page 66: Joel Gordon;
page 78: Lynn Lennon/Photo Researchers, Inc.; page 97: Georg Gerster/Photo Researchers, Inc.; page 118: Joel Gordon; page 130: Joel Gordon; page 134: Joel Gordon; page
147: Joel Gordon; page 153: Sybil Shelton/Peter Arnold, Inc.; page 174: Franklynn Peter-
son/Black Star; page 187: Joel Gordon; page 200: Russ Kinne/Photo Researchers, Inc.;
page 216: Joel Gordon; page 221: Christa Armstrong/Rapho/Photo Researchers, Inc.;
page 232: Sybil Shelton/Peter Arnold, Inc.; page 238: Lizabeth Corlett/DPI, Inc.; page
254: Dennis Black/Black Star; page 274: Sybil Shelton/Peter Arnold, Inc.; page 292: Joel
Gordon. Picture research by Rosemary Eakins and Barbara Hatcher, Research Reports,
New York.

Preface

This textbook has developed over a number of years, growing out of our approach to communication and our teaching of a particular course, Communication 100 at Michigan State University. Like the course, the book has the dual purpose of conveying information that will be immediately useful to beginning students and at the same time will provide a solid basis for further study in the field of communication. Used in tandem with the activities, games, and simulations in the accompanying *Instructor's Resource Manual*, the chapters not only offer basic principles but involve students actively in a variety of communication experiences, including large-group discussions, small-group interaction, interviews, and public presentations.

The text is divided into three parts—principles, contexts, and skills. Part One, chapters 1 through 3, covers basic principles of communication. Chapter 1 identifies the major characteristics of the communication process. Chapter 2 discusses language development as the creation and understanding of symbols and explores both verbal and nonverbal communication. Chapter 3 presents the principles of building and organizing arguments into persuasive and informative messages.

Part Two, chapters 4 through 7, examines interpersonal, group, organizational, and mass communication. The principles from chapters 1, 2, and 3 are applied to those four contexts, which vary according to the types of networks and the numbers of communicators involved. Part Three, chapters 8 and 9, puts the principles into action by presenting the skills of interviewing and public speaking. The appendix further applies communication principles to writing.

A comprehensive glossary defines important terms and concepts in communication. Other useful pedagogical aids are featured in each chapter. Chapter outlines and learning objectives preview the material. Chapters conclude with terms and concepts for review, references, and review questions.

Few texts can have been more exhaustively classroom-tested than this one. Prior to its formal publication, it has gone through numerous preliminary editions and been used by thousands of students. The students have varied enormously in their communication skills and experience. Their motives in taking the course have ranged from grudging fulfillment of a graduation requirement to enthusiastic choice of communication as a major field. We are indebted to all of our students, whose responses have improved this book in important ways.

Many other people—more than could possibly be named here—deserve special appreciation for their hard work in making the publication of this book possible. The clerical staff of the Department of Communication at Michigan State University was most cooperative, skillful, and efficient in typing and preparing the many drafts of the manuscript. Josephine Barnett, Sherry Carman, Julie Dingee, Janet Hoel, Paula Place, and Michelle Torres are especially to be credited. Our graduate teaching assistants deserve credit for their patience and resourcefulness in pilot testing the book and providing suggestions for the improvement of previous versions. Karen Krzanowski helped by proofreading the chapters; Anita Covert has our special thanks for coordinating, proofing, and editing various parts of the book efficiently and dependably.

About the Authors

Terrance L. Albrecht (Chapter 8, with Cassandra L. Book) is Assistant Professor at the University of Washington, Seattle, Washington. She holds M.A. and Ph.D. degrees in communication as well as a master's degree from the School of Labor and Industrial Relations at Michigan State University. Her major areas of teaching and research are organizational communication, persuasion, and interpersonal communication. She has had extensive experience in interviewing, both in her work as a former newspaper reporter and as a social-science researcher.

Charles Atkin (Chapter 7, with Bradley S. Greenberg) is Professor of Communication at Michigan State University. He teaches courses in mass-media effects and conducts research on children's responses to television and political communication. Dr. Atkin has testified at a number of federal government hearings on public policy issues involving the media. He is writing a textbook on the social effects of mass communication.

Erwin P. Bettinghaus (Chapter 2, with Mark Milkovich, and Chapter 3, with Ted J. Smith III) is Professor of Communication and Dean of the College of Communication Arts and Sciences at Michigan State University. He received a BA. degree from the University of Illinois, an M.A. from Bradley University, and a Ph.D. from the University of Illinois. He is the author of *The Nature of Proof* and *Persuasive Communication*, as well as numerous research articles in communication. His research has been concentrated in persuasion and language behavior.

Cassandra L. Book (General Editor, and author of Chapter 8 with Terrance L. Albrecht) is Associate Professor at Michigan State University, where she has directed the basic communication course since 1974. She holds three degrees in communication education: a B.A. from Michigan State University, M.A. from Northwestern University, and Ph.D. from Purdue University. Her major research has been in instructional development and classroom communication, and she has co-authored several books and papers in these areas.

William A. Donohue (Chapter 5) is Assistant Professor of Communication at Michigan State University. His research is focused in the area of interaction patterns in negotiation and other organizational settings. He received his B.S. from Bowling Green University, and his M.A. and Ph.D. in communication at Ohio State University.

Richard V. Farace (Chapter 6) is Professor of Communication and Director of Graduate Studies at Michigan State University. He received his Ph.D. in communication from the University of Iowa in 1965. His area of academic interest is organizational communication. He has conducted research and consulted for state and federal agencies and private industry. These organizations include departments of education, major banks, publishing firms, construction companies, and space-related agencies. He is co-author of *Communicating and Organizing*, as well as a number of articles and convention papers on organizational communication topics.

Bradley S. Greenberg (Chapter 7, with Charles Atkin) is Professor of Communication and Telecommunication and Chairman of the Department of Communication at Michigan State University. He received his Ph.D. in mass communication from the University of Wisconsin. His major research focus has been on the social effects of mass communication. He is the author of an array of published work dealing with the diffusion of news; minorities and the media; and children and television.

Hal W. Hepler (Appendix: Concepts for Writers) was educated at the University of Toledo, New York University, and Michigan State University, from which he received his Ph.D. in communication. He teaches business communication and research utilization courses in the Department of Communication at Michigan State. He serves as the Director of the Knowledge Utilization Master's program. He is an active consultant to business, industry, government, and education in the areas of communication, management, writing skills, and market research. His research interests are in the measurement of literacy and in organizational behavior.

Mark Milkovich (Chapter 2, with Erwin P. Bettinghaus) is Assistant Professor at the University of Utah. He received his Ph.D. in communication at Michigan State University. He holds M.A. and B.A. degrees from the University of Montana. His major area of academic interest is language, about which he has written several articles.

Gerald R. Miller (Chapters 1 and 4), who received his B.A. and M.A. in political science and his Ph.D. in communication from the University of Iowa, is Professor of Communication at Michigan State University. Dr.

Miller's major research and teaching areas include communication theory, interpersonal communication, persuasion, and communication in the legal system. He has written or edited seven books and has written numerous articles for journals of communication, psychology, and law. He is the former editor of the journal *Human Communication Research* and is presently the President of the International Communication Association.

David C. Ralph (Chapter 9) is Professor of Communication and Director of Undergraduate Education at Michigan State University. He received his Ph.D. in rhetoric and public address from Northwestern University. His area of academic interest is public speaking. He is co-author of *Principles of Speaking,* third edition.

Ted J. Smith III (Chapter 3, with Erwin P. Bettinghaus) is currently Assistant Professor of General Studies at Warrnambool Institute of Advanced Education, Australia. He received his Ph.D. in communication from Michigan State University. His primary areas of interest are the philosophy of the social sciences, practical reasoning, interpersonal persuasion, and the effects of television news and entertainment programs. He is currently conducting research on the development-of-the-self concept through interaction, the uses of informal fallacies, and television coverage of human rights.

Contents

Preface   v
About the Authors   vii

Part One
PRINCIPLES OF COMMUNICATION   1

Chapter 1
Introduction to Communication   4
 Outline   4
 Objectives   5
 Defining the Characteristics of Communication   8
 Three Critical Communicative Concepts   20
 Modeling the Communication Process   30
 Conclusion   36
  Terms and Concepts for Review   36
  Review Questions   37
  References   37

Chapter 2
*Codes and Code Systems: Verbal and
    Nonverbal*   40
 Outline   40
 Objectives   41
 Code Systems and Meaning   42
 Verbal Code Systems   45
 Nonverbal Code Systems   58
 Conclusion   67
  Terms and Concepts for Review   67
  Review Questions   68
  References   68

Chapter 3
Message Construction   70
 Outline   70
 Objectives   71

Informative Messages   73
Persuasive Messages   76
Rational Appeals   77
Motivational Appeals   96
Conclusion   101
   Terms and Concepts for Review   101
   Review Questions   102
   References   102

Part Two
CONTEXTS OF COMMUNICATION   103

Chapter 4
Interpersonal Communication   106
   Outline   106
   Objectives   107
The Situational View   109
The Developmental View   113
Strategies for Gathering Information   123
The Role of Trust in Communicative
      Relationships   128
Conflict in Communicative Relationships   132
Conclusion   137
   Terms and Concepts for Review   137
   Review Questions   137
   References   138

Chapter 5
Small-Group Communication   140
   Outline   140
   Objectives   141
What Is a Small Group?   142
How Are Groups Formed?   145
How Do Groups Work?   149
The Social Environment of the Group   153
The Task Environment of the Group   161
Conclusion   162
   Terms and Concepts for Review   164
   Review Questions   164
   References   164

Chapter 6
Organizational Communication   166
   Outline   166
   Objectives   167
Definition of an Organization   170
Functions of Organizational Communication   170

Information Processing   171
Communication Rules   176
Communication Flows   180
Organizational Communication Networks   183
The Organization as a Form of Culture   188
Conclusion   192
  Terms and Concepts for Review   193
  Review Questions   193
  References   193

Chapter 7

Effects of the Mass Media   194
  Outline   194
  Objectives   195
The Mass-Communication Process   197
Audience Exposure Patterns   199
Dimensions of Audience Effects   202
Effects of Informational Content   205
Impact of Persuasive Content   209
Impact of Entertainment Content   215
Conclusion   222
  Terms and Concepts for Review   222
  Review Questions   223
  References   223

Part Three
COMMUNICATION SKILLS   225

Chapter 8

Interviewing   228
  Outline   228
  Objectives   229
The Interview Defined   230
Interviewing Purposes   231
Distortion of Information: Causes and
    Preventions   232
Managing the Interview   234
Steps in Interviewing   237
Conclusion   248
  Terms and Concepts for Review   248
  Review Questions   249
  References   249

Chapter 9

Public Speaking   250
  Outline   250
  Objectives   251

Step "X": Analyzing and Adapting to Your
Receivers   252
Step One: Choosing and Adapting Your Subject and
Purpose   256
Step Two: Developing the Content of Your
Speech   259
Step Three: Structuring Your Speech   268
Step Four: Delivering Your Speech   272
Step Five: Evaluating Your Speech   279
Conclusion   280
Speech Evaluation Form   280
A Sample Deductive Speech Plan   283
  Terms and Concepts for Review   284
  Review Questions   285
  References   285

Appendix
Concepts for Writers   286

Glossary   297
Index   313

Human Communication: Principles, Contexts, and Skills

Part One
PRINCIPLES OF COMMUNICATION

The principles of communication discussed in chapters 1, 2, and 3 are so fundamental that they transcend all contexts in which communication occurs. This overview will highlight the key concepts of those three chapters, show relationships among them, and forecast the application of the concepts to interpersonal, group, organizational, and mass communication contexts.

Chapter 1 defines communication as a transactional, symbolic process which allows people to relate to and manage their environments by (1) establishing human contact, (2) exchanging information, (3) reinforcing the attitudes and behaviors of others, and (4) changing the attitudes and behaviors of others. This definition contains significant principles which are developed in the chapter and referred to throughout the book.

The transactional nature of communi-cation means that all people in a communication exchange affect and are affected by the communication and their relationships in that interaction. You may think that the source, or initiator, of the message is not changed because he or she creates the message, and delivers it, with the purpose of changing or at least reinforcing the attitudes or behaviors of the receiver(s). However, the source, in choosing to communicate, runs the risk of being changed too. If the receiver rejects the message, the source may have to adjust it and try again. Or he may reassess his own view and agree with the receiver that the message should be rejected. Or he may give up trying to communicate that message to that receiver. On the other hand, if the receiver enthusiastically accepts the source's message, the source again may change, for he may be reinforced in his belief and more firmly support his own cause. The principle here is that as source and receivers engage in communication, both sides may be altered by the communication experience to varying degrees.

The notion of communication being a process is critical as we begin to understand that our past experiences; our knowledge of topic, persons, and general information; our attitudes, language skills, socioeconomic background, and demographic characteristics all affect our ability to create and respond to messages. In other words, an unlimited number of factors affect the way in which we generate, understand, and act upon messages. There is no beginning to a communication event, since all that occurred before it can affect the event. Similarly, there is no end to a communication exchange; it will subtly affect the interpretation of, or directly contribute to, future exchanges. For the purpose of studying a communication event, however, we put artificial boundaries on the event by identifying when it began and when it ended, who the participants were, and what inputs and outputs were considered pertinent to the exchange. When we draw a model of a communication exchange, we necessarily start and stop the process. The concept of communication as a process helps us to understand and alleviate communication barriers, since it reminds us that what each person brings to and takes from the communication exchange is different. The process notion also reminds us of the fleeting nature of communication.

The symbolic nature of communication helps us define—or at least question—the uniqueness of the human animal. As discussed in chapters 1 and 2, humans have the ability to use language,

or symbols that stand for other things, both physical and nonphysical. We use words as well as gestures and other nonverbal symbols to send messages. This ability to communicate about something which is not present may be unique to humans or may be shared (as evidenced by recent research) with other higher-level primates.

Many models of communication have been devised. Chapter 1 provides a brief discussion of the nature and purpose of studying and creating these models. Each context of communication can be described by various models. The differences in the number of communicators and immediacy of feedback available help determine which models best describe communication in interpersonal, group, organizational, and mass communication contexts.

Communication is constrained by cultural, sociological, and psychological contexts. Chapter 1 describes how these critical contexts affect and are affected by language. The basic idea is that by understanding the cultural, sociological, or psychological context, we can make predictions about what communicative approaches are most likely to be effective and adapt our messages accordingly. Chapter 2 develops the idea that a person's language is affected by the culture or social class to which he or she belongs. In addition, communicators need to be aware that people ascribe different meanings, and react in different ways, to even the most common words and concepts. As the saying goes, "meanings are in people."

The way in which language is structured and learned has many implications for the student of communication. Hence chapter 2 devotes considerable time to theories of language development. The theories of Skinner, Osgood, and Chomsky provide interesting insights into the role of language in human interaction.

The omnipresence of nonverbal communication in our lives makes it an important concept in the communication process. Chapter 2 suggests that since nonverbal communication can support or contradict verbal messages sent and is often more intense or more attended to than the verbal message, communicators are well advised to increase their knowledge of nonverbal codes. Competent communicators will have a repertoire of nonverbal behaviors and use those that most appropriately convey their meanings.

As with verbal messages, the meaning of nonverbal messages often varies according to the cultural, sociological, and psychological contexts. Certain gestures or use of time and space differ in meaning from one country to another. Similarly, various groups within a society create nonverbal codes (e.g., making the sign of the cross) that take on specific meaning for them. Finally, individuals use nonverbal codes to convey a particular message (e.g., Johnny Cash wearing dark clothing to indicate his protest of the Vietnam war). The more attentive communicators are to nonverbal messages used in different critical contexts, the better they will be at creating and interpreting messages in those contexts.

The actual construction of effective verbal messages is taken up by chapter 3. Sources should strive to achieve a "goodness of fit" between the message and the audience. Since the source has more control over the message than over the audience, he needs to carefully analyze receivers according to their cultural, sociological, and psychological characteristics. Then he must (1) develop logical arguments they can understand; (2) use sufficient and appropriate evidence they will believe; (3) appeal to needs that motivate them; (4) link data and claims with warrants they will accept; and (5) organize the message in a way that they will find clear and persuasive.

While the principles of message construction are used most obviously in public speaking, they are fundamental to communication in all contexts, including interpersonal, group, organizational, and mass communication contexts. Indeed, the competent source will use information from each setting to construct the most effective message. It is important, however, regardless of setting, for sources to know precisely what their goal of communication is and to communicate that to their receivers.

Defining the Characteristics of Communication

A TRANSACTIONAL, SYMBOLIC PROCESS

ALLOWS PEOPLE TO RELATE TO AND MANAGE THEIR ENVIRONMENTS
Establishing human contact
Exchanging information
Reinforcing others' attitudes and behaviors
Changing others' attitudes and behaviors

Three Critical Communication Contexts

CULTURAL CONTEXT
Characteristics of a culture
Communication as cause and effect of culture
Cultural rules

SOCIOLOGICAL CONTEXT
People's group memberships
Role behaviors and expectations
Changes in role behaviors over time

PSYCHOLOGICAL CONTEXT
Grounded in people's uniqueness
Relies on stimulus discrimination
Rules grown out of relationship

Modeling the Communication Process

DEFINITION OF MODEL

FUNCTIONS OF MODELS
To organize thoughts
To generate research
To aid prediction

A MODEL OF THE COMMUNICATION PROCESS

1

Introduction to Communication

After reading this chapter, you should be able to:

1. Explain the concept of process.
2. Differentiate between a transactional and linear view of communication.
3. Give examples of symbolic and nonsymbolic behaviors.
4. Describe common examples of people's efforts to control the environment by communication.
5. List ways that communication is used for environmental management.
6. Distinguish between the cultural, sociological, and psychological contexts of communication.
7. Construct a simple model of the communication process.
8. Compare Miller's model of communication with Berlo's model of communication.

"I don't know what I'd do without you!"

"The square of the hypotenuse is equal to the sum of the squares of the other two sides."

"There's nothing that would give me more satisfaction than punching you out!"

"Buy Brand X Aspirin for the fastest relief from headaches."

"Did you hear about the butcher who backed into a meat grinder and got a little behind in his work?"

Communication enables us to share our innermost feelings, to express love, hate, happiness, and despair. Through communication we grow and learn; we enrich our understanding of ourselves and the world in which we live. We use communication in our attempts to influence others; indeed, reliance on the spoken word rather than a smoking gun to persuade others is often viewed as a way of distinguishing civilized persons from barbarians. Our funnybone is tickled by communication, be it a network television comedy or an exchange of jokes between two acquaintances. Loving, learning, loathing, leading, and laughing—the five Ls captured by our introductory quotations—are either manifested in or triggered by the marvelous gift of communication.

Yet our attempts to communicate often fall far short of success. Words fail us when we try to express our affection for a loved one, or we seethe in silent fury while longing to shout our contempt for another's actions. The magic phrases about hypotenuses, multiplier effects, or Othello's tragic flaw elude us, either over a friendly glass of beer or in a crucial examination. Our advertising campaign fails to boost sales for our product. And like the comedian Rodney Dangerfield, we sometimes regretfully conclude that "We don't get no respect" for our jokes, mirth-provoking as they seem to us. It is a rare person who has not at one time or another lamented his inability to communicate effectively.

This book seeks to increase your understanding of the communication process and to assist you in becoming a more effective communicator. Communication is a vital human activity; in fact, people's chances of leading happy, productive lives are directly related to their communicative abilities. Moreover, the fact that everyone does a lot of communicating does not imply that everyone does a lot of *effective* communicating; communicators suffer from bad habits, just like tennis players or opera singers. Good communication requires constant attention to effective communicative skills and strategies, just as good tennis requires constant attention to proper grip and footwork and good opera singing requires constant attention to proper breathing and intonation. Everyone, including the authors of this book, is capable of becoming a more effective communicator if he or she is willing to expend the time and effort.

The development of effective communicative skills does not, of course, provide a magic solution to all of life's quandaries. Despite what some writers would have us believe, not all problems are problems of communication; people and nations often understand quite clearly what they are disagreeing about and still continue to disagree. To say that two bitter political foes would become warm personal friends or that the United States and the Soviet Union would become kindred political spirits if they could only communicate more effectively would be naive, for the social, economic, and political issues dividing individuals and countries far transcend their symbolic exchanges. Yet even in these instances effective communication is important to both sides, since it is the vehicle used to identify the consequences which will result from various courses of action. If a war breaks out in the Middle East, both the United States and the Soviet Union take great pains to indicate how they will respond to possible military and political moves by the other. Indeed, so important is good communication that these two superpowers have installed a hot line which permits their respective leaderships to clarify intentions and to explain actions at an instant's notice.

Just as not all problems are communication problems, not everything a person does is communication. Watzlawick, Beavin, and Jackson have intrigued many readers with their observation, "You cannot not communicate" (1967, pp. 48–51). Certainly, in a very broad sense of the term, every behavior (or absence of behavior) "communicates" something to other persons. For example, if you are walking down the street preoccupied in thought and fail to greet an acquaintance, she may infer that you are angry or put-out at her; your failure to speak has communicated a negative personal attitude to your acquaintance. Similarly, if you chance to wear a loud tie some morning (just because you feel like wearing a bright color) and you encounter a person who believes clothing should be conservative and understated, your choice of a tie will likely communicate your lack of good clothing judgment to him. Or say you are racing through a field and stub your toe on a rock. You may irrationally kick the rock a second time, and by doing so, you communicate the pain and anger you experienced upon initially hurting your foot. The problem with the "You cannot not communicate" viewpoint, however, is this: *While communication can be defined broadly enough to embrace almost all human activities, such an approach deprives us of any central focus; to write about communication literally becomes a task of writing about everything.*

In this chapter, we will undertake the more modest and manageable task of attaching some defining characteristics to the term communication. In addition, we will consider several important contexts in which communicative transactions occur. Finally, we will briefly examine some possible ways of modeling the communication process.

Defining the Characteristics of Communication

As we conceive of the term, **communication** *is a transactional, symbolic process which allows people to relate to and manage their environments by (1) establishing human contact, (2) exchanging information, (3) reinforcing the attitudes and behaviors of others, and (4) changing the attitudes and behaviors of others.*

Communication Is a Process

To say communication is a **process** implies two important considerations. First, a process is continuous and ongoing; when applied to communication, this continuity means that efforts to fix the beginning and end of a communicative transaction are arbitrary and to some extent artificial. The communication theorist David Berlo puts it this way:

> If we accept the concept of process, we view events and relationships as dynamic, on-going, ever-changing, continuous. When we label something as a process, we also mean that it does not have *a* beginning, *an* end, a fixed sequence of events. It is not static, at rest. It is moving. The ingredients within a process interact; each affects all others (Berlo, 1960, p. 24).

To illustrate, consider the communicative transaction which we, the authors, are presently engaged in with you, the reader. When did it begin? It perhaps appears to have started when you picked up the book and started to read. But to take this position ignores many things that have happened to you, the events that have shaped your life. Obviously, had you not spent many years using and studying the English language, you would be unable to interpret our messages. At a more subtle level, you have developed beliefs and attitudes about the way communication functions, as well as its relative importance to you. Moreover, other readers have acquired beliefs and attitudes that diverge from yours, and as a result, their interpretations of many of the things we say will differ from yours. By the same token, the thoughts and ideas about communication expresssed in this book have been molded by years of study and experience. Furthermore, in formulating our ideas, we have tried to anticipate some of your experiences and concerns—to predict *what* things to say and *how* to say them. If we have been partially successful (total success with all readers is impossible), some effective communication will occur; if we have anticipated poorly, our ideas will have little impact. Thus this communicative transaction had no beginning, since it is influenced by everything that has happened to the participants since birth and, for that matter, genetic factors which preceded birth.

When will this communicative transaction end? Again, it is tempting to say it will terminate when you finish this chapter, or at term's end, when you retire this volume to your bookshelf or rush to the local bookstore to resell it. But once more, these end points are arbitrary and misleading. Some of the ideas you discover may have a lasting impact on the way you communicate; as a result of them, you will be a changed person. We too will change; we will subscribe to some ideas more enthusiastically and discard or modify others because of feedback we receive from the book's readers. Thus, just as our communicative exchanges have no clearly defined beginning, they have no readily discernible end.

The second major consideration associated with the process concept concerns the potential complexity of communicative exchanges: *Process implies that what occurs during a communicative transaction, as well as the outcomes that accrue from it, are influenced by many factors.* In other words, communicative transactions and their outcomes usually defy simple explanation. Consider again our efforts to communicate with you via the pages of this book. A simplistic approach leads to the belief that if we just select the appropriate words and organize them carefully into sentences, paragraphs, and chapters, we will be successful. True, wisely chosen words and clearly organized paragraphs will aid us in communicating, but the matter is not that simple. Suppose you are suffering from a bad headache and you are forcing yourself to read this chapter because a quiz is scheduled tomorrow. Or suppose you have just had a violent quarrel with a close friend or romantic partner. Or suppose you have always hated communication because you have often sought to express yourself to others and have been rebuffed or ridiculed. Might not such conditions affect the way you interpret and respond to our messages?

The same questions can be raised about our activities. Perhaps we have just had a heated argument with a colleague. Perhaps we are worried about a relative's or friend's health. Or perhaps (and this is, in fact, the case) these words are being written on a hot, muggy day, which encourages thoughts of the swimming pool or the movie theater. All these factors, and a host of others, influence the messages we produce.

Thus the concept of process implies both that communication has no beginning or end and that it is extremely complex. Both implications might make it seem futile to study communication. After all, if a phenomenon has no temporal boundaries and is influenced by innumerable factors, how can we hope to acquire much understanding of it?

Fortunately, subscribing to the process concept does not force us to abandon the quest for knowledge and understanding about communication. Even though beginning and end points are arbitrary and somewhat artificial, we can establish such points to mark off a communicative exchange. If you want to persuade a professor to reconsider your examination grade, you must eventually decide upon the strategies and arguments to be used, although you realize that whatever happens in the conversation will be influenced by many things which preceded it. Indeed, when the student or practitioner of communication assigns temporal boundaries to events of interest, he is not behaving any differently than the historian or biological scientist. History and biology are also processes, but since the whole field of history or biology is impossible to study, students of these areas must stake a claim on a small portion of the total process. Thus a historian may study the causes of World War I or a biologist the factors that lead to damage of the cardiovascular system, even though such investigations involve simplifying the situation and in a sense "stopping" the process.

Acceptance of a process viewpoint does involve two requirements. First, communicators must engage in **communicative analysis**—i.e., anticipate some of the things preceding a particular communicative transaction which may affect its progression or outcomes. Second, they must assume **communicative responsibility**—i.e., consider some of the possible enduring effects which may result from a particular communicative transaction. The former requirement is likely to produce a more effective communicator; the latter a more ethical one. Hence a major value of the process perspective is to remind us that each communicative transaction has both a history and a future.

But what of the complexity aspect of process? What seems to have been overlooked by many writers is that although each communicative transaction may be influenced by many unique factors, *powerful general factors exert a strong impact on all or at least most communicative transactions.* One can grant each communicative transaction its many uniquenesses and at the same time argue that certain regularities persist from transaction to transaction, some of which consistently affect both the transactions themselves and their outcomes. Thus, in our earlier example, we suggested that if the words we used in this book failed to express our intended meanings or if our thoughts were unclearly organized, our communication would probably be ineffective, regardless of whether you the reader were suffering a bad headache or feeling in top form.

This entire book is largely concerned with such regularities, but let us cite two other examples. Surely all communicative transactions are to some extent influenced by the participants' perceptions of each other's **credibility**. Communicators who are perceived as incompetent or untrustworthy are not likely to be very effective, unless they have considerable raw power at their disposal. Similarly, the **prior attitudes** of a participant enter into play, particularly since they exert a strong impact on the way messages are processed and interpreted. For example, a person with liberal attitudes about sexual norms may be easily persuaded to attend a pornographic movie, while one with conservative leanings is likely to be adamant in his refusal.

In summary, then, allegiance to the concept of process does not preclude useful and systematic analysis of communication. Rather, the process concept keeps us on our analytic toes; it forces us to remember that all descriptions and explanations of communicative transactions are likely to be incomplete. Moreover, it reminds us that communication is not static, but an ever-changing psychical and behavioral phenomenon.

Communication Is Transactional

To say communication is **transactional** suggests it is more appropriately viewed from a *relational* perspective. Save for intrapersonal communication, or "talking to oneself," communication is a cooperative social enterprise requiring two or more participants. When these participants are engaged in communicative transactions, they also comprise a relationship; they reciprocally affect each other's behavior as well as mutually develop rules which define the structure and content of their transactions.

To illustrate, consider the following three statements:

"Ed is quite dominant."

"Jack is very submissive."

"Ed certainly bosses Jack around a lot."

The first two assertions identify one aspect of Ed's and Jack's personalities from an individual perspective; i.e., they declare that Ed is a dominant person and Jack a submissive one, apart from any consideration of specific relationships that the two may have with other people. The third statement, however, says something about Ed's and Jack's *relationship*; it indicates that Ed assumes the dominant and Jack the submissive role; or, in Watzlawick, Beavin, and Jackson's (1967) terms, that a **complementary relationship** exists with Ed in the one-up position and Jack in the one-down position. Note that if the statement read, "Ed is always trying to boss Jack around, but Jack doesn't take it," it would imply a **symmetrical relationship**, with one of the parties (Ed) striving to alter it to a relational state of complementarity.

A transactional view of communication also endorses the importance of both the nature of the environment and the perceptions of the communicators in determining communicative outcomes. Some approaches to communication focus only on the environment, arguing that people's communicative behaviors are shaped and guided solely by the forces of external events. Other schools of thought contend that communicative behaviors are controlled by the communicators themselves, since their motives and intentions determine the actions to be taken. A transactional perspective prefers to focus on the *interaction*, or conjunctive relationships, between environment and perception. Thus throughout this book you will encounter discussions of the ways environment affects communicative behavior, the ways motives and intentions influence communicative actions, and the ways the two areas operate together to shape ongoing communication relationships.

Until recently, few students of communication have tried to approach it from a transactional stance, opting instead to adopt an individualistic, linear approach. As a result, it has been customary to speak of the **source** and the **receiver** of communication and to focus primary attention on *the effect the source has on the receiver(s)*. The transactional view conceives of communicators, rather than sources and receivers, and of effects as reciprocal and frequently simultaneous, rather than linear and unidirectional. In a communicative relationship all participants are both affecting and being affected, even when one *appears* to be sending many more messages than the other(s). As much as possible, we will analyze communication from this set of assumptions.

The cautious tone of the preceding pledge results from one potential problem in adopting a transactional perspective. The language available for *communicating about communication*—or **metacommunication**—is itself largely linear and unidirectional. In everyday conversations we usually talk about someone having an effect on someone else—e.g., "Mary really made Anne angry when she accused Anne of gossiping about her"—rather than speaking in terms of reciprocal effects. We also make observations about communication as if it were a process involving sources and receivers—e.g., "Bob called Nancy and told her off for standing him up the other night." We have no effective language to describe simultaneous effects. The best we can usually do is a serial listing of communicative exchanges: Mary made Anne angry; Anne scowled and called Mary a liar, which infuriated Mary; Mary said she ought to pull Anne's hair out, which frightened Anne, etc. Because of such deficiencies in our language tools, we shall sometimes have to resort to analyses and explanations that depart radically from our transactional ideal. Nevertheless, we shall continue to remind you of the importance of adopting a transactional perspective toward communication.

Communication Is Symbolic

Communicative transactions symbolize, or stand for, something else. The **symbolic** dimension of our definition limits the domain we will consider as communication, since much of our behavior is not symbolic. For instance, downing a cold glass of beer is not symbolic behavior, nor is consuming a thick cut of rare prime rib. But the expressions "Boy, a cold beer would taste good on a hot day like today!" or "I could go for some of that prime rib they serve at the Little Embers!" are symbolic because they use words which stand for the events described, making them instances of communicative behavior.

The symbol set which first comes to mind for most people is language. Considering the time and effort we devote to learning this symbol set, its primacy is hardly surprising. Moreover, the ability to use language is one of the things that most sharply distinguishes human beings from other animal forms. Fascinating research with dolphins (Lilly, 1961, 1967) and primates (Premack, 1971, 1976) notwithstanding, humans have a capacity for linguistic symbolizing that far outstrips that of other species.

As important as verbal code systems are to communication, symbolizing is not limited to verbalizing. Nonverbal code systems contribute heavily to our symbolic activities; in fact, some communication researchers (e.g., Mehrabian, 1971; Knapp, 1972) argue that more meaning is communicated nonverbally than verbally. Certainly, when the nonverbal and verbal codes conflict, most people tend to attach more importance to the former than the latter. Thus the statement "I've never had a more enjoyable evening in my life" is not likely to be very persuasive if delivered in a flat bored tone accompanied by several yawns.

Nonverbal code systems do pose one difficulty for the symbolic dimension of our definition of communication. Unlike language, which is by definition symbolic, some nonverbal behaviors are symbolic and some are not; e.g., a punch in the nose is not symbolic but a clenched fist raised in defiance is. How do we decide when a nonverbal act is symbolic? Some students of communication subscribe to a general view, preferring to see almost any nonverbal behavior as potentially symbolic. The major shortcoming of this approach has been mentioned earlier; it

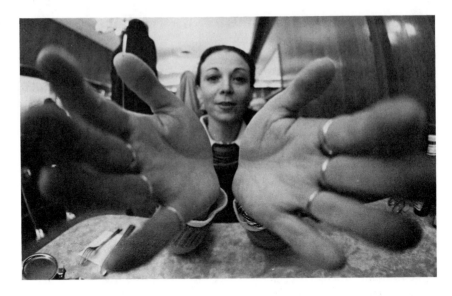

opens the door for almost everything to be labeled communication. Other, more conservative writers limit nonverbal communication to sets of behaviors which can be grouped under general labels designating particular nonverbal code systems. For example, *paralinguistics* is a set of vocal behaviors accompanying language which are not themselves strictly linguistic, and *proxemics* is a set of behaviors having to do with the way people position themselves in relation to other people. These two code systems will be explored more fully in the material dealing with nonverbal communication.

Communication Allows People to Relate to and Manage Their Environments

Communication is the bridge between people's thoughts, feelings, and needs and their external world. The baby experiences a prick of pain or a pang of hunger, responds by uttering the vocalic noises commonly labeled "crying," and is rewarded by the presence of a concerned parent who eases the pain by clasping the open diaper pin or makes the hunger vanish with a warm bottle. Undifferentiated crying becomes "Hurts!" or "Hungry!" as the child learns to associate labels with feelings and experiences; in turn these sounds are supplemented by "Stove hot!" or "Want cereal!" as the child masters ways of labeling external objects or events related to its subjective experiences. Early in life the child discovers that success in being recognized, responded to, and rewarded by its environment hinges on the development of its communicative skills.

So pervasive is the role of communication in relating to and managing our environments that we take it almost for granted. Like water for fish or soil for earthworms, communication is an essential ingredient of our existence, and like those creatures, we would probably be the last to realize this fact were it not for our ability *to communicate* about it. Our unquestioning acceptance of the gift to communicate is most apparent when things are going smoothly in our daily lives. When trouble erupts—when we are unable to relate to and manage our environments in functional, satisfying ways—we quickly become conscious of our communicative limitations, or perhaps even more commonly, of the perceived communicative shortcomings of others. "You haven't heard a word I've said!" laments an angry spouse or a disgruntled roommate, and the words testify to the frustration experienced when communication fails to produce the desired environmental outcomes.

Stated differently, communication is our chief vehicle for exercising **control** over our environments. While for many the term "control" smacks of Machiavellian manipulation, we use the term broadly, holding that "one has successfully controlled his environment whenever there is at least some correspondence between his desired and his obtained outcomes" (Miller and Steinberg, 1975, p. 65). Moreover, as these writers go on to assert, *"When used in this sense, control per se can be viewed as bad only if one believes there is something wrong with people preferring one set of outcomes to another"* (p. 65, italics in original). Viewed in this light, control is one of the staples of humanity's daily existence; for everyone, save perhaps the most emotionally unstable, prefers friendly recognition to cruel rebuff, intellectual acceptance to intellectual rejection, or need satisfaction to need deprivation. And as we have already emphasized, friendly recognition, intellectual acceptance, and need satisfaction are closely wed to our ability to communicate.

Terms such as "relate," "manage," and "control" constitute a very general perspective for discussing the functions of communication. What are some of the ways we seek to relate to and manage our environments—to exert maximum control over our external world and the people in it? Our definition of communication stipulates four important ones.

Establishing Human Contact

Human beings are social animals, and people do in fact need people. Great novels explore the theme of loneliness; distinguished sociologists warn of the dangers of anomie; "solitary confinement" is a hated phrase to inmates of penal institutions, who regard it as the ultimate indignity for real or imagined transgressions. Popular expressions such as "the brushoff" and "the cold shoulder" reveal our awareness of the destructive impact of failing to reciprocate social overtures. Recently, while enjoying a late evening beer at one of East Lansing's finest, we saw an obviously inebriated man approach a woman seated at the bar. "Aren't you the woman who brushed me off about a half-hour ago?" he inquired.

"Yes," she responded in a tone of feigned sweetness, "What's the matter; didn't I do it right?" Unquestionably, her cutting retort penetrated the alcoholic haze, causing the man to experience pain and rejection. Without a word he turned and left the bar.

Most of us have known the humiliation of such a rebuff. At times, of course, we realize that we brought it on ourselves. The woman in the bar was surely within her rights to discourage the man's overtures; nothing about the situation required her to converse with him. Moreover, her skill at inserting the verbal scalpel did not go unnoticed, for several people in the bar commented that it was the best put-down they had heard in some time. But even though we may not approve of the man's behavior, we can still empathize with him, largely because we have at some time shared his feeling of rejection.

The importance of communication in establishing human contact is forcefully illustrated by the plight of those persons who find it difficult, if not impossible, to initiate such contacts. Shyness can be excruciatingly painful. Followers of the comic strip "Peanuts" will recall Charlie Brown attempting to screw up enough courage to go over and introduce himself to the new girl in the class. Charlie fantasizes, rationalizes, and self-criticizes, but he never acts; and each failure to act further heightens his agony and contributes to his self-doubts. Recently the social psychologist Philip Zimbardo, along with a group of his colleagues, completed an extensive series of studies on shyness. Zimbardo characterizes some of the problems of shy persons in the following way:

> There are some shy people who have both the desire and the know-how to do a particular thing, but are held back from taking action. . . . They go to a dance, they know how to do the dance steps, yet something within keeps them from asking anyone to dance or accepting an invitation. Similarly, in the classroom, there are students who know the answer and want to make a good impression on the teacher, but something keeps their hands down and stifles their voices. They are inhibited from answering because of inner commands from the guard-self: "You'll look ridiculous; people will laugh at you; this is not the place to do that; I won't allow you the liberty to be spontaneous; do not raise your hand, volunteer, dance, sing, or make yourself obvious; you'll be safe only if you're not seen and not heard." And the prisoner-within decides not to risk the dangerous freedom of a spontaneous life and meekly complies (Zimbardo, 1977, pp. 4–5).

Exchanging Information

Establishing human contact is important not only in its own right but is also a necessary first step for accomplishing other communicative goals. Information exchange is one such goal, for without needed information, our attempts to manage our environment are doomed to failure. Baking a cake, passing a test, winning a football game, engineering a complicated stock merger, getting elected to public office—success in these undertakings, as well as in countless others, depends on our ability to amass relevant information, to get the facts. Indeed, information *is* power, and communication opens the door to its acquisition.

There are at least three ways in which information confers power on its possessors (Miller and Steinberg, 1975). First, persons perceived to have substantial information at their disposal are usually viewed as more credible communicators, thus paving the way for successful management and control of their environments. People listen carefully to, and frequently comply with, individuals who are in the know. By contrast, persons who never seem to have the answers are usually frustrated in their efforts at environmental management. Indeed, in late twentieth-century society, when information grows by exponential leaps, vague allusions to informational expertise may themselves be sufficient to ensure an acceptable level of control. For instance, it has become commonplace, if not democratically desirable, for governmental officials to justify policy decisions on the grounds that they are privy to items of "sensitive" information which are unavailable to the general public or to prate learnedly about the "complexities" of the social, economic, and political issues which face the country.

Second, information can be bartered for other social or economic objectives, thereby increasing its possessor's power. Sometimes the use of this tactic is reprehensible, as in the case of blackmail. But in general our society accepts this bartering principle and uses it extensively. People pursue educations so that they will be able to trade their information expertise for increased social status, added economic security, and more rewarding and challenging personal relationships. The material poverty of the economically and socially disadvantaged stems from a poverty of information; they lack the informational chips needed to ensure upward mobility. Thus the rich do, indeed, get richer and the poor get poorer, for just as it takes money to make money, it takes information to acquire information.

Finally, information confers power by expanding the available resources for problem solving. Problem solving ranges from making a railroad run to making a relationship run. Indeed, these two enterprises suggest a convenient analogy: keeping a train on track and keeping a marriage on track both impose heavy informational demands on the involved parties, demands that can only be achieved by effective communication. Lack of information limits our depth of understanding and our available alternatives, deficiencies which in turn seriously hamper our efforts at environmental management. If we are ignorant of the techniques of mouth-to-mouth resuscitation, we can only gaze helplessly at the accident victim or cry out for assistance; if we possess the needed information, we can literally breathe life back into the victim's dying body. By the same token, possession of the necessary information—or knowledge of the required communicative skills to obtain it—sometimes permits us to breathe life back into a dying relationship or to enhance the vigor of a reasonably healthy one.

Exchanging information is seldom a communicative end in itself; rather it usually serves as a *means* to the end of better management and control of one's environment. To say this in no way demeans the importance of information exchange; it is difficult to conceive of management without adequate information. Even more important, it is impossible to imagine adequate information in the absence of effective communication, since we accumulate most of our information through communicative exchanges with others.

Reinforcing the Attitudes and Behaviors of Others

To borrow from an old saying, the most effective environmental managers understand the importance of both "making new friends and keeping the old." Keeping old friends depends on continued communicative contacts with them, contacts aimed at reinforcing existing attitudes and behaviors deemed congruent with the communicator's goals. In short, it is vital to provide support for those who already agree with us or who find us attractive:

> Rather than aiming at changes in attitudes and behaviors, much persuasive communication seeks to reinforce currently held convictions and to make them more resistant to change. Most Sunday sermons serve this function, as do keynote speeches at political conventions and presidential addresses at meetings of scholarly societies. In such cases, emphasis is on making the persuadees more devout Methodists, more active Democrats, or more committed psychologists, not on converting them to Unitarianism, the Socialist Workers Party, or romance languages (Miller and Burgoon, 1973, p. 5).

People often overlook this aspect of communication in their everyday activities. As we noted earlier, most of us are essentially trouble-shooters who primarily occupy our minds with the things that are not going well. Suddenly, however, an unexpected crisis erupts; a supportive colleague deserts to the opposition or a close friend accuses us of taking her for granted. Immediately we engage in a flurry of communicative activity to repair our broken relational fences. If we are lucky, our efforts bear fruit and the relationship is reestablished; if not, we end up sadder, wiser, and with one less friendship.

Such crises in environmental management can be reduced by devoting adequate time to nurturing and supporting those who nurture and support us. Although it is impossible to specify a precise figure, part of each communicative day should be allocated to these activities. We are constantly bombarded with competing messages from groups and individuals seeking to expand their areas of environmental control. The mass media are the most obvious example of this highly competitive communicative marketplace. To induce people to buy a particular product or to support a specific political party is insufficient to ensure effective management and control of the environment. In addition, loyal customers and party supporters must continue to be rewarded for their actions, and communication remains an effective vehicle for extending this reward.

The same principle applies to interpersonal relationships. For many people, being taken for granted constitutes the supreme indignity. According to many clinical psychologists and marriage counselors, a chief cause of marital conflict is the failure of one or both parties to reinforce the other adequately. Such failures range from an absence of communication—the domestic cliché of the spouse whose attention is constantly glued to the newspaper or the television set—to communicative exchanges that wound and destroy, rather than reward and authenticate. Assuming that the relationship continues to be meaningful to the participants, it could benefit greatly from more effective environmental management.

Changing the Attitudes and Behaviors of Others

Traditionally students of communication have stressed the communicative importance of changing the attitudes and behaviors of others— the "making new friends" aspect of the saying that began the previous section. Since the days of Plato and Aristotle, treatises about communication have explored the persuasive function, with persuasion typically viewed as a change-oriented process. Hence this way of managing and controlling the environment is likely to be more familiar to you than the others we have considered.

All of us frequently seek to institute changes in our surroundings. If we are committed ecologists, we may champion various policies aimed at reducing environmental pollution—tougher standards for automobile emission systems, say, or reduced dumping of chemical pollutants into streams and rivers. If we are dissatisfied college students, we may campaign for measures to eliminate the depersonalization in higher education—smaller class sizes, more out-of-class contact between students and professors, and the like. If we are disgruntled professors, we may argue vigorously for policies that will improve our professional circumstances, such as higher salaries or more released time for research.

Nor are the changes we seek restricted to collective causes. Change is also one of the dominant facts of our personal lives. When people consciously pursue a search for a wider circle of friends and acquaintances, they are usually motivated by a felt need for change in their daily social lives. When one roommate informs another that continuance of their communal arrangement hinges on some changes in the way things are done, she underscores the centrality of attitudinal and behavioral change to effective environmental management. "I wish you'd stop cracking your knuckles constantly!" remarks an annoyed wife to her husband, and her commonplace complaint underscores the pervasiveness of change as a sought-after commodity in our daily activities.

When other avenues are closed, people sometimes resort to force to bring about changes. While such coercive actions are frequently dramatic and colorful—the stuff of which newspaper headlines and television news reports are made—they constitute a tiny minority of the everyday attempts at change. Unquestionably, communication is the means most frequently employed to change the attitudes and behaviors of others; for every loaded pistol, there are hundreds of loaded sentences. Consequently, good environmental managers know how to employ communication to modify others' behaviors and attitudes.

A concluding word of precaution is necessary. Earlier we noted that students of communication have usually opted for a linear, unidirectional view of the communication process. To a great extent, preoccupation with attitude and behavior change has stimulated the continued interest in this source-oriented perspective; after all, when the objective is change, we typically think of someone trying to influence the thoughts or actions of someone else. Although it sometimes may be convenient to think in these terms, this book, to repeat, subscribes to a transactional view of changes; seldom, if ever, do changes affect only one of the parties to a communicative transaction. A person's success or failure in changing the attitudes and behaviors of others is almost certain to result in changes in him.

Three Critical Communicative Contexts

Communicative transactions always occur within, and are constrained by, several critical contexts. By contexts we mean the environments where communication takes place, including the other communicators involved in the transaction. Since effective management of one's own environment is virtually impossible without an understanding of these critical contexts, we will now discuss them briefly.

The Cultural Context

Cultural influences are an inherent aspect of all communicative transactions. The term "culture" refers to the sum of language, values, beliefs, habits, and practices shared by a large group of people. These characteristics comprise the **cultural context** of communication. Cultures sometimes correspond with the political boundaries of nations, but this is not always the case. For instance, countries like the United States and the Soviet Union are *pluralistic societies*, meaning that more than one culture exists within their borders. Within any large American metropolitan area, one discovers numerous ethnic groups, each with its own cultural characteristics. During the past few decades, members of certain cultures have evinced renewed interest in their cultural identities. Phrases such as "black power" or "black pride," along with the phenomenal popularity of literary and television works such as Alex Haley's *Roots*, attest to the contemporary pride of black people in their cultural heritage.

The uniting force of a culture lies in its common language, values, norms, and shared historical experiences. Taken together, these four factors form the basis of an *ideology*, a rationale consisting of a blend of factual statements and value judgments which motivates individuals and confers a sense of cultural identity on them. The celebration of America's Bicentennial serves as an excellent example of ideological refurbishment. During 1976 citizens of the United States renewed traditional values, rejoiced in their history, and recommitted themselves to the preservation and growth of the society. Following on the heels of the divisiveness and social strife of Watergate, the Bicentennial was hailed as an opportunity to heal cultural wounds.

Communication both determines culture and is determined by it. Values, common language, and shared historical experiences are transmitted within and between generations via communication. In this way communication determines culture. At the same time, the culture determines communication; it defines, at least partially, appropriate and inappropriate strategies for conducting communicative transactions. Understanding the cultural context contributes greatly to effective environmental management, for without some appreciation of the cultural milieu, communication is doomed to failure.

Nowhere is this fact more forcefully illustrated than in cross-cultural communication. The most obvious, and occasionally amusing, deficiency lies in the lack of a common language. Recently, several of us attended an international communication conference held in West Berlin. Since none of us could speak German, we hoped that the folklore about "everyone in Europe speaking English" would prove true. Unfortunately, it did not, and as a result, we were severely handicapped communicatively during our week in West Berlin. Moreover, we returned frustrated by the realization that our language inadequacies seriously limited our capacity to appreciate the German culture.

Cross-cultural differences also intrude on the communicative scene in more subtle ways. Anthropologist Edward Hall (1959) has described how cultural variations in nonverbal communication—e.g., differences

in orientation toward space and time—hinder communicative effectiveness. Consider, for instance, a situation involving two parties from cultures with different norms about the appropriate social distance for casual conversation. When such meetings occur, it is not unusual to witness a slow, well-coordinated "dance" across the room: one party moves closer; the second retreats; the first reapproaches; the second moves back, etc., until escape is blocked by some immovable object such as a wall, a piece of furniture, or a group of people. At that point, the person who feels his personal space is being violated usually terminates the conversation. Furthermore, he will go on believing the other party is "pushy" or even "weird." Conversely, the other person is likely to think his conversational partner is cold and aloof, that he does not "warm up to other people."

Cross-cultural communication problems can be catalogued almost indefinitely. But we are even more concerned with what transpires between members of a common culture, for in this context, too, cultural factors exert a powerful influence. Indeed, if communicators violate certain cultural rules associated with the transaction, their chances for successful environmental management are dramatically reduced.

Since the concept *rules* is crucial to understanding many communicative exchanges, we will take a moment to define and illustrate it. By **rules** we mean *consensual agreements, shared at varying levels of generality, concerning the procedural, structural, and content factors which direct and shape a communicative relationship* (Miller, 1978). Cultural rules reflect agreements shared by most members of a particular culture. Sometimes these rules are articulated explicitly (e.g., a grammar text specifies numerous rules governing the use of the English language), while at other times they exist as implicit shared understandings (e.g., until recently it would have been difficult to discover a written description of the previously mentioned rules for appropriate social distance in various communicative transactions). But in either case, they strongly affect the process and the outcomes of communication.

To illustrate, consider the cultural rules governing greeting exchanges. When people encounter an acquaintance they have not seen for a period of time, they typically offer a few words of greeting. Although they have some choice about the content of the greeting—"Hi!"; "How's it going?"; "How are you?"—their options are relatively limited. For instance, one does not say, "Are you still fighting with your wife (or husband)?" or "Have you made any dishonest stock market deals lately?" The acquaintance is expected to respond to the greeting in kind— "Hi!"; "Great! How about yourself?"; "Fine, how are you?" Often this terminates the exchange, though the original greeter may respond with a few final words.

Such exchanges are so routine that students of communication refer to them as **phatic communication**, i.e., ritualized, rule-governed transactions that are second nature to the transactors. But suppose someone disrupts the ritualized sequence or, stated differently, violates the cultural rules of greeting exchanges. If the acquaintance fails to acknowledge the greeter, the latter may think the acquaintance is cold or arrogant; or she may become concerned that she has done something to offend or irritate the acquaintance. If the acquaintance responds to "Hi! How are you?" with a twenty-minute discourse about his health problems, he is likely to be branded an insufferable bore or a total ignoramus regarding cultural greeting rules. Yet were it not for these cultural rules, such a response would be reasonable; after all, when a doctor asks a patient how he feels, it is perfectly appropriate for the patient to recite physical symptoms and feelings.

Cultural rules strongly influence the content of many messages. To be effective, messages often must be congruent with the values of the culture. This requirement poses an interesting dilemma for the mass media, which try to bring about the conformity of a large heterogeneous audience while at the same time paying lip service to the American values of independence and individuality. Thus we are treated to a logically absurd yet persuasively effective diet of perfume commercials extolling the virtues of a fragrance that "interacts with normal body chemistry" to produce a unique scent for each wearer. If uniqueness is truly the goal, why shouldn't each person settle for his or her "normal body chemistry"? Obviously this alternative would not satisfy the perfume company or its advertising agency. Instead they want to establish control over the purchasing behaviors of as many consumers as possible. To accomplish this goal, they appeal to the American consumer's desire to be different. In a culture that did not value individuality, such commercials would be ineffective.

Astute environmental managers strive to comprehend the cultural rules governing communicative exchanges and to take advantage of them when mapping message strategies. Although understanding these rules does not ensure successful outcomes, it contributes markedly to a communicator's potential effectiveness.

The Sociological Context

Just as everyone belongs to a culture, each person also belongs to many groups within the culture. The **sociological context** of communication refers to the sum of the individual's group memberships as well as the *roles* associated with those memberships. The membership of these groups may be quite specific and limited—e.g., "Marble School PTA" or "Ingham County Medical Association"—or it may be broad and nebulous—e.g., "college students" or "fathers." Either way, certain roles are inevitably associated with each membership. As we use the term, **roles** refers both to behaviors and expectations concerning them. Thus the position of father traditionally entails role behaviors which provide financial support for the family, and the society expects fathers to perform these behaviors. Of course, the extent to which others' expectations mandate the performance of certain role behaviors varies (Sarbin, 1954; Sarbin and Allen, 1969; Turner, 1970). For example, the fatherly role behaviors of providing financial support for the family and moral guidance for the children are typically demanded, while engaging in recreational activities with the children is desirable but not necessarily demanded. Similarly, professors must assist students in mastering an area of study, but having a cup of coffee with students after class is merely desirable.

Like communication, roles are relational: without the position of child, there would be no position of father; without the position of student, there would be no position of professor. Because of the relational nature of roles, much role behavior is inextricably bound up in communication. For this reason an understanding of the sociological context is essential to effective communication.

Take the position of college student. Many appropriate role behaviors associated with this position are both rule-governed and communicative. These include rules of address (a student addresses a professor as "Doctor" or "Professor," not "G. R." or "Beech Street Fats"), rules of appropriate content (a student fills examination bluebooks with relevant ideas, not irrelevant jokes or excuses), and rules of ethical conduct (a student fills examination bluebooks with his or her own thoughts and ideas, not those of a roommate). To be sure, our society permits flexibility in the performance of these role behaviors. Some professors may not object to being addressed by their first names, and some may appreciate a few humorous quips interspersed with the answers to test questions. Still, upon entering an unfamiliar situation, a cautious "proper" strategy is most likely to pay dividends, and knowledge of the sociological context aids in selecting that strategy.

Status considerations are intimately related to many roles. Status is sometimes communicated and acknowledged verbally: the statement "I'm Carole Evans, Chairperson of the Board of Directors at IBM" communicates something about the status of the speaker, while the salutation "Good morning, General Parsons" acknowledges the status of the individual being greeted. More frequently, however, status distinctions are communicated nonverbally. Clothing, ranging from uniforms to expensive suits or dresses, is often used to engender status perceptions, as are automobiles or dwellings. It may sometimes be difficult to determine whether these personal artifacts were purchased with an eye toward symbolizing status or whether they merely reflect the personal tastes of the purchaser. Nevertheless, there is no doubt that clothing stores, car dealers, and realtors often stress the status dimension in their advertisements. "For the man on the way up," trumpets an ad for a three-piece suit by an "established designer," though, of course, the man who "has arrived" wears custom-made suits designed and fitted by his private tailor. And nowhere is status striving more apparent than in the world of women's fashion, where eager buyers pay thousands of dollars for a Saint Laurent or a Galanos gown that is worn on several occasions and then discarded for next year's creation. Indeed, status consciousness is largely responsible for the recent phenomenon of "cut label" stores: shops that remove the labels (the chief badge of status) from garments and sell them for considerably less than their original prices.

The large formal organization stands as a prime example of the use of nonverbal status trappings. Status rules determine office size, office furnishings, restroom prerogatives, and a host of other matters. At many universities, individuals with the rank of dean or other high position merit carpeted offices at university expense, while those with a lower rank—specifically, the teaching and research faculty—either pay for their own carpeting or do without. This example illustrates the sociological inconsistencies that often arise between verbal and nonverbal symbols. The official rhetoric of most universities advertises that faculty are the heart and soul of the campus, with administrators existing solely to facilitate the faculty's important work. Yet even a cursory analysis of the sociological context of these institutions leads quickly to the conclusion that the nonverbal accoutrements are sharply at odds with commonly verbalized status distinctions. Furthermore, one gets the feeling that such nonverbal trappings are often retained for their status value alone, even when other evidence suggests they are counterproductive. In the case of carpeting, maintenance experts hold that custodial and upkeep costs would drop sharply if all offices were carpeted, but we are not going to hold our breath until this change takes place.

Understanding the sociological context of communication requires constant diligence, for appropriate role behaviors change with the ideological ebb and flow of society. Until a decade ago, desks were common status barriers in communicative transactions between students and professors. During the social and political turmoil of the late 1960s, many professors became convinced their roles precluded the erection of such status barriers, and it became fashionable to position desks against the rear walls of offices, so that conversations with students would be uninhibited by office furnishings. Today the trend is toward a more conservative view of role relationships between students and professors, and desks are being moved back to the middle of the office. Even an institution like the military, which imposes relatively strict, inflexible rules on the communicative behaviors of members of varying status, has learned it must bend with the times; while exchanges between military personnel of differing ranks are still far from casual, enlisted personnel can claim more role latitude today than once was the case.

The sociological context pervades our daily communicative exchanges. Indeed, as we will argue in a later chapter, most of the communicative strategies aimed at environmental management are rooted in sociological considerations: because the communicative activities associated with most roles are clearly specified, *the best initial predictors of effective communication stem from an awareness of the sociological context in which the transaction takes place.* By combining an understanding of cultural and sociological factors, communicators can take a giant step toward the goal of effective environmental management and control.

The Psychological Context

Although the preceding two contexts of communication are critically important, they do not impose an iron hand on individual behavior. People *do* violate cultural values, and group members *do* refuse to conform with the norms and the role expectations of the group. Though individuals are partially a product of cultural and sociological conditioning, they are strongly influenced by individual learning experiences. The sum of these individual learning experiences constitutes the **psychological context** of communication.

As it relates to individual learning, the term "psychological" can be used in two senses. First, it can refer to learning experiences shared by a large number of people, experiences that combine to produce a general trait or characteristic. For example, concepts such as *authoritarian, dogmatic, cognitively complex*, and *low self-esteem* are shorthand labels for general psychological traits assumed to evolve from shared learning experiences. In terms of the goal of environmental management, preferred communicative strategies for dealing with persons who manifest these general traits can be suggested. Thus if one believed that most of the other communicators in a transaction were highly dogmatic (Rokeach, 1960), one might tailor a message to contain numerous references to positive authorities, since high dogmatics are known to be strongly influenced by authority-based appeals (Powell, 1962). Conversely, if most of the other communicators were low dogmatics, messages might rely more heavily on logic and sound argument, since low dogmatics pay more heed to message content to reach positions concerning an issue.

In addition to general traits, the term psychological also refers to the unique learning experiences of individuals, the many factors contributing to the individual differences that exist among members of the same cultural and social groups. Until now, the various contexts we have discussed encourage **stimulus generalization** as a way of determining effective communicative strategies; i.e., these contexts focus on the ways that members of particular cultures and groups are *similar*. Emphasizing individual differences shifts the focus to **stimulus discrimination**, i.e., the key to devising effective message strategies lies in determining how individual members of particular cultures and groups *differ* from their fellow members. Obviously the ability to make such discriminations can markedly increase one's potential for environmental management, since the individual, rather than the group, becomes the unit of strategic analysis:

> Stimulus generalization is closely akin to abstraction; one observes a group of objects and notes aspects they have in common. For instance, on the basis of knowledge about one professor, a person could generalize that all college professors have advanced degrees, are committed to scholarship, and control certain rewards of importance to most students. But suppose a particular professor has not earned an advanced degree, and moreover, he is touchy about this fact. To address him as "doctor" may cause him to assume an intended slight and to react negatively. Another professor may have earned an advanced degree but may have an aversion to the status barriers erected by the title "doctor." In either case, continued use of the formal title may produce undesirable

communication outcomes for the student.... If predictions are based on stimulus discrimination, the amount of predictive error can be greatly reduced. Were you to rely on stimulus discrimination rather than on stimulus generalization in dealing with a particular professor, you might ask yourself how he is different from other professors with whom you have studied. Some professors encourage disagreement with their positions, while others abhor it; some professors encourage out-of-class contact, while others avoid it. How does this one feel? In what ways will he behave like other professors? Most importantly, does he vary in ways you cannot now predict? (Miller and Steinberg, 1975, p. 24).

The benefits to be gained from basing predictions on stimulus discrimination can be realized only if the communicator has developed an appreciation for the psychological context of the communicative transaction.

Communication rules based on psychological considerations differ significantly from their cultural and sociological counterparts. In the latter two areas, rules are externally imposed and exist as givens at the relationship's outset. By contrast, psychologically based rules are internally derived and are defined and negotiated as the relationship progresses. Thus the two types of rules permit varying degrees of choice. Although relational participants must accept culturally and sociologically based rules more or less as they find them, they have broad latitude in choosing the psychologically derived rules that will govern their relationship.

To illustrate, consider the relationship between a new employee and his supervisor. Initially the relationship is largely guided by existing sociologically based rules describing the structure, procedures, and content of employee/supervisor communicative exchanges. Thus both participants understand that the supervisor is in the "one-up" high-status position, while the employee occupies the "one-down" low-status position (structural rule); that the supervisor usually initiates communication and the employee responds to it (procedural rule); and that the supervisor gives orders and the employee accepts them (content rule). Given these initial agreements, exchanges such as the following are highly predictable:

SUPERVISOR: Fred, will you come in here for a minute.
EMPLOYEE: Certainly, Mr. Jones.
SUPERVISOR: There seems to be some delay on that shipment to Acme Bolt Company. Will you see if you can straighten things out.
EMPLOYEE: Yes sir, I'll get right on it!
SUPERVISOR: Thanks, let me know when you've spotted the hitch.

Marked communicative departures from this scenario are likely to create relational strains. Note, for instance, that while Mr. Jones's opening message is phrased interrogatively, no question mark appears at the end of the sentence. This omission is intentional, for the statement acts as a command, not a query. If Fred were to respond, "No, I'm busy right now, but I'll come in when I have time," serious relational strain would result. Of course, Fred will not respond this way (at least, not if he wants to succeed in his new job), because he knows that such behavior would constitute a flagrant violation of sociologically derived rules.

Suppose, however, that Mr. Jones (Bob) and Fred discover that they share many interests and that they heartily enjoy each other's company. If this happens, the two men may develop a close personal relationship and begin to spend considerable time together during leisure hours. Under these circumstances, a transaction such as the following would not be surprising:

BOB: Damn, Fred, it's always the same! You catch your limit and I go home empty-handed.

FRED: As I've told you before, you don't bait the hook right. Here, let me show you how to do it.

BOB: Yeah, I wish you would. I don't want to get skunked again today.

FRED: There, you see you've got to hook the pork rind close to the end, not in the middle. Now why don't you cast right over there. And try to get a little more rod action. . . .

The radical change in the communicative rule structure governing the relationship is readily apparent. As a result of continued interaction, Bob and Fred have negotiated a different set of rules to guide their social relationship, rules derived from the psychological context of the relationship.

The preceding example underscores another important point: in some situations cultural and sociological rules take precedence, while in others psychological rules prevail. The ability to discern which rule set has priority constitutes an important dimension of understanding the three crucial communicative contexts. If Fred continues to address Bob (Mr. Jones) in a dominant, assertive way at the office, he is sure to encounter trouble either from Mr. Jones or from other members of the organization who consider such behavior inappropriate. Furthermore, should Mr. Jones permit this to happen, he will also be sanctioned by his colleagues. Consequently, both Fred and Mr. Jones (Bob) must be adaptive in managing their professional and social relationships.

Knowledge about the psychological context of communication dramatically enhances a communicator's potential for effective environmental management. In addition, since psychological factors are often unique to particular situations and relationships, they allow communicators the greatest amount of inventiveness when devising message strategies. We will have more to say about the psychological context of communication in later chapters.

Modeling the Communication Process

Numerous models of the communication process have been devised; indeed, there are almost as many models as there are writers about communication (e.g., Shannon and Weaver, 1949; Westley and MacLean, 1957; Berlo, 1960; Kelman, 1961; Miller, 1966, 1972; Dance, 1967). Introductory chapters of communication texts typically contain several of the authors' pet models, including verbal descriptions and visual depictions. In our brief discussion of modeling, we shall adopt a different strategy. Rather than providing a capsule overview of a number of models, we shall consider the nature and functions of models, concluding with one possible way of modeling the communication process as we have defined it in this chapter. A rudimentary acquaintance with the logic of model-building should help you to select the most appropriate models for various communicative purposes and even to construct models of your own to fit the task at hand.

A Definition of Model

Several years ago a noted psychologist presented a convention paper dealing with various ways of modeling the process of language learning. The paper was titled, "Models I Have Tried and Found Wanting." On the eve of the convention a local paper ran a story about the psychologist's presentation, including the title of the paper. The next morning a party called him at his hotel to inquire if his presentation would deal with fashion models. "Oh no," said the psychologist, who possesses a ready sense of humor, "If I planned to talk about that area, I would have titled my paper, 'Models I Have Wanted and Found Trying.' "

Obviously, as used here, the term "model" does not refer to the fashion world. Neither does it mean a miniature replica of some larger object, a common usage for hobby buffs who build models of planes or cars. A model of the communication process represents a complex human process. To produce an exact replica of this process would be impossible. Any model of the communication process requires **abstraction**; i.e., it forces the model builder to select certain parts of the total process for inclusion in the model and to ignore others. *What the model builder chooses to include and to ignore depends largely on his or her purpose(s) for devising the model.* For instance, someone who wished to study the influence of nonverbal code systems on communication outcomes would construct a very different model from someone who wanted to investigate the influence of media programming on aggressive behavior. Although one could ask whether the two models achieve the purposes sought by the model builders, it would be useless to argue over which one represents the most "correct" or "true" view of communication, for both models are abstractions of the total process. This characteristic of models implies, first, that any number of models may be helpful in illuminating various aspects of the communication process; and, second, that when evaluating a model, utility, not truth, is the primary ground for judgment. Thus a model of a two-person transaction will probably differ markedly from a model dealing with mass communication, or a model of some aspect of small-group communication may depart radically from a model of certain communication activities in formal organizations.

Having established these limiting considerations, we offer this definition of **model**: *a systematic representation which abstracts and classifies/describes certain potentially relevant aspects of a process.*

Functions of Communication Models

A model of communication can serve an **organizational function**; i.e., it can help people order their thoughts about communication and communicate more effectively with others about the process. By constructing a model, students of communication focus attention on certain relevant aspects of the process, and this simplifying act organizes and clarifies the "total picture" so others can engage in meaningful, coherent interaction about it.

To illustrate this function, consider the communication model depicted in Figure 1–1, the SMCR model first presented by David Berlo

Figure 1–1
Berlo's SMCR Model

S SOURCE	M MESSAGE	C CHANNEL	R RECEIVER
Comm. skills	Elements	Seeing	Comm. skills
Attitudes	Structure	Hearing	Attitudes
Knowledge	Content	Touching	Knowledge
Social system	Treatment	Smelling	Social system
Culture	Code	Tasting	Culture

Source: David Berlo, *The Process of Communication.* Copyright © 1960 by Holt, Rinehart and Winston, Inc.

(1960). As our earlier remarks about the nature of communication suggest, this model is not immune from criticism. For instance, it clearly embodies a linear, unidirectional perspective of communication: sources (S) transmit messages (M) through channels (C) to receivers (R), with no feedback mechanism included in the model. Nevertheless, the model identifies and organizes certain potentially relevant aspects of the communication process. Intuitively it provides a vocabulary for talking about communication that many people find sensible and useful. In particular, it coincides fairly closely with the communicative goal of effective environmental management, identifying various factors that may influence a communicator's relative success or failure in achieving that goal. Hence, the model fulfills the organizational function nicely.

A model of communication can also perform a **research-generating function**; i.e., it can suggest questions and hypotheses for students of communication to investigate. Research constitutes one of the most effective tools for increasing our understanding of the communication process; in fact, much of the information in this book was gleaned from the scholarly efforts of researchers from communication and related fields. Consequently, anything that stimulates question asking and answering is valuable, and most models of communication have this potential.

The research-generating function is illustrated by the simple model (Miller, 1966, 1972) in Figure 1–2. Although rudimentary, the model suggests a number of research hypotheses. After you have considered the examples in the list below, it might be instructive for you to try to formulate some additional hypotheses.

1. As listener attitudes toward the speaker become less favorable, a greater quantity of negative feedback will occur.
2. The kind of feedback that a speaker receives will subsequently affect his attitudes and his encoding behaviors.

Figure 1–2
A Simple Model of the Speech Communication Process

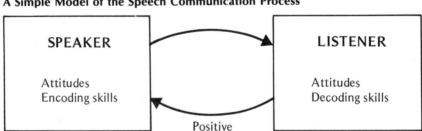

Source: G. R. Miller, *Speech Communication: A Behavioral Approach* and *An Introduction to Speech Communication.* Copyright © 1966 and © 1972 by the Bobbs-Merrill Company, Inc.

3. If feedback is predominantly negative, the speaker will manifest a less favorable attitude toward the proposition he advocates; if it is predominantly positive, the converse will occur.
4. Positive feedback will facilitate encoding behavior and negative feedback
will have a disruptive effect on this variable.
5. The more similar the initial attitudes of the speaker and the listener toward the position advocated, the greater the amount of positive feedback
(Miller, 1972, p. 59).

Granted, all these hypotheses could be derived without relying on a
model. But the model organizes and classifies variables, in some cases
making things explicit that were formerly implicit. Moreover, by omit-
ting certain variables, the model identifies things that may not merit attention. To use research time and energy wisely, it is sometimes as important to define what *not* to study as it is to hit upon things to
investigate.

Finally, a communication model can fulfill a **practical predictive** function. Not all students of communication are concerned with research;
many are interested in applying knowledge about communication to
practical situations. Stated differently, they are interested in the ways
communication can aid in achieving effective environmental management. Often, a model of communication provides some tentative predictions about the probable success of certain communicative strategies.

To acquire an appreciation for this practical function of models, examine Herbert Kelman's (1961) three processes of social influence, a
model detailed in Table 1-1. In constructing this model, Kelman was
primarily interested in specifying the processes communicators can use
to influence others—or, as we have termed it, to exert environmental
control. Suppose a communicator is trying to decide whether coercion is
likely to be an effective strategy. By studying "compliance"—the process
most closely akin to coercion—the communicator can determine the
necessary conditions for this strategy to succeed. For instance, he can
see that for compliance to work, he must have *means-control* over the persuadee; i.e., he must control some rewards or punishments that are important to the persuadee. Moreover, if the communicator wants the persuadee to continue to behave in a certain way, choice of the compliance
process entails ability to exercise continued surveillance over the persuadee's behavior, since the model predicts the desired behavior will occur only when the persuadee believes he is being monitored by the communicator. By examining the other social influence processes, similar
predictions can be generated, predictions that can help the communicator to become a more effective environmental manager.

Obviously, none of the three models described above is limited to a
single function; e.g., just as the SMCR model helps to organize ideas
about communication, it also generates research and suggests practical
predictions about communicative outcomes. What is important to re-

Table 1–1
Three Processes of Social Influence

Antecedents	Compliance	Identification	Internalization
1. Basis for the importance of the induction	Concern with social effect of behavior	Concern with social anchorage of behavior	Concern with value congruence of behavior
2. Source of power of the influencing agent	Means-control	Attractiveness	Credibility
3. Manner of achieving prepotency of the induced response	Limitation of choice behavior	Delineation of role requirements	Reorganization of means-ends framework

Consequents	Compliance	Identification	Internalization
1. Conditions of performance of induced response	Surveillance by influencing agent	Salience of relationship to agent	Relevance of values to issue
2. Conditions of change and extinction of induced response	Changed perception of conditions for social rewards	Changed perception of conditions for satisfying self-defining relationships	Changed perception of conditions for value maximization
3. Type of behavior system in which induced response is embedded	External demands of a specific setting	Expectations defining a specific role	Person's value system

Source: H. C. Kelman, "Processes of Opinion Change," *Public Opinion Quarterly*, 25 (1961).

member is that the contribution of a model is determined by its **utility**—the extent to which it enhances theoretical and practical understanding of the communication process.

A Model of the Communication Process

Figure 1–3 contains a model designed to capture some of the characteristics of communication discussed in this chapter. For the sake of simplicity, we have depicted a dyadic, or two-person, model, though the model could easily be expanded to include more than two people. We have labeled the two individuals "communicator 1" and "communicator 2" to underscore the transactional nature of communication; rather than conceiving of sources and receivers of communication, we view these two individuals as communicators who are sending and receiving many verbal and nonverbal messages simultaneously.

The three critical contexts of communication are also reflected in this model. We have placed the psychological context within the two boxes representing the communicators to illustrate the unique, idiosyncratic character of this context and to suggest that it often evolves from features of the ongoing relationship itself. By contrast, the cultural and sociological contexts are external to the communicators and always impinge upon the relationship at its outset. Finally, we have pictured three paths for verbal and nonverbal messages to emphasize that these messages can be based primarily on factors associated with any of the three contexts or on a combination of factors associated with all three.

The model satisfies the organizational function by pulling together many of the concepts discussed in this chapter in a relatively simple, or-

Figure 1–3
A Model of the Communication Process

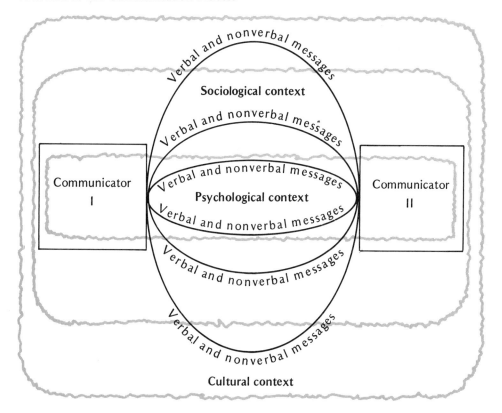

ganized manner. Although some research questions can be generated from the model, it is too general to fulfill this function satisfactorily. To identify a number of questions for investigation, it would be necessary to focus on a particular aspect of the model and to state explicitly some of the anticipated relationships existing between variables. This same limitation holds for the practical predictive function. Nevertheless, the model does suggest some probable practical outcomes; for instance, it implies that primary reliance on the psychological context will result in more effective environmental management. We are not bothered by the model's restricted utility in the research and predictive areas, since it was primarily constructed to serve an organizational function. Thus if our model provides a relatively good picture of the communication process and facilitates effective communication about this process in later chapters, it serves our purpose satisfactorily.

Conclusion

Communication plays a vital role in all the events of our lives, from how we conduct our day-to-day affairs to how we achieve our ultimate goals in life. It should be viewed as a process that is affected by all that goes before and after it, one that links us to our fellow human beings and relies to a large extent on symbols. It is inextricably bound up with cultural, social, and psychological factors that must be understood if we are to use communication strategies effectively. Communication models can help us analyze the process and anticipate probable outcomes. Together, the foregoing concepts lay the foundation for the discussion of communication contained in this volume.

TERMS AND CONCEPTS FOR REVIEW

abstraction
communication
communicative analysis
communicative responsibility
complementary relationship
control
credibility
cultural context
Kelman's model
metacommunication
Miller's model
model

organizational function
phatic communication
practical predictive function
prior attitudes
process
psychological context
receiver
research-generating function
roles
rules
SMCR Model (Berlo)
sociological context

source
stimulus discrimination
stimulus generalization
symbolic

symmetrical relationship
transactional
utility of a model

REVIEW QUESTIONS

1. What is the concept of process?
2. What are the differences between a transactional and linear view of communication?
3. Distinguish between symbolic and nonsymbolic behaviors by giving examples.
4. How do people commonly try to control the environment by communication?
5. In what ways is communication used for environmental management?
6. What are the differences between the cultural, sociological, and psychological contexts of communication?
7. Construct a simple model of the communication process.
8. How does Miller's model of communication compare with Berlo's?

REFERENCES

Berlo, D. K. *The Process of Communication.* New York: Holt, Rinehart & Winston, 1960.

Dance, F. E. X. "Toward a Theory of Human Communication." In F. E. X. Dance (ed.), *Human Communication Theory: Original Essays.* New York: Holt, Rinehart & Winston, 1967, pp. 288–309.

Hall, E. T. *The Silent Language.* New York: Fawcett, 1959.

Kelman, H. C. "Processes of Opinion Change." *Public Opinion Quarterly,* 1961, 25, 57–78.

Knapp, M. L. *Nonverbal Communication in Human Interaction.* New York: Holt, Rinehart & Winston, 1972.

Lilly, J. C. *Man and Dolphin.* Garden City, N.Y.: Doubleday, 1961.

———. *The Mind of the Dolphin.* Garden City, N.Y.: Doubleday, 1967.

Mehrabian, A. *Silent Messages.* Belmont, Calif.: Wadsworth, 1971.

Miller, G. R. *Speech Communication: A Behavioral Approach.* Indianapolis: Bobbs-Merrill, 1966.

———. *An Introduction to Speech Communication.* Indianapolis: Bobbs-Merrill, 1972.

———. "The Current Status of Theory and Research in Interpersonal Communication." *Human Communication Research,* Winter 1978, 4, 168–178.

————, and M. Burgoon. *New Techniques of Persuasion.* New York: Harper & Row, 1973.

————, and M. Steinberg. *Between People: A New Analysis of Interpersonal Communication.* Chicago: Science Research Associates, 1975.

Powell, F. A. "Open-and-Closed-Mindedness and the Ability to Differentiate Source and Message." *Journal of Abnormal and Social Psychology*, 1962, 65, 61–64.

Premack, D. "Language in Chimpanzee?" *Science*, 1971, 172, 808–822.

————. *Intelligence in Ape and Man.* New York: John Wiley & Sons, 1976.

Rokeach, M. *The Open and Closed Mind.* New York: Basic Books, 1960.

Sarbin, T. R. "Role Theory." In G. Lindzey (ed.), *Handbook of Social Psychology.* Vol. 1. Reading, Mass.: Addison-Wesley, 1954, pp. 223–258.

————, and V. L. Allen. "Role Theory." In G. Lindzey and E. Aronson (eds.), *Handbook of Social Psychology.* 2nd ed., vol. 1. Reading, Mass.: Addison-Wesley, 1969, pp. 488–597.

Shannon, C., and W. Weaver. *Mathematical Theory of Human Communication.* Urbana, Ill.: University of Illinois Press, 1949.

Turner, R. *Family Interaction.* New York: John Wiley & Sons, 1970.

Watzlawick, P., J. H. Beavin, and D. D. Jackson. *Pragmatics of Human Communication.* New York: W. W. Norton, 1967.

Westley, B. H., and M. MacLean, Jr. "A Conceptual Model for Communication Research." *Journalism Quarterly*, 1957, 34, 31–38.

Zimbardo, P. G. *Shyness: What It Is and What to Do About It.* Reading, Mass.: Addison-Wesley, 1977.

Code Systems and Meaning

ELEMENTS

PATTERNS
  Syntactic rules
  Semantic rules

Verbal Code Systems

ROLE OF LANGUAGE IN HUMAN
INTERACTION
  To learn about the world around us
  To conduct our relations with others
  To create coherence in our lives

EXAMINING THE VERBAL CODE SYSTEM
  Linguistics
  Chomsky's ideas

LEARNING VERBAL CODES
  Skinner—behaviorist approach
  Osgood—mediation theory
  Chomsky—cognitive theory

VERBAL CODES AND COGNITION

VERBAL CODES, SOCIETIES, AND
CULTURES
  Whorf-Sapir hypothesis
  Sociolinguistic theory

Nonverbal Code Systems

INTERACTION OF VERBAL AND
NONVERBAL CODES

PERFORMANCE CODES
  Paralinguistics
  Emblems
  Illustrators
  Regulators
  Affect displays

ARTIFACTUAL CODES
  Personal artifacts
  Shared artifacts
  Public artifacts

MEDIATORY CODES

SPATIO-TEMPORAL CODES
  Hall's interaction zones

Codes and Code Systems:
Verbal and Nonverbal

After reading this chapter, you should be able to:

1. Give examples of syntactic rules and semantic rules.
2. Explain the difference between denotative meaning and connotative meaning.
3. Explain the difference between linguistic performance and linguistic competence.
4. Compare the learning of verbal codes according to the behaviorist approach, mediation theory, and cognitive theory.
5. Explain the Whorf-Sapir hypothesis.
6. Explain the difference between restricted code and elaborated code according to Bernstein.
7. List the six ways in which nonverbal communication interacts with verbal communication.
8. Give examples of paralinguistic features, emblems, illustrators, regulators, and affect displays.
9. Give examples of personal, shared, and public artifacts.
10. Give examples of mediatory codes.
11. Give examples of spatio-temporal codes.
12. Differentiate among intimate, personal, social, and public distances.

We have suggested that the ability of mankind to use symbols may well be the distinguishing factor between animal communication and human communication. Animals *do* communicate. They use touch, taste, smell, and sound to acquire information about the world and to convey information to other members of their species. But humans are different. We do not need to rely on our senses to convey or receive information. We can communicate through *symbols*. In many ways, understanding this ability to symbolize is the most important part of the study of communication.

The study of symbolic behavior is most commonly thought of as the study of "language." The term, however, has come to mean a number of different things. We can talk about having a language, knowing a language, speaking a language, or reading a language. For that reason, we are going to use the term **code system** as a more general term that can be precisely developed. Code systems include all the spoken and written languages, such as English, German, or French. But there are many other code systems that are extremely important to communication. These include the gestures we use in talking to one another, the ways in which we dress, the cars we drive, and the places where we live. These are *nonverbal* code systems, and we will contrast their use with the more familiar *verbal* systems.

Achieving success in our communication relationships is frequently a matter of carefully observing and accurately evaluating verbal and nonverbal coding behavior. This should not be surprising. The words and actions of others are used to assess their desirability as friends, instructors, roommates, or co-workers. The verbal and nonverbal messages we send and receive determine what we learn and how we learn it. The purpose of this chapter is to examine the process of coding and the role it plays in our daily lives.

Code Systems and Meanings

For most of us the terms "code" and "code behavior" bring to mind the secret codes that children get from cereal boxes, the Morse code, the work of the CIA, or Edgar Allan Poe's *The Gold Bug*. The Morse code *is* a code system, but so is English, Spanish, or Japanese; each is composed of a series of stimuli which can evoke specific responses in a receiver. Whether the code be the English language or a complex numerical code used to protect military secrets, certain characteristics can be identified.

First, all code systems possess a set of identifiable **elements**. The elements in Morse code are dots and dashes. In written English the elements are twenty-six letters and punctuation marks like commas, periods, and apostrophes. By themselves, elements have no meaning. But they are the building blocks we use to create symbols which express our meaning to a receiver. The elements may differ from system to system, may be many or few, but to say we have a code system is to imply that it is composed of a set of elements.

Second, all code systems have rules which allow the elements of the system to be arranged into **patterns**. For instance, SOS in Morse code isn't just composed of six dots and three dashes; it is composed of a unique pattern of three dots, followed by three dashes, followed again by three dots. If we were to change the pattern, we would be changing the meaning. The users of a code system agree on what the rules are going to be for the combination of elements into larger, patterned structures. For example, in written English there are no words beginning with *ff*. If the occurrence of elements in larger structures were completely arbitrary, one would expect to find examples of all possible combinations. However, the combination of elements is governed by a set of **syntactic rules**, which specify the ways elements can be ordered into acceptable patterns.

Syntactic rules may govern more than one level in a complex code system. In a verbal code they specify not only how letters are arranged into words, but also how words are arranged into sentences. Changes in word order can produce changes in meaning, even though the words remain the same. For instance, although the sentences "John hit the car" and "The car hit John" contain identical words, we assign different meanings to the sentences. Thus it is possible to identify a kind of meaning which arises directly from the operation of syntactic rules in the language. We call this type of meaning **syntactic meaning**, and it simply refers to the understanding gained from the patterns we use rather than the elements themselves. Each of us ascribes a meaning to the words "John," "hit," and "car," but different meanings emerge depending on how we arrange these words. One of the major interests of scholars who study verbal and nonverbal codes is isolating the syntactic rules people actually use, whether consciously or not.

A final characteristic of all code systems is a set of rules called **semantic rules**. These are the rules we use in assigning meanings. Semantic rules reflect the ways in which members of a common culture respond to a particular language stimulus. People who live in any culture develop behaviors that are held in common with all other members of the culture. Thus everyone living in East Lansing, Michigan, might expect to recognize street names, appropriately respond to traffic signs, and be able to understand other people living in the same city. But each person comes to the communication situation with a unique set of experiences and values as well. The difference between common and unique experiences suggests that we can assign **semantic meanings** to symbols in two ways: (1) as reflecting our membership in a culture and group and (2) as reflecting our own individuality. Language scholars have taken both into account by distinguishing between denotative and connotative meanings.

Denotative meaning is the meaning assigned to symbols strictly on the basis of cultural commonality. Thus when any English speaker sees a sign reading "Stop," the response expected is clear and uniform across the culture. We have come to expect that pattern of elements to elicit a specific and limited type of meaning. On the other hand, a word like "divorce" also has denotative meaning but may elicit different responses from different subgroups within the population. In our culture divorce usually refers to (i.e., denotes) the dissolution of a marriage by law. It would be difficult to say exactly how that particular set of letters came to represent this particular set of events and legal procedures because the denotative association between the word and what the word represents is purely arbitrary. We can only say that, at some time, our culture agreed upon a fairly definite interpretation of divorce and this became the way in which everyone within the culture has been taught to use and understand it.

When we hear the word divorce, however, we think of more than the defining phrase "the dissolution of a marriage by law." If we happen to be going through these legal procedures ourselves, the word may make us feel awkward; we may think of the unpleasantries involved or feel relieved that we can soon begin a new way of life. If we are strongly religious, we may respond negatively, because we feel that divorce is unthinkable or should be made illegal. If we are attorneys, we may have mixed reactions: divorce may mean a sizeable fee for us, but at the same time, we can feel sorry for the couple involved. Somehow, this sort of reaction to the word—the personal feelings of attitude and emotion—seems different from the meanings we described as denotative. This type of meaning, which varies from person to person and can be directly tied to the individual rather than the culture, is known as **connotative meaning**. It can be defined as the meaning assigned to symbols on the basis of attitudes and emotions.

If we are to understand human communication, it is important to realize the part that meaning plays in the success or failure of any communication situation. Failure to recognize that meanings are learned and that they are in people's minds, not words, may lead to communication breakdowns. At an international level, the difference between the way the Russians and the Americans define the term "human rights" has increased tensions between the two superpowers. At an individual level, the varied attitudes toward the term "abortion" may lead to breakdowns in communication between the source and receiver. It is probable that differences in the meanings held by people—whether they be connotative, denotative, or syntactic meanings—are the primary cause of problems that people have in interacting together.

All code systems, then, are composed of elements that can be structured into patterns. As people learn code systems, the patterns come to acquire connotative, denotative, and syntactic meanings. Success in communication transactions can come only when people have acquired common meanings for the code systems they learn.

Verbal Code Systems

Verbal codes are those codes used to transmit messages utilizing sets of words. If I do not use words, if I use gestures, or pictures, or drawings, or cries, or screeches, I am using a nonverbal code. Verbal codes use a **language**, which can be defined as the *set of all grammatically acceptable sentences that can be constructed from a particular set of words*. This definition assumes a set of words associated with individual natural languages, like the set of all English words or all German words.

The Role of Language in Human Interaction

Most of us acquire the ability to speak at a very early age, so early that we cannot remember the process. Learning to ride a bicycle or learning to swim usually occurs when we are old enough to remember the trials, the problems, and the successes we had. Language seems to have always been with us.

However, languages as individual verbal codes and communication did not just happen. They evolved in response to human needs and developed because there were functions which had to be served. What are these functions? Language has many different functions, but at least three are crucial to successful communication: (1) to learn about the world around us; (2) to conduct our relations with others; and (3) to create coherence in our lives.

The first function views language as the primary medium of information exchange within society. It is difficult to overstate the importance of this role. Because of language, the human animal, unlike all other animals, does not need to directly experience an event to know about the event. You can learn about Russia, its language, economics, politics, psychology, geography, and religions without ever going to Russia or even talking to a Russian. Language enables us to acquire and transmit information in a way that is unique on this planet. As an informal exercise, keep a log for one day, and try to estimate how much new information you acquired. Then estimate how much of that new information came through language and how much through direct experience.

The second function of language serves our interpersonal needs. It allows us to define our roles for the people around us. It is the image function described by Goffman (1959) in his book *The Presentation of Self in Everyday Life*. It may seem trite to say that what others think of us depends on how we use language when interacting with them. However, we often consider this variable only in terms of relationships among individuals rather than in relationships among larger groups like social groups, subcultures, and cultures. This variable will be discussed with respect to social groups later in the chapter. Here let us consider how it can operate in the interaction between cultures. Two examples will illustrate the problem.

A major problem facing Canada has been the possible secession of the Province of Quebec, led by a French Separatist movement, from the Canadian federation. Quebec's French-speaking population has not been content to present itself as a minority group whose tongue differs from that of the English-speaking majority. This is predictable, given the importance of language to a people's cultural heritage. Such problems are not always resolved without bloodshed. In a second situation, the spark which ignited recent race riots in South Africa was the government's insistence that the blacks give up their individual tribal languages in favor of a Dutch-language derivative, Afrikaans. You and I would probably go to similar lengths rather than give up our mother tongue. There can be little doubt about the importance of our language in determining our image of ourselves and others' image of us.

The third function of language, that of providing coherence, is different from either the learning or relating functions. Language need not take the form it does. Instead of constructing sentences as we know them, we could simply string words together in any order we choose. Similarly, sentences in a long message like a speech or essay do not necessarily have to relate to one another in a logical fashion. However, by allowing certain word orders but not others and by demanding that sentences in long messages focus on a particular topic, we can help our audience make better sense of what we are trying to communicate. We can make it easier to learn or respond by using language to make life more organized.

The possession of language does not, of course, guarantee that the three functions described above are always successfully served. We transmit information about the world through language. But "the word is not the object," as S. I. Hayakawa (1964) has pointed out. When meanings are different for different people, information will be imperfectly transmitted. When the phrase "down the road a little bit" means ten miles to the speaker, and one mile to the listener, a communication problem is likely to occur. When a person's reaction to a casual obscenity is so strong that the next ten words of a speaker are not really heard, the message tends to be ineffective. Differences in the way we acquire and use the verbal code system raise serious problems for society as a whole and for us as individuals. Thus one of the communication scholar's goals is to understand language in its relationships with people, objects, and social contexts.

Examining the Verbal Code System

If we are to study the way in which language relates to different aspects of our environment and behavior, it is necessary to understand language as a system in and of itself.

Linguistics is the study of language per se. Traditionally this field focused more on language structure than on the function of language in human communication. Linguists typically spent much of their time collecting samples of actual spoken language and then analyzed the characteristics of the samples. They would painstakingly record the phonetic (or sound) characteristics of the language and look for common patterns or arrangements. The goal was to isolate all the *rules* a native speaker of the language used in combining sounds into sentences and to use the rules to describe the language. It was felt that once all the phonetic and syntactic rules had been identified, a series of principles for effective communication might be identified.

We have learned a great deal about our language from application of the "native speaker" method to the analysis of language. But the application also entailed a lot of problems. It is extremely tedious work. It requires the linguist to be able to identify native speakers and justify their use as representative of all speakers of the language. Most important, it requires the linguist to collect enough samples of the language to be assured that *all* the rules have been identified. This is extremely difficult to do, since most language examples are unique, that is, they have never been said before and may never be said again. The need for examples of all possible combinations proved to be a distinct stumbling block for the traditional linguist.

In the 1950s **Noam Chomsky** (1957) upset the linguistic applecart. He built a linguistic system on two major ideas. First he proposed to distinguish betwen **linguistic performance** and **linguistic competence**. Linguistic performance is the actual use of language in real situations. Linguistic competence is the speaker's underlying knowledge of the language. Chomsky argues that it is our linguistic competence that makes it possible for us to understand and to create sentences that we have never heard before. He suggests that if we did not have such an underlying competence, each time we heard a sentence we would have to hear it again and again until we finally learned it. We do have to operate in such a fashion when we learn to play golf or learn to swim. But our underlying knowledge of the language helps us to understand and communicate.

Chomsky's second major contribution to linguistics was to propose a set of rules which would allow the linguist not only to describe the language, but to take the elements of the language, apply the rules, and actually create grammatically correct sentences. Essentially the system, known as generative-transformational grammar, means that even the most complex sentence can be reduced to a simpler form known as a **kernel sentence**. For example, "It was John who was hit by the car" is reduced or simplified to "The car hit John." By the same token, by applying the generative-transformational rules proposed by Chomsky, the one kernel sentence can be transformed into many complex sentences like "Did the car hit John?" or "John was hit by the car" or "Was it not John who was hit by the car?" In each case, the words of the new sentence are not randomly arranged. There is an underlying rule in the language that allows for the generation of each new, grammatically correct sentence.

In many ways, this approach is like a chess game. When we begin the contest, all the pieces are arranged in a certain pattern on the board much like the linguistic elements in a kernel sentence. Whenever we make a move on the chess board, we rearrange the pieces, but we do it in a manner governed by a set of rules. The bishop can move only in certain ways, while the knight can move only in another set of directions. There are some moves which result in the loss of a piece and others, such as moving a pawn to the other end of the board, which result in the addition of a piece. Similarly, Chomsky's rules prescribe ways of adding, deleting, and rearranging linguistic elements as we move from a kernel sentence to more complex sentences. There are only a small number of rules that govern the game of chess. The board has only sixty-four spaces on it. Yet an almost infinite number of patterns can occur in chess, and for any particular situation, a large number of moves can be made. In similar fashion, Chomsky's postulation of a fairly small set of rules still allows the formulation of an almost infinite number of sentences. The rules of chess and the sequence of their employment result in one of two things—we either win the game or we don't. The same goes when applying Chomsky's rules. If the rules are correctly applied in an acceptable order, the sentence produced will be grammatically acceptable; if they are not, the sentence will be grammatically unacceptable.

Chomsky's work has had tremendous impact for several reasons. First, it demonstrated the enormous complexity and creative potential of language. As speakers, we seldom give much thought to the fact that many of the sentences we construct are unique. They have never been uttered by anyone. Second, given this complexity, our basic knowledge of our language must be phenomenal. In spite of the difficulties most of us have learning about our language in formal grammar classes, all of us use a wide variety of grammatical structures without a moment's hesitation. Third, Chomsky's work brought into focus the issue of how we learn a language. Given the complexity of language and our vast knowledge of it, how are very young children consistently able to master it so quickly? If we can understand the language learning process, we can also hope to improve our abilities as adults.

Learning Verbal Codes

In spite of the complexities involved in English or French or Spanish, a two-year-old child can and usually does master such a language and correctly uses it as a tool for communication. If we could understand just how the child is able to learn a language, it might enable us to help adults improve their communication ability. Three theories propose to account for this amazing ability of children.

At the one extreme is the *behaviorist approach* of B. F. Skinner (1957), which rigorously avoids any discussion of cognitive (thought) processes. Somewhat in the middle are *mediation theories* as represented by Charles Osgood (1963), which examine observable stimuli and responses and on that basis try to explain what is going on in the language user's head. And at the other extreme, some *cognitive theories* focus on and attempt to explain the thought processes involved in the use of language codes.

B. F. Skinner has become famous for his **behaviorist approach** to human learning, the idea that all human behavior can be explained by examining the ways in which the behavior was first conditioned. He suggests that future behavior is dependent on the ways that past behavior was rewarded when it occurred. Thus Skinner takes *operant conditioning* rather than cognitive processes as the basis for language learning.

In **operant conditioning**, when the organism correctly responds to a stimulus, the organism is rewarded, or reinforced, for that behavior. In many, but not all instances, the reward is controlled by someone other than the organism itself. When an infant begins uttering sounds, some of the sounds will be similar to words acceptable to that particular language, and the baby's parents are likely to "reward" the baby with hugs, kisses, and food. Skinner argues that such rewards will increase the probability that the baby will make similar sounds again and again, until the sound comes to be firmly associated with an object or action. Thus the baby may first say "mama" as an accidental set of sounds during a babbling period. If the mother picks up the baby and hugs it immediately afterward, the baby will associate the sound making with the pleasure of being hugged and will repeat the sound again.

Skinner argues that language learning is an operant conditioning pro-

cess from start to finish. It is easy to see how the child might learn "mama" and "dada" through the operant learning process. It is far harder to see how the human being would learn to correctly say complex sentences that have never been said before. It is hard to see how operant conditioning can account for the large vocabulary that children acquire at an early age if reward is needed for the first time the word is uttered. It is difficult to see how Skinner can account for the large passive vocabulary that people acquire where the word is understood but has never been used. Skinner does attempt to provide answers for these questions. He talks about the child learning a number of general language functions through operant conditioning and then just applying other words to those functions when appropriate.

Are Skinner's ideas about language and communication worth arguing about? Most scholars feel strongly that they *are*. If Skinner is correct, we can develop a system of operant conditioning to improve the language behavior of people, to improve vocabulary growth, to improve communication breakdowns among people. The fact that operant conditioning is a relatively simple system and easy to use suggests that considerable attention ought to be given to Skinner's ideas. The reader is referred to Skinner's *Beyond Freedom and Dignity* (1971) as an excellent source for some of the social implications of this position.

Charles Osgood (1963) agrees with Skinner that the ability to use the expression system and to encode and decode messages is gained through a conditioning process. In terms of decoding messages, he argues that we are conditioned to distinguish between the sounds of language and all other sounds. When encoding, we translate nerve impulses we have created within ourselves into learned movements of our articulatory or vocalizing faculties.

Osgood departs from a strict behaviorist position, however, when he attempts to account for the internal cognitive behaviors which take place between the time we decode a message and the time we encode a response to it. His scheme, known as **mediation theory**, is based on the same general principles of stimulus-response-reward advanced by Skinner. But Osgood argues that in addition to those stimuli and responses which are external and observable, there are those involving internal mental processes which occur as a result of perceiving words. An example will help clarify mediation theory.

A baby responds to wet diapers by crying, kicking, and screaming. When the baby's mother hears the baby crying, or sees it kicking, the mother might say "wet diaper" and then proceed to change the baby. The child has now been rewarded, since the child feels comfortable. What has happened in conditioning terms is that the sounds "wet diaper" have been paired with the sensations that accompany such a condition. If the paired situation occurs several more times, the child will soon learn that the sound "wet diaper" can come to stand for the feelings experienced. Osgood would argue that the child has thereby acquired a meaning for the sounds. Since the child learned the words by pairing them with the real thing, Osgood says, his cognitive response to the words will always retain parts of his original external response to wet diapers themselves. As an adult, he might experience this retention as a generalized feeling of discomfort. This internal response can lead to an internal self-stimulation which, in turn, often results in an external response, such as entering the nursery to make sure his own child has dry pants. The important point here is that he is responding to the meaning—the internal response and consequent self-stimulus he has for the words "wet diaper"—rather than to wet diapers themselves. Osgood would argue that one of the strong points about his theory is that it seems to account for the different connotative meanings we each develop, pointing out that our original experiences with cats, dogs, snakes, and roses are different and thus the things that will be internalized as connotative meanings are also going to be different for each of us.

The mediation hypothesis seems to be able to explain how we learn the meaning of a word like "wet" in relation to objects other than diapers. There are wet floors, water is wet, and so forth. A Skinnerian has difficulty handling this problem realistically. The mediation theory would suggest that first we respond internally to the individual words in the message, then to the way they are ordered in the message, and finally to all words in the message. This allows us to respond differently to

"Mary hit Jim" and "Jim hit Mary," even though both have the same linguistic elements. The theory is also able to explain cases where our response is so well learned that we do not have to go through these complex procedures, such as when we hear "Duck!" or "Watch out!" We have so completely internalized the message that mediation is automatic and our response habitual.

Osgood's theory represents an important attempt to relate language and thought. And it has proven to be directly useful in developing practical methods of communication analysis.

One alternative to the stimulus-response theories advanced by Osgood and Skinner are the **cognitive theories** set forth by some psychologists. Cognitive psychologists who are concerned about language behavior often adopt the work of Chomsky as a basis for theories of language development and focus on the things a speaker would need to know to *use* language. In other words, they focus on linguistic competence rather than on linguistic performance. While Skinner examined language without considering thought processes and Osgood attempted to show a direct relationship between language and thought, a cognitive approach would argue that we actually think in kernel sentences. For example, if we hear the sentence "Didn't John drink the beer?" we will store the kernel sentence "John drank the beer." Somewhere along the line we must account for our ability to reproduce the sentence as stated rather than just the kernel sentence form. One explanation of this ability suggests that along with the kernel sentence, we abstract and store certain clues from the original sentence which remind us that it was negative, interrogative, and so on.

If this is really what people do when they perceive sentences, where did they acquire the ability to perform these seemingly complex tasks? If we sit down with a paper and pencil, it takes a fair amount of time to go through the process of reducing a sentence to its kernel form and then translating it back to its original form. There are many transformational rules; just to describe the ones for English would take a book larger than this one. There are also different rules for different languages. How are we to account for the ability that nearly all human beings have to be able to use language appropriately?

One answer Chomsky gives is that there is a biologically innate ability to learn language which is peculiar to humans. This position was also maintained by the late Eric Lenneberg (1964), who pointed out that even children who were isolated for long periods of time were able to acquire language with minimal effort. Chomsky and Lenneberg argue that the types of learning theories advanced by Osgood and Skinner require so much effort and time that no child could learn to speak as rapidly as children actually do. They hold that the only possible explanation for language acquisition is some biological built-in mechanisms that predispose the human being to speech.

We have examined the three currently most popular psychological theories of language development and use. What conclusions can be drawn? Although these theories differ in certain respects, they all agree that learning *is* important (though it may not be the only thing that takes place in language development and use). This consensus suggests that it is possible to improve one's communication behavior and that attention paid to learning theory principles can help. There is also agreement between the mediation theorists and the cognitive theorists on the importance of meaning to communication.

Once again we come back to meaning as a critical issue in dealing with verbal codes. There are two areas in which it must be examined. The first is meaning in relation to language and cognition (i.e., how we assign meanings to the ongoing interactions in which we are engaged), and the second is meaning in relation to language and social structure (how our meanings and language are associated with our social environment).

Verbal Codes and Cognition

There has been a great deal of research on how people cognitively process a single sentence. Our concern, however, is more often with connected discourse, sets of connected sentences, than with individual sentences. A communicator needs to know how a receiver makes sense of what is said from the beginning of a message to the end. Frequently this involves more than a single sentence, and the meaning assigned is different from the sum of meanings assigned to the individual sentences.

The notion that we might seek to assign meanings to messages longer than a sentence has been around a long time. The first systematic research on how that might be done began with a distinction made by Michael Halliday (1967). He proposed that sentences contain two kinds of information: given information—information the listener is assumed to have; and new information—information the listener is assumed *not* to have. Speakers were thought to adapt to their listeners in part by anticipating which information the listener did indeed already possess and then help the listener by stressing the new information in the sentence. Consider the sentence "John painted the barn." If the speaker places stress on the word "John," he assumes that the listener knows someone painted the barn but does not know who did it. If the speaker stresses "painted," it implies that the listener knows that John did something to the barn but is not sure exactly what. Finally, if "the barn" is stressed, the listener is assumed to know that John painted something but not to know what it was.

Let's extend this idea to connected discourse as has been done by Herbert Clark (1973). Consider the sentences "John spent three days trying to contact his travel agent. He was finally able to arrange his itinerary." Notice that the second sentence presupposes that John had already spent time trying to arrange his itinerary. What the speaker has done is provide the background information so that the second sentence will make sense. Clark argues that we all subscribe to a "social contract" in which we agree to structure information in this way for the listener. It makes comprehension and recall easy because all the listener has to do is keep adding the new information in succeeding sentences to the old information already received from earlier sentences. If the order of the sentences were reversed, processing the information would be much more difficult. After hearing that "He was finally able to arrange his itinerary," the listener would be faced with several questions which need answers for comprehension to occur (e.g., Who was? What was the problem? How long did he try?). The processing is actually more complex than this, but the critical idea is that we actually have a system which makes it easier for listeners to assign meaning to what we are saying. Among other things, this sytem suggests that becoming competent as a communicator involves more than learning to construct grammatically acceptable sentences. Research conducted since Clark published his findings consistently shows that listeners do attempt to find a theme or central meaning for messages. Thus the advice to systematically develop the ideas in a public speech is no simple nicety but a key factor in communicating with an audience.

Verbal Codes, Societies, and Cultures

Experience tells us that people with different social and cultural backgrounds talk differently. People from the North do not talk the same as do those from the South or those from the Far West. Engineers do not use the same terminology as do insurance salespersons. Do these differences make a difference in the ways people communicate? Do cultural language differences make a difference in the ways people think about the world? Let us briefly examine some of the effects of the sociocultural context.

Some anthropologists argue that our language is a determining factor in the way we perceive the world. Such an approach would argue, for example, that skiers can perceive "powder" and "popcorn" as different types of snow because they have developed an individual word to describe each. In other words, those concepts have no meaning without labels. The implication is that if a culture has developed a rich language and extensive vocabulary, people in the culture will be able to perceive far more things in the world around them than will the culture which has a limited language. This view of language has even made it possible to contend that a thorough psychological examination of a culture could be made using that culture's language as the source of data.

The central source for an anthropological view of language behavior is stated in the **Whorf-Sapir hypothesis**. This hypothesis, first advanced by Benjamin Lee Whorf (1956) and Edward Sapir, posits that (1) without language we cannot think; (2) language influences perception; and (3) language influences thinking patterns. Think for just a minute about the evidence you might want to gather to prove that any of these three hypotheses were true.

The first idea's correctness depends partly on a definition of thinking and partly on being able to find someone who has no language at all. There seems to be no way, given available scientific techniques, to either prove or to disprove this point. Whorf and Sapir posited the second point when they found that some languages did not contain words for objects found in other languages. For example, some languages do not contain words for certain colors. More recent studies, however, have shown that people have no trouble in distinguishing between colors even when they do not have a specific word for the color. Research *has* supported the final point and thus provided us with a needed link between psychological, sociological, and cultural aspects of language.

The support for Whorf and Sapir's third idea came in a simple but ingenious experiment. It was noted that in the Navajo language verb endings are dependent on the physical shape of the subject of the sentence. The researcher reasoned that if Navajo-speaking children were given a set of objects which could be grouped according to either shape or color, they would match the objects on the basis of shape. On the other hand, English-speaking Navajo children would classify the objects on the basis of color, since the verb endings and subject shapes are independent in the English language. Both of the hypotheses were supported. The conclusion is obvious. The language of the individual was responsible, in part, for the thought processes which led to the way in which the children grouped the objects. While there may be some other language-related factors that could be advanced to account for some of these differences, differences in language between the children do seem important.

The Whorf-Sapir hypothesis was developed largely through the efforts of anthropologists, who take entire cultures for their area of concern. Sociologists, on the other hand, take a single culture but look at the differences that might be created within the culture by social, economic, and educational variables. The sociologists would not disagree with the anthropologists about the importance of culture in language. But they suggest that many of the more important differences among people may be caused by the differences *within* a culture, not the language differences between cultures.

Sociolinguistics is the study of the relationship between language and society which posits that social structure and context determine language. Although this is the reverse of the anthropologists' basic assumption, both are to some degree accurate. Social structure, culture, and language all influence one another in a wide variety of ways. Much of the seminal work in the area stems from Basil Bernstein's (1973) research, which compared the language styles of middle-class and working-class (e.g., factory worker) families. Bernstein and his colleagues have consistently found two differences in the linguistic codes employed by the two groups. First, middle-class speakers tend to use more of the available syntactic structures than do working-class families. The differences in the number of syntactic structures employed is not large, but it is noticeable. Given the many syntactic structures available in any language, the failure to employ some of them does not prevent working-class speakers from expressing any ideas they may choose. Second, working-class speakers express context-bound meanings while middle-class speakers attempt to make expressed meanings more context free. For example, the sentence "Isn't that wonderful" expresses a context-bound meaning. The listener is required to know what "that" refers to if the sentence is to make sense. The meaning could be made more context free if it were expressed as "Isn't it wonderful that tuition at Michigan State has been reduced." Bernstein found that working-class speakers express meanings which are context bound in two senses: (1) the speakers assume the listener's familiarity with the current situation rather than using language to make the context explicit and clear; and (2) the exact operations involved in performing a behavior and the reasons why it should be performed (i.e., the principles underlying the behavior) are implicit. The middle-class speaker tends to make them explicit for the listener. Bernstein referred to the language used by working-class individuals as a **restricted code** and the language used by middle-class speakers as an **elaborated code**.

Given these conceptions of elaborated and restricted codes, it should not be surprising that there was a great deal of controversy about whether the restricted code was inferior to the elaborated code (the deficit hypothesis) or merely different from it (the difference hypothesis). As long as the language code used meets the needs of the speaker, there is no reason to consider it deficient. This is not to say that the differences do not matter in day-to-day affairs. For example, in this country it has been shown that students who typically employ a linguistic code different from that used by the middle class receive lower grades for equivalent answers on tests.

There are four areas in which social groups seem to use language differently. Bernstein calls these the regulative, the instructional, the imaginative, and the interpersonal.

The regulative, or control, function refers to the strategies employed by individuals to control the behavior of others. In Bernstein's research it refers almost exclusively to the ways mothers control their young children and the ways these children then use language to control others. Middle-class children and mothers were found more likely to provide the listener with some principle or rationale to guide future behavior. The working-class mothers and children placed a greater reliance on "simple rule-announcing statements."

The instructional function refers to the use of language in teaching children. The researchers found that middle-class mothers placed a greater reliance on words while working-class mothers tended to employ actions rather than words for teaching complex activities. Further, working-class mothers had a greater tendency to avoid answering difficult questions posed by the children.

The imaginative function refers to the use of language as it relates to fantasy. Fantasy and play are critical to developing a creative imagination in the child. There is some evidence to indicate that middle-class mothers encourage such behavior more and see its relevance for education more than working-class mothers.

The interpersonal context refers to the uses to which language is put when interacting with others. Bernstein's colleagues found that working-class mothers used language for teaching basic motor skills while middle-class mothers tended to emphasize language use for dealing with persons, e.g., "letting them know what you are feeling" and "dealing with them when they are unhappy."

There are obvious advantages and disadvantages to both working- and middle-class socialization processes. We will leave these for you to consider. There are two points to keep in mind, however. First, the way we are spoken to as children helps determine our attitudes and our connotative meanings concerning fantasy, social relations versus skills, interpersonal control, and the like. Second, the communication styles we eventually adopt as adults are highly influenced by those styles our parents employed in dealing with us.

We have yet to consider the social circumstances which give rise to the code differences and their implications. Bernstein suggests the following antecedent conditions. First, restricted codes will emerge in situations where there are strongly shared assumptions and expectations. To the extent that assumptions are not shared by members of a given family or group, elaborated codes will emerge. Second, restricted codes emerge in situations where there are high levels of social solidarity; a lack of solidarity requires elaborated codes. Third, a restricted code "presupposes a generalized other," i.e., one who can be categorized, while an elaborated code presupposes a sharp boundary between self and other, a differentiated or unique other. Fourth, when the principles and operations underlying behavior must be made explicit, elaborated codes will be used. When they need not be explicit, restricted codes will emerge.

Bernstein's work seems to pinpoint some of the major problems that people have in communicating. Almost everyone has noted that it is difficult to communicate with someone who is vastly different from oneself. If you come from an upper-class family, have gone to private schools, and are a corporation lawyer, you will likely have a problem talking with an individual coming from a working-class family, who didn't complete high school, and works as a dishwasher. If we realize that some of these difficulties in communicating may come from the nature of the code systems we use, efforts can be made to alleviate them. If we know that some children have trouble learning in school simply because of their code system, efforts can be made to help them.

The sociologist and anthropologist do not disagree with the linguist or psychologist. What they have done for the study of langauge is to point out the consequences of differences in our social and cultural systems. Thus, with the addition of materials from anthropology and sociology, we have come full circle. We have shown that our verbal code systems can be described in terms of their elements and a set of rules for combining those elements. We have shown that it is possible to speculate on the ways in which we acquire both the elements and the rules. And we have shown that the people we live with, and the experiences we have, affect our language performance and that our language performance is affected by our experiences.

Nonverbal Code Systems

If words are not involved in a communication situation, we can say that we are dealing with a **nonverbal code** system. Theories about verbal code systems are not necessarily confined to verbal behavior. Nonverbal codes, as we shall see, may have elements as well as rules which allow for the combination of elements. However, scholars have been formally concerned with verbal codes for far longer than they have with nonverbal codes, and we know far more about their structure. In recent years the number of scholars studying nonverbal communication has dramatically increased. They can be found not only in departments of communication but also in departments of anthropology, sociology, psychology, and medicine. Interest in this area probably began in 1873 with Charles Darwin (1955), who wrote an early treatise on facial expression. Since then, many people have commented on the importance of nonverbal code systems to the success of human communication.

Figure 2–1
Relationship of Verbal and Nonverbal Code Systems in Human Interaction

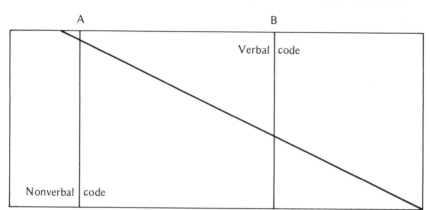

Just how important nonverbal code systems are in our daily life can be seen in some of the following situations. If you walked or drove to get to class, you were guided by traffic signs. Many traffic signs bear no words, but you have learned to interpret the nonverbal clues they display. The dress of the people around you may be a good indicator of the role they play in society. The businessman wears a suit during the week. On the weekend he may wear shorts and a T-shirt, thus signifying the change in his role from work to play. You would communicate differently with him depending on the nonverbal messages given off by dress. The newspaper you read this morning directs your attention to important stories via the size of the headline and the placement of the items. In the supermarket, manufacturers use colors, shapes, and sizes to attract customers to their products. And the supermarket manager places items on the shelves in ways he hopes will attract buyers to the more expensive products. Nonverbal code systems help govern our daily lives. Harrison (1974) suggests that we can look at any communication situation as a blend of verbal and nonverbal communication. Figure 2–1 illustrates the overlap between the two kinds of communication. The line drawn through the chart at Point A suggests a situation in which most of the message is being carried through the nonverbal code, while the line at Point B indicates a communication situation where more of the message is being carried by the verbal band.

Interaction of Verbal and Nonverbal Codes

Nonverbal behavior interacts with and consequently affects the interpretation of verbal messages. Knapp (1978) summarizes the work of several people in stating that nonverbal behavior can repeat, contradict, substitute for, complement, accent, or regulate verbal behavior. The gesture of pointing to a building and saying, "That is the library," in response to the question "Where is the library?" exemplifies a nonverbal behavior repeating the verbal message. Frowning, looking at one's watch, and edging toward an exit while saying to another person, "Yes, I have time to talk with you," illustrates nonverbal behaviors contradicting the verbal communication. An example of nonverbal behaviors substituting for verbal behaviors would be the common waving of greetings or goodbyes, particularly when at a large distance from the person, without the accompanying words of "Hi" or "Bye." The media use nonverbal codes to complement meanings conveyed via the spoken message. For example, soft background music and dimmed lights during a passionate embrace by lovers on the movie set add to the verbal endearments they may be exchanging. Pounding on the lectern may help a speaker accent certain points in his speech. Finally, students are adept at forcing a professor to conclude a lecture by putting on their coats and collecting their books, thus regulating the communication. Many other types of nonverbal behaviors from facial expressions to use of space can affect the flow and meaning of communication interactions.

Many communication situations do not involve verbal communication at all. Because it takes less formal education to interpret the nonverbal code, a larger number of people are dependent on the nonverbal system for their information.

One reason the nonverbal code requires less formal education has to do with the concept of iconicity. **Iconicity** is the degree to which code elements and patterns resemble their referents (the things to which they refer). An example will clarify. You could say, "I was walking down the street and suddenly I stumbled," while actually going through the motions of walking and stumbling. Your actions of walking and stumbling would resemble what happened on the street more closely than the words themselves would. The actions are more iconic than words. Or you may be asked for directions and respond by saying, "It is straight north of here." At the same time, you point to the north. The pointing action is a more iconic symbol than the word and can be understood by someone who may not know what direction north is.

Verbal codes are characteristically less iconic than nonverbal codes. However, there is a range of iconicity among the nonverbal codes. For example, the fact that we stop on the red and go on the green traffic signal is arbitrary. The color red does not in any way resemble a lack of movement and thus has a very low iconicity. The arrow on a traffic sign indicating a sharp curve has a high degree of iconicity and requires almost no training to understand.

Nonverbal codes have been categorized in several different ways. Some ways look at the relationship of the nonverbal system to the verbal by examining the "paralinguistic," or nonverbal, elements of the verbal code. Other systems examine portions of the nonverbal band, e.g., facial movements or dance movements. The category scheme we will use was first set forth by Harrison (1974). It has the advantage of categorizing a lot of nonverbal behavior with just four types of codes. These are: (1) **performance codes**, which the body produces; (2) **artifactual codes**, which involve the arrangement and manipulation of inanimate objects such as clothing and furniture; (3) **mediatory codes**, which deal with the ways people like artists, photographers, and film makers get us to perceive specific things in their works; and (4) **spatio-temporal codes**, which pertain to the use of space and time in communicating.

Performance Codes

Cries, shouts, and screams are nonverbal messages which fall into the category of performance codes. Also in this category are aspects of a vocal message that are nonverbal, or **paralinguistic**—e.g., the rate, pitch, and intensity with which we speak. From one speaking situation to another we vary the pitch and control of our voice and the rate of word production. While these features of our speech are closely related to the verbal system, they must be considered part of the nonverbal code. They tell us how important the speaker feels the message is, how confident or how nervous the speaker is, and, in general, how speakers communicate emotional states.

The paralinguistic aspects of vocal messages are often crucial to a full understanding of what is being communicated. To look at some other performance codes, we shall consider a category system first developed by Paul Ekman and Wallace Friesen (1969).

Emblems are learned, highly stylized nonverbal symbols having a certain meaning within a culture or subculture. They include elements which are low in iconicity such as the "peace sign" and the "thumbs up" signal of the hitchhiker. Emblems can be used either with or without verbal accompaniment, and the same signal can vary in meaning from one culture or time to another. For example, the peace sign is used by young people to designate freedom from war, but its use in that fashion may be confusing to people who learned it as a gesture for victory in World War II. Emblems are often used in place of a verbal message. The hitchhiker doesn't have time to ask passing motorists for a lift. But his signal is so well known that almost every driver in the country knows what he wants.

While emblems do not require the use of a verbal message, **illustrators** make little or no sense without an accompanying verbal message. They are defined as the nonverbal signs used to clarify verbal messages. The most familiar illustrators are those we call "talking with the hands." The use of illustrators, like emblems, varies from country to country. In this country we indicate height by holding our hand in the air with the

palm facing down. In some South American countries, the palm faces down when indicating the height of animals and faces upward when indicating the height of people. This type of illustrator is called a *spatial* and is primarily used to indicate size. Other illustrators include *pointers*, which are simply used to point out objects, and *batons*, which pound out a beat for a verbal message. Ministers sometimes use batons when they wish to be particularly forceful, such as when they say, "You (pound) must (pound) repent (pound)!"

Notice that illustrators are more iconic than emblems. Although we often use them unconsciously, they can be effective communication aids. We can provide additional information when verbal code systems fail us. We use illustrators to indicate the height of people, size of fish, and direction to a town. In each case, the verbal element may well be rather vague (such as the use of the word "tall"), and the use of an illustrator helps specify what is meant.

Regulators are the nonverbal signs we use to control (or at least guide) the behavior of others when we interact with them. For example, if you are at a party and wish to talk with a specific person, you could let him know your intentions by catching and holding his gaze for a moment. You might also raise your eyebrows and nod slightly. Much like illustrators, the use of regulators varies from culture to culture and are often used unconsciously. The next time you're talking with someone, see if you don't wait until they look directly at you before you respond to their last statement. In our culture, when someone looks off to the side or down at the floor, it usually means that he or she is thinking about what to say next rather than seeking a response. If you really want to see regulators in action, engage someone in a conversation when he is in a hurry to get somewhere else. Generally, he will look at his watch, tap his feet, look at everyone in the room but you, and start inching toward the door.

The final kind of performance code is **affect displays**. These are the nonverbal behaviors we use to convey emotions. We smile, frown, wrinkle up our face, open our mouth, expand our nostrils, and widen our eyes to show happiness, sadness, disgust, and a whole range of emotions. Different cultures vary in their use of affect displays during communication situations. Thus in one culture people will refrain from showing sadness in public upon the death of a loved one but exhibit sadness when talking to close relatives. In other cultures "keeping a stiff upper lip" is not expected, and an individual not showing sadness would be thought peculiar. Although cultures may differ in terms of when it is appropriate to display emotion, there does seem to be a basic set of emotions, including happiness, surprise, sadness, fear, and disgust, which elicit the same facial expressions in all societies.

Facial expressions are not the only means of showing emotions; gestures, body movements, and paralinguistics are other means. It is also interesting to note that people have differing abilities to correctly identify the emotions being expressed nonverbally. This suggests that performance codes are learned, and that although there may be some basic facial expressions for different emotions, we can learn through experience and training to improve our abilities at deciphering a particular expression.

Artifactual Codes

Archeologists often learn much about past cultures by examining the things they produced—their artifacts. We gather similar information from the artifacts utilized by individuals, institutions, cities, and even countries. Harrison suggests that there are three types of artifacts important to human communication: (1) *personal artifacts* such as clothing, cosmetics, jewelry, and hair styles; (2) *shared artifacts* such as furniture; and (3) *public artifacts* such as municipal buildings and monuments.

Personal artifacts are important in creating impressions and thus in aiding the communication process. A man wearing a fashionable suit is responded to by salespeople, police officers, and students in a different way from a man wearing a set of bib overalls. We may not like to believe that we communicate differently to people because of the way in which they dress, but test the premise yourself; watch closely what happens when you get dressed up versus what happens when you appear in very casual clothes.

Shared artifacts and public artifacts also help indicate the ways in which we expect communication to take place. On any campus we can frequently tell the graduate students from the faculty simply by the furnishings in their office. And we can frequently tell the status of a public agency by the newness of the office building in which the department is housed.

Mediatory Codes

The various media, especially film and television, are often able to work with nonverbal patterns all their own. Interesting examples of how artists have used mediatory codes can be found every month in the ads placed by the Book-of-the-Month Club for their "Art Seminars in the Home." One of these relates the story of King Henry VIII and his search for a fourth wife. It seems the king wasn't willing to make the trip across Europe to meet his two prospective brides in person. Therefore he sent Holbein the Younger to paint and bring back their portraits. To convey the intelligence and vivaciousness of Christina of Denmark, the artist painted her in dark clothes which would not take attention away from the princess herself. Anne of Cleves was a rather bland individual; Holbein made this apparent in the painting by her gaudy costume, which takes the viewer's attention away from her plain face and downcast eyes.

Modern television producers make use of mediatory codes to carry their message. The dress of a character may indicate whether the audience is supposed to like or dislike the character. The way in which one scene follows another, i.e., the cuts, fades, and dissolves, may indicate the passage of time, the importance of the scene, the status of the actor, and other elements that would take many minutes to explain using a verbal code. Try watching television with the sound off. You will find that often little of a message is lost by the absence of a verbal code. This is particularly true of commercials, where the advertiser has little time to convey his message and frequently does so with minimum use of the verbal band and much use of mediatory code systems.

Spatio-temporal Codes

Since we have no alternative but to exist in time and space, it is difficult to stand back and objectively view them as means of communication. Perhaps a few examples can help us see just how we use temporal and spatial relationships to express our messages.

When we have an important appointment, such as a job interview, we make every effort to arrive on time. The message we are trying to communicate is the image of an industrious person who is eager to work. When we go to a party, on the other hand, we never arrive early and rarely on time. Heaven forbid that others should think we don't know enough to be "socially late." These are examples of using time to communicate an impression of ourselves.

There is another side of the coin—how long a wait are we willing to tolerate due to the tardiness of others? To communicate some measure of respect, students will generally wait longer for a full professor who doesn't arrive in class on time than they will for a graduate assistant. In similar fashion, if the mayor is late for a meeting, one worries less about it than if the mayor's secretary is late for a meeting. In some cultures, status is precisely indicated by the lateness of an individual's arrival at a meeting, with the persons of highest status expected to be extremely late.

Time can communicate; so can space. Edward T. Hall, in his book *The Silent Language* (1959), has shown that white middle-class Americans use four different **interaction zones**, which are the distances people attempt to keep between themselves and others on different occasions. The zone chosen is regulated by the nature of the discussion and the relationship of the people involved. The first zone, *intimate distance*, ranges from physical contact to about eighteen inches. Adults usually do not use this zone in public settings unless they are in a crowded elevator or similar situation. The second zone, *personal distance*, extends from eighteen inches to four feet. At any party, notice that couples tend to maintain this distance; others move together in order to discuss some personal matter. The third zone, *social distance*, runs from four feet to twelve feet and is often used to transact business. The fourth zone, *public distance*, begins at twelve feet and extends to the limits of our voices and hearing. Teachers, ministers, and public speakers are about the only individuals who make extensive use of this zone.

Although the use of space is learned by the members of a culture, it can become an important part of any communication situation. A failure to observe the distances for particular kinds of communication can result in a complete communication failure. If you don't think so, try a simple experiment. Go shopping and approach a salesperson in a department store to ask for the location of the furniture department. Ap-

proach the salesperson so that you are only two feet away before you begin asking about the furniture department. In nine cases out of ten, the salesperson will back hastily away from you. You have used an intimate distance to communicate when you would be expected to use a social distance.

Spatio-temporal codes differ widely from culture to culture. For example, when we have an appointment in someone's office, we get irritated if we have to sit waiting for more than five or ten minutes. In some foreign countries, however, it is nothing to wait for up to an hour. It is often assumed that you will arrive at least forty minutes late anyway. In such a situation, the individual arriving "on time" is considered the peculiar one.

Knowing something about nonverbal codes will aid the communicator in improving overall communication. It works in two ways. As a receiver of communication, we should be able to recognize the messages being transmitted through the nonverbal band as well as those being transmitted through the verbal band. At times, people send conflicting messages. They say one thing, but their bodily movements say another. Being able to interpret the nonverbal code is important if the receiver is to make an accurate assessment of the messages being sent.

When we are the source of communication, the nonverbal messages we send are just as important as the verbal messages. Are we saying one thing and signaling another? Is the message we have important, but the clothes we wear tell the receiver another story? What setting should we pick in order to be maximally effective? How we answer these questions can mean the difference between success and failure in our communicative ventures.

Conclusion

Typically, when we think of the word "message" we think of words. Words may well be used, but they are only part of the story. Before any individual can exhibit some aspect of linguistic performance, there has to be linguistic competence. The message that is eventually created is complex. Its reception may depend on both linguistic and paralinguistic elements present within the message. And the receiver may have individual or cultural characteristics that help or hinder the reception of the message.

Successful communication is not simply a matter of "sending a message." The type of message sent, the way it is sent, the form it takes, and the nature of the communication situation itself may all play a part in the eventual success of communication. In our next chapter we shall look at some principles to aid us in effective message composition, using either speech or writing.

TERMS AND CONCEPTS FOR REVIEW

affect displays
artifactual codes
behaviorist approach (Skinner)
Chomsky's theories
code system
cognitive theories

connotative meaning
denotative meaning
elaborated code
elements
emblems
iconicity

illustrators
interaction zones (Hall)
kernel sentence
language
linguistic competence
linguistic performance
linguistics
mediation theory (Osgood)
mediatory codes
nonverbal codes
operant conditioning
paralinguistics
patterns

performance codes
personal artifacts
public artifacts
regulators
restricted code
semantic rules and meaning
shared artifacts
sociolinguistic theory (Bernstein)
spatio-temporal codes
syntactic rules and meaning
verbal codes
Whorf-Sapir hypothesis

REVIEW QUESTIONS

1. What are syntactic rules and semantic rules? Give examples.
2. What is the difference between denotative meaning and connotative meaning?
3. What is the difference between linguistic performance and linguistic competence?
4. How do the behaviorist approach, mediation theory, and cognitive theory differ in explaining the learning of verbal codes?
5. What is the Whorf-Sapir hypothesis?
6. According to Bernstein, what is the difference between restricted codes and elaborated codes?
7. What are six ways in which nonverbal communication interacts with verbal communication?
8. What are paralinguistic features, emblems, illustrators, regulators, and affect displays? Give examples.
9. What are personal, shared, and public artifacts? Give examples.
10. What are mediatory codes? Give examples.
11. What are spatio-temporal codes? Give examples.
12. What are the differences among intimate, personal, social, and public distances?

REFERENCES

Bernstein, B. (ed.). *Class, Codes, and Control.* Vol. 2. London: Routledge and Kegan Paul, 1973.

Clark, H. H. "Comprehension and the Given-new Contract." Paper presented at the conference on "The Role of Grammar in Interdisciplinary Linguistic Research," University of Bielefeld, Bielefeld, Germany, December 1973.

Chomsky, N. *Syntactic Structures*. The Hague: Mouton, 1957.

――――. *Aspects of the Theory of Syntax*. Cambridge, Mass.: M.I.T. Press, 1965.

Darwin, Charles. *The Expression of the Emotions in Man and Animals*. New York: Philosophical Library, 1955.

Ekman, P., and W. V. Friesen. "The Repertoire of Nonverbal Behavior: Categories, Origins, Usage, and Coding." *Semiotica*, 1969, 1, 49–98.

Goffman, E. *The Presentation of Self in Everyday Life*. New York: Doubleday, 1959.

Hall, E. T. *The Silent Language*. Greenwich, Conn.: Fawcett, 1959.

Halliday, M. A. K. "Notes on Transitivity and Theme in English: II." *Journal of Linguistics*, 1967, 3, 199–244.

――――. *Learning How to Mean: Explorations in the Development of Language*. London: Edward Arnold, 1975.

Harrison, R. P. *Beyond Words: An Introduction to Nonverbal Communication*. Englewood Cliffs, N.J.: Prentice-Hall, 1974.

Hayakawa, S. I. *Language in Thought and Action*. 4th ed. New York: Harcourt Brace Jovanovich, 1978.

Knapp, Mark L. *Nonverbal Communication in Human Interaction*. 2nd ed. New York: Holt, Rinehart & Winston, 1978.

Lenneberg, E. H. "A Biological Perspective of Language." In E. H. Lenneberg (ed.), *New Directions in the Study of Language*. Cambridge, Mass.: M.I.T. Press, 1964.

Osgood, C. E. "On Understanding and Creating Sentences." *American Psychologist*, 1963, 18, 735–75.

Skinner, B. F. *Verbal Behavior*. New York: Appleton-Century-Crofts, 1957.

――――. *Beyond Freedom and Dignity*. New York: Alfred A. Knopf, 1971.

Whorf, B. L. *Language, Thought, and Reality*. New York: John Wiley & Sons, 1956.

Informative Messages
PRINCIPLES

ORGANIZATION PATTERNS
    Time
    Space

Persuasive Messages
THE PROPOSITION, OR THESIS

RATIONAL APPEALS
    Principles
    Toulmin model of argument
    Organizing Arguments into Messages

MOTIVATIONAL APPEALS
    Biological drives
    Learned motives
    Motivated sequence
    Problem-solution pattern

3

Message Construction

After reading this chapter, you should be able to:

1. Organize persuasive and informative messages according to the patterns discussed in the text.
2. Evaluate and construct informative messages according to the seven principles discussed in the text.
3. Break down simple arguments into their component parts according to the Toulmin model of argument.
4. Evaluate evidence, or data, offered in support of a claim according to five general standards, or tests of evidence.
5. Construct simple and complex arguments following the pattern of the full Toulmin model of argument.

In chapter 1 we argued that communication allows people to manage their environment in a number of important ways. In chapter 2 we discussed some of the code systems that people have developed to be able to send and receive messages. Even when we have acquired a set of code systems, however, and have learned how to use them, sources and receivers can improve their abilities by learning how to tie code systems to communication goals. Some messages are designed to induce learning, some to change attitudes, some to maintain social relations, and some to directly affect the behavior of receivers. We will use code systems differently in arriving at the messages we construct for different situations.

The purpose of this chapter is to outline a series of principles which will aid in constructing certain types of messages. Our focus will be restricted to two types of messages: those intended to induce learning and those intended to produce attitude or behavior changes. These will be called informative messages and persuasive messages.

There are similarities in the messages people construct, even though sources and receivers are attempting to meet different needs and goals. For example, you have learned that all messages use code systems, either verbal or nonverbal, and the symbols in those systems are usually common to all members of a given culture. Although the messages will differ, the basic patterns of organization used in message construction are much the same for all informative and persuasive messages.

The first section of the chapter looks at the nature and organization of informative messages. The second is concerned with persuasive messages. It looks first at "rational appeals," including a discussion of rationality, the structure of rational arguments, and some of the ways in which individual arguments can be organized into more complex messages. We then examine the nature of "motivational appeals" and the ways in which they can be organized into more complex messages. We feel strongly that receivers as well as sources should know something about how messages are organized. After all, we are all exposed to far more messages sent to us than we can ever send to others. Understanding how people may be affected by message organization can help us understand our own response to a message.

The distinction between informative and persuasive messages is not as easy to make as it might seem. All messages seek to have an effect, either to change or reinforce knowledge, attitudes, or behaviors. Information exchanged in informative messages is generally used as a means to some other end. Thus, for example, one person might inform another of the rules of chess, but only as a means of getting the other to be willing to play a game. But, in general, informative and persuasive messages can be distinguished by the *intent* of the source and how specific the goal of the message is. Persuasive messages have an explicit goal of trying to change or maintain a particular attitude or behavior of the receiver. A purely informative message seeks only to transmit information accurately, without specifying what use the receiver should make of that information. For example, a newspaper might provide its readers with information about the voting record of a political candidate but stop short of suggesting what they should do with the information. A persuasive message might use the same information but would combine it with an appeal to vote for or against the candidate. Newspapers provide persuasive messages of this type in their endorsements of candidates at the end of a political campaign. As this example indicates, however, the dividing line between informative and persuasive messages is fuzzy, and a skilled persuader can hide a powerful appeal in what appears to be a purely informative message. We will therefore point out additional means of distinguishing between the two types of messages as we develop our discussion.

Informative Messages

As indicated, persuasive and informative messages can be differentiated on the basis of how specific the goal of the messages is. Persuasive messages tend to be centered on a particular goal a source would like to achieve. Informative messages are much more diffuse. They are concerned primarily with receivers *learning* some body of information. The use the receivers make of that information is usually of secondary importance. In fact, receivers may behave the same toward a persuasive message as they do toward an informative one. The central criterion for judging the quality of an informative message, and for guiding the construction of informative messages, is *accuracy*.

Unfortunately, we have not yet discovered any completely effective method of insuring the accurate reception of a message. A source cannot just *pour* a message into the ears of a receiver and expect that perfect understanding will take place. Receivers differ in their interests, motivations, and abilities, all of which will affect whether an information exchange will succeed or fail. Nevertheless, some guidelines can be offered to help communicators create messages that will be received accurately.

Principles

Communication is a transactional process, and there has to be a mutual understanding on the part of both source and receiver as to the nature of the informational process. The following principles, if applied sensitively and intelligently, will allow sources to construct informative messages which will be accurately received by at least most people of average interests, motivations, and abilities:

1. Make the message as simple as possible with a clear purpose statement. One of the major problems many of us encounter in constructing informative messages is that we try to tell our receivers everything we know about a subject. This may make us appear learned to them, but unnecessary details obscure the accurate transmittal of information. At the same time, we must be careful not to simplify our message to the point that it becomes boring to the audience or interferes with an accurate understanding of the subject.

2. Phrase the message in the language of the receivers. Avoid using jargon and technical terms whenever possible. These may seem important, even necessary, to describe the subject, but a little reflection will generally reveal more common ways of saying the same things.

3. Illustrate every major point with an example or an analogy. Most people feel much more comfortable with a new idea if they have some concrete referent for it. Purely abstract descriptions tend to fade and merge into an undifferentiated mass of memories. At the same time, make sure that the example or analogy clearly illustrates the point—it may be the only thing many receivers remember.

4. Use repetition to drive the point home. You cannot expect perfect attention and comprehension on the part of receivers. Minds wander, and they may wander at the most important point in the message. Again, however, don't repeat ideas to the point of boredom.

5. Use summaries and presummaries to fix the major points of the message in the minds of the receivers. A presummary is merely a brief statement of what will be accomplished in the next section of the message. The summary should confirm for the receivers that they have understood at least the most important part of the message. The old teaching adage puts the point well: "Tell them what you're going to say, say it, then tell them what you said."

6. Allow opportunities for interaction with and feedback from the audience whenever possible. Among other benefits, this will enable you to discover just how effective the communication process has been. Remember—there is no such thing as a dumb question.

7. Select an organizational pattern that will provide the maximum amount of clarity for the subject.

The best type of organizational pattern to use for an informative message will depend on the subject. The two major patterns that are useful primarily in informative messages are time patterns and space patterns.

Time Patterns

A time pattern organizes material according to the time frame in which a series of events occurred. An example might be:

I. The development of the railroad in the United States in the nineteenth century.
II. The development of the automobile in the early twentieth century.
III. The development of the airplane in the mid-twentieth century.

Here the intent is to present the receiver with a history of major forms of transportation, and an easy organizational format is to place them in chronological order. It is possible to use this kind of sequence as a framework for a persuasive message. Using the three points outlined above, a speaker might add a fourth point to make a proposal:

IV. The necessity for the development of new forms of mass transportation.

This last point would seem to turn a regular time-order message into a problem-solution message and illustrates the point that there is nothing "magic" about any of the organization patterns we are going to discuss.

Space Patterns

Material can also be organized according to spatial or geographic categories. An example might be:

I. Problems in juvenile delinquency on the Eastern Seaboard
II. Problems in juvenile delinquency in the Midwest
III. Problems in juvenile delinquency in the South
IV. Problems in juvenile delinquency in the West

Note that here a major problem is simply broken down into more manageable chunks, by looking at different areas of the country. This sort of pattern will work for the listener or the reader only if there are some natural consequences or differences based on the geographic division. If the problem in each area is the same, there is no reason to organize material in this way.

Time and space patterns are not related to the analysis of arguments.

They are not meant to be used as substantive analysis frameworks, but rather as convenient and familiar ways of organizing messages. Additional organizational patterns are discussed in the appendix. Also, many of the organizational patterns discussed in the next section can be easily adapted for informative messages.

Persuasive Messages

The Proposition

Every argumentative, or persuasive, message has a **proposition**, or **thesis**, as its foundation. Stated simply, *the proposition is what a source wants a receiver to do as the result of attending to the message.* Some typical propositions are listed below:

1. Vote for Mayor Blake.
2. Buy this ten-speed bicycle.
3. Stop rapes on campus.
4. Buy an Oldsmobile.
5. Send a check to your local cancer society.
6. Continue to support your local public television station.
7. Maintain your confidence in the ability of the president.
8. Adopt a more humane attitude toward homosexuals.
9. Change your definition of success from money to happiness.
10. Love your neighbor.

Some of these propositions will be explicitly stated in the message; others may not be formally stated. Regardless of whether the proposition is explicit or implicit, *every* persuasive message has a central proposition. Thus an analysis of persuasive messages by either source or receiver begins with the attempt to identify its underlying proposition(s).

Similarly, the first step in constructing a persuasive message is to formulate a specific proposition. It may not be used in the actual message, but unless the source has a clear understanding of the desired outcome, he or she can hardly expect a receiver to respond in any particular way. Furthermore, attempting to actually write a proposition may demonstrate to the source that his thinking is still a bit ambiguous, and that further thought is needed before continuing with the construction of the message itself.

Many propositions can be constructed for almost any topic. Propositions can also take many different forms, but for persuasive messages four types of propositions can be identified. These types can be expressed in terms of four possible responses a source might desire a receiver to make: (1) to change or maintain opinions or attitudes, (2) to change or maintain overt behaviors, (3) to change or maintain perceptions, and (4) to change or maintain emotional states. Thus, for example, the proposition "Vote for Mayor Blake" asks the receiver to change or maintain a behavior (depending on whether the receiver has voted for Blake in the past). The proposition "Maintain your confidence in the ability of the president" asks the receiver to maintain an attitude; "Change your definition of success from money to happiness" asks for a change in perception; and "Love your neighbor" asks for a change in emotional state.

Selecting the proposition is only the first step in constructing a persuasive message. People do not change their behaviors unless they are given some *reason* for so doing. Why should a man send a check to a cancer society simply because we have told him to do so? Why should he vote for a political candidate simply because we said, "Vote for Candidate X"? Why shouldn't he vote for the candidate's opponent, or why should he vote at all? Unless we can give the receiver some rationale for taking an action, or changing an attitude or an emotion, our message is likely to leave the receiver unchanged. The **appeal**, or *the justification for expecting some particular response*, must be made an integral part of the message itself.

There are two general types of appeals, *rational* appeals and *motivational* appeals. A **rational appeal** is built on one or more *arguments* and seeks to intellectually *convince* the receiver to accept a proposition; that is, it requires or authorizes a conclusion on intellectually defensible grounds. A **motivational appeal** seeks to *stimulate* the receiver to accept a proposition by linking it to one or more of the biological drives or learned motives of the receiver; that is, it generates a conclusion on psychologically or physically satisfying grounds. The distinction between rational and motivational appeals is not clear in all cases. A predominantly rational appeal will frequently and validly include purely motivational components, and a predominantly motivational appeal will often incorporate rational aspects. Keeping this overlap in mind, let us turn to a closer examination of rational appeals.

Rational Appeals

Anytime you read a newspaper, or listen to a television news broadcast, you are acting as a receiver of a message. As you do so, you are deciding whether or not you *believe* in the statements made. You may go through this process either consciously or unconsciously, but you cannot avoid engaging in it whenever you act as the receiver of a message.

your flag...
your future

join the U.S. ARMY

If we asked you on what basis you made your decisions about the truth or falsity of the messages you receive, you might well tell us that you try to be *rational* in those decisions. In everyday conversation people use the terms "rational" and "irrational" rather indiscriminately and therefore ambiguously. Most of us feel that our *own* behaviors and decisions are made rationally. We are not as sure about the behaviors and decisions of other people. When someone does something that is very different from what we would have done, we are likely to say that the individual's behavior was irrational. Thus it seems necessary to define what is meant by the term "rational." As with any definition, this one will not be ultimately "correct," but it is what we will mean as we discuss using arguments in messages.

To begin with, we argue that to "think rationally" is to think in accordance with four general principles:

1. *Rationality is linked to objectivity.* Objectivity is an ideal, and like all ideals, it can never be fully reached. But rational thinkers attempt to be objective in the way they view the world. Objectivity demands that we do not make a decision without examining all the available evidence relating to the decision. Objectivity demands that we do not decide on the

truth or falsity of a statement simply on the basis of what we want to be so or what might feel comfortable to us. We all face the world with certain attitudes, memories, past experiences, and beliefs which help condition the way in which we view new issues. But as rational thinkers, we should experience a certain sense of guilt if we accept or reject an idea or position without fully studying it.

2. *Rationality requires critical detachment.* By critical detachment we mean the attempt to reflectively examine our own thinking processes. All of us get in a rut from time to time. Decisions are made because they are easy, or because we have always made decisions in a particular way. Assumptions are used to arrive at conclusions, and we fail to ascertain whether we really believe the assumptions anymore. The rational thinker stops from time to time to mentally step back and review the ways in which evidence is judged, issues are handled, and decisions are made.

3. *Rationality demands standards.* If you are asked to vote for a particular political candidate, how do you decide whether the candidate will make a good officeholder? A rational response demands a set of standards that can be applied to determine what will count as acceptable evidence and what conclusions may be drawn from a particular body of evidence. Over the centuries mankind has developed a number of sets of standards that people have argued for or against. To be valid, the components of any set of standards must be mutually consistent and capable of being defended if challenged. These two requirements—consistency and defensibility—stand at the heart of the concept of rational argument. Every rational person must adhere to a set of standards and be willing to submit the set to critical examination. Only in this way can standards be improved and rationality maintained.

4. *Rationality implies the use of evidence.* It is not necessary to search for evidence in making decisions. Decisions can be made, and actions taken, on the basis of intuition, or personal preference, or prejudice. But the rational person has made a strong commitment to base actions, beliefs, and decisions on a consideration of the available evidence, rather than on intuition or preference. Further, this commitment obligates the rational person to modify a position when faced with superior evidence or argument contradicting the position.

Viewed with these four principles in mind, rationality emerges as an idealized method of thinking, based on the values of objectivity, reflectiveness, consistency, defensibility, and reasonableness. Because it is an idealized method, we cannot expect to find any completely rational persons. Because it accepts any consistent and defensible set of standards of evidence and inference, we can expect to find different and even contradictory systems of beliefs to be equally rational.

Rationality has come under recent attack in our society. There are those who reject the analytical aspects of rationality on the grounds that such a method destroys creativity and spontaneity. Others argue that because it is impossible to be completely rational, the method is somehow flawed, and other answers should be found. Still others argue against rationality because they feel it is opposed to humanistic values.

We would argue that opposition to rationality on any of these bases exposes a basic misconception about the nature of the method. The rational person recognizes that some ideas and information can be clearly articulated and analyzed, and therefore welcomes intuitive insight and understanding. The rational person, however, does insist on labeling these as intuitive and weighs them accordingly in communication and decision-making situations. Similarly, creativity and spontaneity are encouraged and valued, but their products must still be submitted to critical scrutiny. Finally, the acceptance and use of rational principles of thought can help free the individual from the control of prejudice, hidden assumptions, and unsupported beliefs. The benefits of rational thinking affect communication whether you are a source or receiver of messages meant to persuade. Constructing rational arguments may help you influence opinions, change attitudes, or affect behavior. And the ability to think rationally may help you avoid being manipulated by those who are skilled in using misinformation, prejudice, and sophistry to achieve their goals.

The Toulmin Model of Argument

Arguments are the vehicles of rational discourse and rational persuasive appeals. That is, both the establishment and expression of rational belief are based on the analysis and evaluation of the arguments drawn up by oneself and others. Therefore this section will outline a model of arguments and discuss methods of constructing, evaluating, and organizing arguments in persuasive messages. Over the centuries mankind has developed a number of ways of constructing arguments that are designed to meet our four criteria for rationality. The early Greek philosophers devised the classical syllogism as an argumentative form. We are going to present an adaptation of the work of Stephen Toulmin (1958). We have chosen the **Toulmin model of argument** over a number of other possibilities for two reasons. First, it is broad enough to encompass all arguments, rather than only those which meet some (essentially arbitrary) standard of validity or rationality. Second, it is simple enough to provide a valuable tool in developing fundamental reasoning skills.

Toulmin argued that while the standards for judging the acceptability of data (evidence) and the validity of arguments may vary from field to field, or from person to person, *the structure of all arguments is the same.* All arguments have three basic components: *claims, data,* and *warrants.* The **claim** is the statement or conclusion which the arguer wishes the audience to accept or believe. It tells the audience *what* to believe. The **data** (or evidence) are facts or reasons which the arguer presents to support

Figure 3-1
The Basic Toulmin Model of Argument

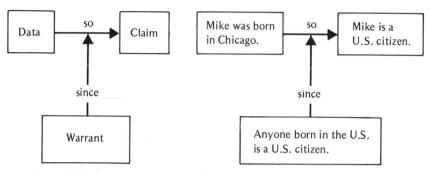

Source: Stephen Toulmin, *The Uses of Argument* (New York: Cambridge University Press, 1958).

the claim. They tell the audience *why* the claim should be believed. The **warrant** is a general hypothetical statement which supports the link from data to claim. It tells the audience *why* the data support the claim. There are other elements of arguments, which we will discuss later in connection with more complex arguments, but they do not disturb the basic model described here.

Figure 3-1 presents the basic Toulmin model and a simple example which applies to the model. Note that in the example the claim functions as the conclusion of the argument, the datum offers a fact in support of the conclusion, and the warrant supplies the bridge which allows us to move from the datum to the claim. We will now examine each component in greater detail.

The Claim

There are two important points to note about the claim of an argument. First, the claim serves the same function in an argument as a proposition does for a persuasive message as a whole. When the persuasive message consists of only a single argument, the claim of that argument is (or should be) the same as the proposition underlying the message. Further, just as we sometimes receive a message that does not state its proposition explicitly, we sometimes encounter an argument in which the claim is omitted and must be filled in by the receiver. This is one example of what Aristotle called an *enthymeme.* Second, we frequently encounter persuasive messages in which we are given *only* a claim—no data or warrants are offered in support of the claim. A claim presented without data or warrant is called an **assertion**. There are a number of situations, especially in emergencies, where it is both necessary and desirable to use an assertion instead of an argument. For example, on the battlefield under enemy fire we would not expect an officer to take the time to explain his reasons for ordering his men to take some action. But, in general, a persuasive message based only on assertions is irrational. Only when the receiver is provided with reasons why a claim should be accepted can the message be called a rational appeal.

The Data

What Toulmin has called data most other writers call evidence. Regardless of which term is used, data, or evidence, is the foundation on which a claim ultimately rests. Speaking broadly, evidence is *anything offered by a speaker or writer in support of a claim.* This definition suggests there are many kinds of evidence, and any particular piece of evidence may be responded to differently by different receivers. One receiver may accept a simple verbal statement from a credible source as evidence and proof of a claim; another receiver may require some physical proof before being willing to accept a claim. Take the claim "You should buy this ten-speed bicycle." A prospective buyer must be given some reasons why he should buy the bicycle. Why not another brand? Why not a motorcycle? Why not a three-speed bicycle? Some or all of the following statements might function as evidence supporting the proposition:

1. This bicycle is nonpolluting.
2. This bicycle is in excellent repair.
3. This bicycle is "Made in America."
4. Parts for this bicycle are cheaper than parts for other brands.
5. A ten-speed bicycle is more versatile than other kinds of bikes.
6. This is the same brand of bicycle ridden by racers in the Olympics.

All these statements are not equally likely to be accepted as evidence by all receivers of the argument. Each supports the claim, but acceptance of a statement as evidence does not depend on the statement, but on the receiver. Receivers decide whether evidence is to be considered true or false, believable or nonbelievable. We will return to this issue later.

Because the range of statements which can be interpreted as evidence is so broad, it will be helpful for us to identify a few basic types of evidence. One common distinction is to divide evidence into direct evidence and indirect, or circumstantial, evidence. Another useful distinction is between verbal evidence and real evidence.

Direct evidence is anything offered as proof which is immediately and directly related to the proposition under consideration. To show that a person was guilty of a hit-and-run accident, the prosecutor might find a witness who makes the statement "I saw the defendant driving the car that hit the boy on the bicycle." This is direct evidence, a statement of knowledge about an event gained from use of the senses. In general, we regard direct evidence as the most convincing. However, as numerous trials have shown, our senses can play tricks on us, and what one individual claims to have seen differs from what another claims to have seen. Direct evidence may also be differentially accepted by various receivers. One way of recognizing direct evidence is that the warrant that links it to the claim will frequently appear to be so obvious that it is trivial.

Indirect, or circumstantial, evidence is anything offered as proof which is only loosely linked to the proposition. Indirect evidence generally functions to increase the probability that a claim is true without conclusively proving it to be true. It is therefore often necessary to present a great amount of indirect evidence to convince a receiver to accept a claim—a single piece of indirect evidence is generally weak. A case in Ann Arbor, Michigan, provides a good example. A number of patients at a veterans' hospital died of breathing failure. The two nurses who were tried and found guilty of poisoning the patients were convicted on the basis of circumstantial evidence. None of the evidence was direct. No one testified that he saw the nurses poison the patients. Instead the prosecution tried to present the nurses as the only people who could have had the opportunity to commit the crime, and the jury apparently convicted the defendants on the basis of that indirect evidence. One way of recognizing indirect evidence is that the warrant that links it to the claim will frequently appear to be so weak and tenuous that it is difficult to see a clear and sufficient connection between the single datum and the claim.

A special type of indirect evidence, known as **negative evidence**, has become increasingly important in recent years because of its use in a wide range of court cases. Negative evidence functions in the following way: It is frequently impossible to find evidence that directly supports a proposition. However, one may be able to show that it is impossible to support the opposite of the proposition and thus argue that the proposition should be accepted. In recent times the charge of racial discrimination has been most frequently supported by the use of negative evidence. It may be impossible to find individuals who will state that they do discriminate against women or against members of minority groups. But if an official finds that a firm has not employed women or minority group members, that fact can be used as negative evidence to support the proposition that the firm does indeed discriminate. In spite of its frequent use, negative evidence skirts very close to being a fallacy. The source who uses negative evidence does not prove a claim, but only shows that the opposition cannot prove *its* claim. Obviously, both sides in such a dispute could use negative evidence to support their claims. Thus negative evidence is suggestive, not conclusive, and should never be used as the sole evidence offered in support of a claim.

Another distinction is between verbal evidence and real evidence. **Verbal evidence** is any statement offered in support of a claim. Verbal evidence includes both observations made by the source himself and observations and data reported by other persons and institutions which are quoted by the source of the persuasive message. Those quotations from persons other than the sources are generally called *testimony*. Most evidence encountered in persuasive messages will be verbal evidence.

One of the major factors which determines whether a receiver will accept verbal evidence is whether the source, or the person or institution quoted by the source, is perceived as *credible*, that is, competent and trustworthy. Thus one of the most effective forms of verbal evidence is **reluctant testimony**. An example is a statement made by a person who testifies as to what he saw even though it damages his interests. Suppose a scientist set up an experiment to test the validity of a theory she has created. We would expect her to want the test to prove the theory correct. Thus if she testified that the experiment showed the theory to be wrong, her statements would conflict with her interests and would be classified as reluctant testimony. Most people will give this sort of testimony more credibility than a statement from someone who stands to gain from testifying for or against an issue.

Real evidence is a thing or artifact offered in support of a claim. Depending on the claim, any type of artifact might be useful as evidence. The power of real evidence derives from the fact that most receivers are inclined to believe in things they can see with their own eyes and touch with their own hands. One familiar example would be the murder weapon introduced as evidence in a trial. Photographs are another type of powerful real evidence. In Michigan, before the U.S. Supreme Court ruling which legalized abortion, a vote was held on the abortion issue. The polls indicated six months before the vote that people generally favored legalized abortion. However, a strong campaign by opponents of legalized abortion was waged, and in the final vote the opponents won a stunning victory. One of the tactics they used was to circulate widely a set of pictures showing aborted fetuses of differing ages. These pictures, obviously gruesome, were touted as being responsible for many people changing their attitudes on the issue. This was effective use of real evidence.

When we discussed the nature of rational thinking, one of the things we stressed was the need to develop a set of consistent and defensible standards for judging the acceptability of evidence. If you are a rational source, you have an obligation to your receivers to construct your persuasive appeal using evidence which meets at least some standard of adequacy. If you are a rational receiver, you have an obligation to yourself to evaluate the quality of the evidence used in such an appeal. The problem is, as was noted briefly earlier, that different persons will use completely different standards for judging evidence. As long as these standards are defensible and consistent, they are perfectly rational. It is possible, however, to identify a set of general standards, or **tests of evidence**, which are used in nearly all rational systems. These standards are: *relevancy, materiality, clarity, credibility,* and *recency*.

Almost everyone has heard speakers use statements that may be interesting but simply do not support the proposition they are talking about. Such evidence does not meet the test of **relevancy**. When a no-fault insurance bill was introduced in Massachusetts several years ago, one speaker supported the bill by arguing that automobile accidents caused many broken teeth, which were expensive to fix. The statement is probably true, but the proposed bill did not call for payments for dental work caused by accidents. The statement was not relevant to the proposition being argued.

On most policy questions there will be many pieces of evidence that could be used to support the proposition. Some evidence, however, is really significant to the issue, while other evidence is more tangential. The more central evidence is to the issue, the better it meets the criterion of **materiality**. In Maine the Army Corps of Engineers discovered that a proposed dam would destroy an isolated clump of about fifty furbish louseworts, a type of wild snapdragon. Supporters of the dam argued that the destruction of the flowers was immaterial compared to the economic and recreational benefits the dam would bestow on the area. This example points to the difficulty involved in determining the materiality of evidence. What is immaterial evidence to one person might be material to another. In the case of the Maine dam, it turned out that the furbish lousewort was on the endangered species list and was fully protected by the federal government. Thus the destruction of what one dam supporter called "a few scraggly weeds" changed from an immaterial piece of evidence against building the dam to a highly material piece of evidence. In general, however, it should be possible for the source of a message to select only that evidence which strongly supports the claim while avoiding peripheral evidence. Receivers must constantly question themselves to see if the evidence presented is sufficiently material to justify their acceptance of the claim.

Another important test of evidence is its **clarity**. We all tend to be a bit sloppy in our communication, and this usually causes us few problems. When we are trying to make a decision based on some set of evidence, however, clarity becomes extremely important. There are an infinite number of ways in which a piece of evidence may be unclear, so we will mention only a few of the most common problems. One arises from the use of vague quasinumerical terms such as "some," "many," "most," "large," "crowd," and so on. For example, a news item in a student newspaper repeatedly referred to a group of people who attended a rally and then marched on the Administration Building as a "large crowd." By actual count, the largest number of persons at either the rally or the march was about 42.

A second problem arises when a piece of evidence includes one or more value-laden terms. In our ideologically divided world, such key terms as "truth," "freedom," "equality," "democracy," and "peace" have acquired a number of different and sometimes contradictory meanings. We cannot simply assume that we know how such terms are meant when we encounter them in a piece of evidence.

Another obstruction to clarity occurs whenever we encounter statistical evidence. Only a small fraction of Americans understands even the most basic statistical concepts, but the use of statistics makes the source appear more credible to many receivers. Thus, for example, the CBS-TV commentators stressed that then-presidential candidate Jimmy Carter had proved his ability to handle domestic problems and issues because of his extensive use of economic statistics in the second presidential debate. Further, certain popular types of statistical data such as public opinion surveys and computer projections of the future are sensitive to numerous forms of error and bias and are thus especially prone to misinterpretation. In general, if statistics are encountered in a persuasive message, there is a good chance that even the source of the message is not completely clear about their precise meaning. Anyone constructing or analyzing a message containing statistical data should be especially careful to understand the accurate meaning of that evidence.

The next test of evidence is the **credibility** of the source of the evidence, either the person who constructed the persuasive appeal or a person quoted in it. In both cases, credibility involves the *competence* and *trustworthiness* of the source.

A source is competent if he or she is capable of recognizing the truth in a matter. Commercials frequently use an entertainer or a sports figure to endorse a product which they are no more competent to judge than anyone else. However, people are often willing to generalize the credibility of an individual from one area of competency to another. Paul Newman may be a competent judge of Hollywood movie making, but he is not necessarily competent to make judgments about the advantages of a given political platform. However, receivers will associate the attributes of his movie success with their desire to share in that success and assign greater weight to his statements about politics than is perhaps rationally justified. In like fashion, it is possible that as a source to link with a message about deodorants, Joe Namath would be perceived as more competent than a chemist or cosmetician.

We say that a source is trustworthy if we believe he would tell us the truth if he knew it. One reason reluctant testimony is so powerful is that the trustworthiness of the source is generally unquestioned. Otherwise, there seems to be a natural tendency for people, consciously or unconsciously, to shape their beliefs and testimony to fit their desires, goals, and past experiences. We should be wary of evidence which serves the interests of a source but which cannot be independently verified by any outside observer. Thus, for example, it seems reasonable to question the trustworthiness of information about domestic conditions in countries such as the Soviet Union and the Peoples' Republic of China which prohibit neutral outside observers from entering the country to examine those conditions firsthand. We should, however, be careful about rejecting evidence merely because we believe the source to be untrustworthy since we may have no rational grounds for that belief. A better course is to examine all evidence carefully, withholding judgment on any evidence that seems untrustworthy and searching for outside sources to verify the accuracy of questionable evidence.

The final test of evidence is its **recency**. We live in a rapidly changing world, and what was true yesterday may not be true tomorrow. Unfortunately, we sometimes make up our minds about a matter based on evidence that is available at the time and then refuse to change when that evidence becomes obsolete. A similar problem arises when we encounter a persuasive appeal based on outdated evidence. Thus, for example, a speaker for the United Front against Racism and Imperialism (remember the problems with value-laden words) "proved" that Puerto Ricans want independence from the United States by pointing to the Puerto Rican revolt against Spanish rule in the 1890s!

Any time evidence is evaluated for use in an argument or message, these five tests of relevancy, materiality, clarity, credibility, and recency should be applied. Their fulfillment does not guarantee that receivers will accept the evidence, but it should improve the probability that they will do so.

The Warrant

The warrant, as we said, is a general statement which links the data and the claim. Because it bridges the two, the warrant is the heart of an argument. Even if we were able to gather "perfect" evidence, that evidence would be useless unless we could also find appropriate warrants authorizing us to take the intellectual leap from the data to the claim. The importance of the warrant is sometimes obscured by the fact that warrants are frequently not stated in the actual argument. That is, they are left implicit and the receiver is expected to fill them in to complete the argument. Consider the following classical syllogistic argument:

Datum: Socrates is a man.

Claim: Socrates is mortal.

In this example the warrant, "All men are mortal," is unstated. As with many simple and familiar arguments, we move naturally from datum to claim, hardly even noticing that we have made an inferential leap. But any fully rational analysis of an argument must begin by isolating and evaluating the implicit or explicit warrant of the argument. Again, however, the acceptability of a warrant will depend on the receivers. There are no warrants which are acceptable to all receivers, and therefore there are no completely universal arguments. At best, we can only expect that a receiver will apply a set of defensible and consistent standards to judge the adequacy of the warrants we use in constructing our arguments.

Relativity of Standards

One of Toulmin's major points is that *all* arguments display the same basic structure of data-warrant-claim. Toulmin also noted, however, that the standards used to judge the data and warrants encountered in arguments will vary from one group of receivers to another and from one field of inquiry to another. This is known as the **relativity of standards** of evidence and inference, or of data and warrants. Thus if we want to construct rational appeals which will be effective with some receiver or group of receivers, we must find some way to discover the standards that will be used to evaluate the data and warrants in our arguments. The search for these standards requires **audience analysis**.

Although many factors may govern how an individual will respond to a particular appeal, one way of beginning audience analysis is to attempt to determine what kinds of people the audience members are. There is a high probability that persons who are firm believers in the principles of the Roman Catholic church will use the same standards to evaluate arguments. Identifying people's characteristics will aid in predicting how those people are likely to respond.

Every individual has a certain number of characteristics simply as a matter of birth. These are **demographic characteristics** and include such distinctions as sex, age, ethnic origin, and native intelligence. A sixty-year-old receiver is likely (although there certainly are exceptions) to have a different set of attitudes and beliefs from a twenty-year-old. A man may respond to a message one way, a woman another. An analysis of demographic characteristics may produce information which will lead to selection of effective appeals to be used in arguments.

Another set of characteristics that receivers have are those they develop by voluntarily aligning themselves with groups. We call these groups **membership groups**. They include social, occupational, political, and religious groups. These voluntary membership groups may exert a strong influence on an individual's reception of a message. A person joins a fraternity or church because of a belief in the principles which the organization or congregation holds to be true. Thus if those beliefs are used as standards in selecting data and warrants in a rational appeal, the individual is more likely to respond favorably to the appeal.

One caution must be mentioned about the use of any membership group in building an appeal. It is probably true that receivers are most affected by membership groups when they are in direct contact with the group itself. We could expect a churchgoer to respond to an appeal based on the values of his religion—*if* the message is delivered in his church on Sunday. However, that same individual attending a meeting of a political party on Monday night may take on the attitudes of the political group—attitudes which may well be in conflict with those of the church group. The source must attempt not only to identify the groups to which receivers belong, but also to determine which group the receiver is likely to use as a reference point in evaluating the message.

More Complex Arguments

Up to this point we have concentrated on simple arguments containing at most a single datum, warrant, and claim. The arguments used in actual persuasive messages tend to be much more complex. This requires us to examine more complex variations of the Toulmin model.

Perhaps the most common form of complex argument is the one in which several pieces of data are used to support a single claim. Such an argument is illustrated in Figure 3–2. Notice that in this argument only one warrant is needed to link all six data to the claim. In other arguments, it may be necessary to use a different warrant to link each datum to the claim. This is frequently the case when we are constructing a persuasive appeal based on circumstantial or indirect evidence. A number of pieces of data are linked through different warrants to produce the same claim. Thus while any single datum may be insufficient to persuade the receiver of the truth of the claim, the cumulative effect of multiple data becomes convincing.

Figure 3–2
The Use of Multiple Data

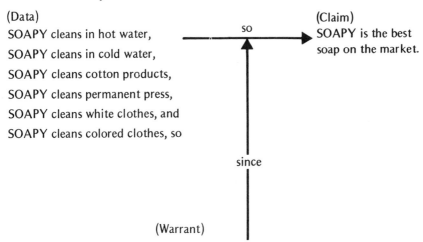

(Data)
SOAPY cleans in hot water,
SOAPY cleans in cold water,
SOAPY cleans cotton products,
SOAPY cleans permanent press,
SOAPY cleans white clothes, and
SOAPY cleans colored clothes, so

so

(Claim)
SOAPY is the best
soap on the market.

since

(Warrant)
The best way to judge a soap is by its
ability to clean under all conditions.

A second type of complex argument might be called a chain argument. Here the claim of the original simple argument is used as a datum in a later argument, and so on through some number of links. Such an argument is illustrated in Figure 3–3. Notice that this figure includes an instance of the use of multiple data such as was ilustrated in Figure 3–2. As with any chain, a chain argument is only as strong as its weakest link—that is, its weakest simple argument.

The Toulmin model can handle arguments that are far more complex than those described thus far. To do so, Toulmin introduces three additional elements: the **backing**, or support, for the warrant; the **rebuttal**, or conditions of exception, to the claim; and the **qualifier**, which indicates the force which the warrant confers upon the claim. Figure 3–4 shows a diagram and a simple application of an argument which uses all six elements.

Note the function of the three new elements we have introduced in Figure 3–4. There may be questions about whether the warrant alone is sufficient justification for the claim. The backing provides additional reasons for a receiver to be willing to accept the reasoning behind the warrant. There may be a situation in which the claim does not apply. So

Figure 3–3
The Use of a Chain Argument

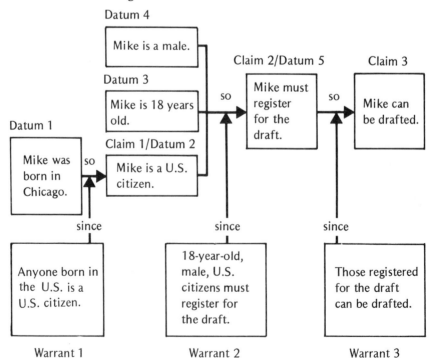

Figure 3–4
Argument with Backing, Rebuttal, and Qualifier

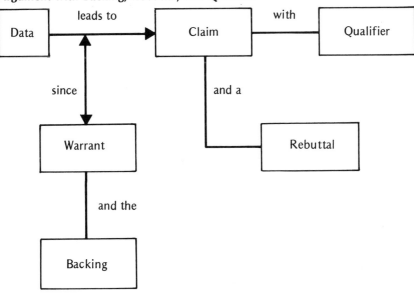

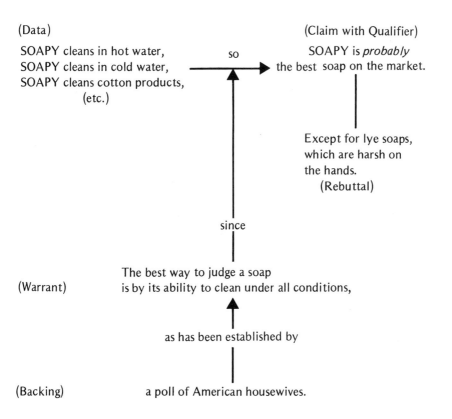

we add a rebuttal or reservation to show the receiver that we are aware of the circumstances that might make the claim untrue. And finally, the claim may seem to be too all-encompassing. Hence we add a qualifier, an adjective placed within the statement serving as the claim. Such adjectives include words like "maybe," "probably," "possibly," "most of the time," or "rarely." A claim that is not acceptable without the qualifier may become acceptable with the qualifier.

Toulmin argues that these six elements are all that is needed either to analyze or to construct an argument. His model does allow great flexibility in examining the arguments of others, as well as in organizing and constructing our own. A more elaborate discussion of the analysis of arguments is contained in Ehninger and Brockriede's book *Decision by Debate* (1963).

Organizing Arguments into Messages

Everyone recognizes that some kind of organization is necessary any time we communicate with one another. The Toulmin model does not specify how elements and arguments should be presented to have a maximum persuasive effect. Thus we will turn to other sources to discover useful methods of organizing arguments into a complete message.

What kinds of data might we look for in attempting to assess the merits of one organizational structure over another? We might ask whether one pattern is more valid, or better accepted by an audience, or easier to learn from than another kind of pattern. Unfortunately, few studies give definitive answers to these questions. There are patterns of organization, however, that attempt to organize materials so that they can be tested against rational criteria. These patterns can be called **logical patterns**, and they are most appropriate for organizing arguments in rational persuasive appeals. Somewhat different patterns of organization will be discussed for motivational appeals. The two logical patterns we shall discuss were chosen for their *familiarity* to most receivers and the *clarity* they provide for most receivers. These criteria suggest that any message using the patterns will require some learning on the part of the receiver and that common patterns may be more effective than new ones.

From the time of the ancient Greek scholars, *deductive* and *inductive* patterns of thought have been used to discover new knowledge by almost every civilization. The **deductive pattern** proceeds from the formulation of a general statement to derive some new conclusion about the world. The classical syllogism about Socrates' mortality is an example of deductive thinking. An **inductive pattern** makes a series of specific observations from which a general observation is drawn. Many of the discoveries of modern science have been made using inductive approaches.

Because these logical patterns of thinking are so well known and understood, messages which use these patterns as their basic organizing principle have proved to be effective. Each pattern deserves elaboration.

Deductive Patterns

In this pattern the source first presents a set of general statements. The source then moves on to specific pieces of data that support the general statements. Figure 3–5 shows a simple deductive argument in the form that Toulmin might use it.

A simple message arranged in the deductive form might be:

The United States should probably (qualifier) not continue to aid South Africa (claim).

South Africa discriminates against its black citizens (data).

South Africa is not supported by other African countries, and we need their support (data).

The United States has no economic interests in South Africa that cannot be supplied elsewhere (data).

Because the United States stands for equality and has an obligation to pursue its own best interests (warrants), we should stop supporting the South Africans (restatement of claim).

Figure 3–5
The Use of a Deductive Pattern

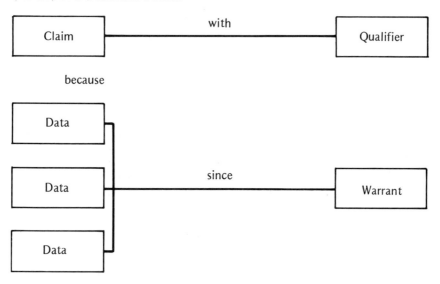

Inductive Patterns

The inductive pattern is perhaps the most familiar one to all receivers. We use it in casual conversations and in formal speeches to large audiences. It is simple but very effective. Figure 3–6 shows the Toulmin elements arranged into an inductive pattern.

An example of a simple argument organized into an inductive pattern is given below.

The Communist revolution in Russia was followed by the slaughter of the middle classes (data).

The Communist revolution in China was followed by the slaughter of the middle classes (data).

The Communist revolution in Cuba was followed by the slaughter or exile of the middle classes (data).

Figure 3–6
The Use of an Inductive Pattern

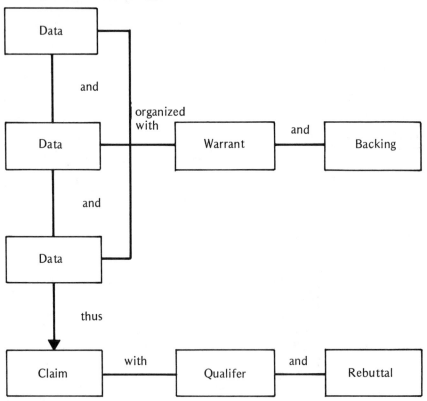

Therefore, if these countries are a representative sample of the results of Communist revolutions (warrant), and these are the clearest examples of Communist revolutions (backing), then the Communist revolution in Cambodia will probably (qualifier) lead to the slaughter or exile of the middle classes (claim), unless the Cambodians are restrained by world opinion (rebuttal).

It is possible to organize much larger arguments into an inductive pattern. Below we show an outline for a speech that makes use of an inductive approach.

I. Delinquency factors in Chicago, Illinois
   A. Summer programs
   B. Unemployment problems
   C. School activities
II. Delinquency factors in Madison, Wisconsin
   A. Summer programs
   B. Unemployment problems
   C. School activities
III. Delinquency factors in Boston, Massachusetts
   A. Summer programs
   B. Unemployment problems
   C. School activities
IV. Recommendations for delinquency problems in Detroit, Michigan
   A. Summer programs
   B. Unemployment problems
   C. School activities

The outline does not specify what the claims are going to be, but it suggests that the speaker is going to review specific pieces of data and then proceed to use them to make a claim for Detroit. That is an inductive approach.

It should be noted that in labeling the deductive and inductive patterns "logical," we do not mean to imply that they are necessarily *valid*. The evidence still has to be supported. The warrant still has to be justified. The patterns are effective in communication simply because they are familiar to the listener, not because of any inherent merit in these over other patterns of organization. We *can* develop rules for determining the validity of an argument, but that process is difficult and well beyond the scope of the average communicator. These patterns are presented here simply as organizing principles for messages.

In this section, we have discussed the nature of rationality and rational arguments. We now turn to the second major type of persuasive appeal—the motivational appeal.

Motivational Appeals

As was recognized in ancient times, humans are not solely or even predominantly intellectual beings. They are a complex blend of intellectual and emotional features. This is why a purely rational appeal, no matter how well constructed and delivered, may fail to have its desired effect. Thus we must examine persuasive appeals which function more to *stimulate* than to convince the receiver to act or believe in certain ways. These motivational appeals attempt to link the proposition of the message with the driving forces of human behavior.

What kinds of factors are likely to make an individual respond favorably to a message? Communication theorists distinguish two general types of motives. The strongest motives we have are **biological drives**. These include hunger, thirst, pain avoidance, and sex. If after working very hard on a hot day, you turn on the television set and see a commercial for a particular brand of soda, your response of going to the refrigerator and getting out a cold can may be motivated by thirst. Seeing the same commercial on a cold winter day when you have been sitting and reading may well not trigger any response.

Most communicators cannot deprive individuals of water before having them listen to a message about a particular brand of soda. But biological motives should not be dismissed as useless by the communicator. The reason lies in what receivers have *learned* about biological motives. Television viewers may be motivated toward action by an advertisement for a beverage not because they are thirsty at the moment, but because they have learned to react to situations involving eating and drinking in particular ways. The advertisement may trigger a behavior even in the absence of actual hunger or thirst. Thus the biological motives become important to the construction of persuasive appeals because they can be used within the appeal as a form of justification for the conclusion.

The second type of motive important to the communicator are those which are learned from the society in which people live. These **learned motives** include loyalty, competition, friendship, love, health, attractiveness, and many more. Unlike biological drives, learned motives differ from culture to culture and from individual to individual. Americans differ from Chinese in their reactions to appeals based on competitiveness. One receiver may be motivated to respond by an appeal to patriotism, while another is motivated by an appeal to health. Thus planning a message to appeal to many different motives emerges as an important goal in constructing motivational appeals.

As an example of the use of learned and biological motives in a simple appeal, imagine that the central proposition is "Buy Soapy Shampoo." It is aimed at persuading the receiver to take a specific action. Imagine further that the message is directed to fourteen-year-old boys. They may be

told, "Use Soapy. You will win more girlfriends with Soapy than any other brand." This appeal may be influential with some members of the audience, but many boys of this age are not typically motivated by appeals to their sexual drives. A larger proportion of that audience may be reached with the statement "Use Soapy! It keeps your hair under control for sports and will help you win the attention of that special girlfriend." In this message, two motives have been addressed, thereby increasing the probability of obtaining a favorable response.

Determining what motives a receiver or group of receivers will be most likely to respond to requires a major portion of the communicator's precommunication analysis. Biological motives differ in their strength, and learned motives vary widely from receiver to receiver. The task of the source is to attempt to ascertain what motives will be likely to be operating in a given situation.

Motivational appeals often occur in the form of arguments. Thus "Buy Soapy Shampoo" is the claim; "It keeps your hair under control for sports and will help you win the attention of that special girlfriend" is the data; and the (implicit) warrant might be "You should buy products which favorably affect your appearance and social life." It is extremely questionable, however, whether such data and warrants would hold up if evaluated on the basis of rational standards of evidence and inference. But this fact is unimportant when examining a motivational appeal, because such an appeal does not claim to be rationally defensible. Instead, it seeks to affect attitudes and behavior by creating some psychological linkage between the proposition and the motives of the receiver.

Another way of making the same point is to say that rational appeals and motivational appeals serve different persuasive functions. Thus it may be that a particular rational argument could also be depicted as a powerful motivational appeal. But the motivational quality of the argument is irrelevant to its quality as a rational appeal. In terms of persuasive effectiveness, however, perhaps the ideal message is one which combines rational and motivational appeals. Consider the following brief message:

> Since the Communist Khmer Rouge seized power in Cambodia in 1975, over 1,000,000 citizens, one out of every seven Cambodians, have been killed (data).

> The senseless slaughter of innocent people demands an outraged response from every decent human being (warrant).

> You must demand that the United States government and the United Nations use all their power to stop this senseless killing in Cambodia (claim).

While this appeal would meet most general standards of rational argument, the wording and the nature of the warrant provides a strong motivational appeal as well. But again it should be stressed that there is no necessity to construct motivational appeals in the form of rationally defensible arguments. The slogan of the French Revolution—"Liberty! Equality! Fraternity!"—is a poor argument but a tremendously moving motivational appeal.

Because most motivational appeals are not constructed in the form of arguments, different organizational patterns are required. We will consider two particularly familiar and clear patterns.

Motivated Sequence

During the 1930s various individuals suggested that there were natural ways in which people made decisions and some specific steps they took when faced with the necessity of making decisions. These studies suggested to Alan H. Monroe (1935) that a persuasive natural pattern of organization would be one that would have the listener travel the same path that he or she might *psychologically* be expected to follow. This pattern was termed the **motivated sequence** and consisted of five steps:

1. Attention step
2. Need step
3. Satisfaction step
4. Visualization step
5. Action step

Essentially, the source attempts to "walk the receiver through" the same steps needed in making any decision regarding a problem. First, materials designed to get the attention of the receiver are presented. Then data are presented which show *why* the receiver should be interested in the problem. Next, the source presents materials which suggest that the solution or desired change will satisfy the receiver's needs. The visualization step shows the receiver *how* the proposed change will work and the advantages for it. Finally, the receiver is told exactly what actions must be taken to achieve the desired result.

This psychological pattern lends itself to messages which are directed toward policy or action changes. Attempting to tell a receiver just why a favorable vote should be cast for increased taxes is difficult at best. But if it can be shown that taxes will provide something the receiver feels a need for, the vote becomes easier to make. Monroe and others argue that use of this sequence maximizes the chance to move receivers to action.

Problem-Solution Pattern

The **problem-solution pattern** is also well adapted to the creation of persuasive messages. It can be used to organize materials in the policy or social change arena. Many receivers come to a common situation faced with the knowledge or realization that there is some problem about which they should be aware, but wondering which of several approaches to the problem ought to be taken. Or they may be aware of a problem, but at a loss as to how to solve the problem. In the problem-solution organizational pattern the source first details the nature of the problem and then proceeds to discuss the steps needed to solve it. An outline for a message organized in problem-solution order might look like this:

I. Six young children have drowned in gravel pits in the Jackson area this year.
   A. No lifeguards or attendants are on duty at any of the pits.
   B. There is no outside swimming pool for any of the children to use.
   C. There is only one organized swimming instructional program in Jackson, and only a few children are eligible for it.
II. Jackson needs to construct an outside pool and begin a "Learn-to-Swim" program available to all youngsters in the community.

Note that there are other possible solutions to the problem that could have been mentioned. The source could have suggested fencing in the gravel pits, using guards, or even draining the pits. Thus we do not imply that the example is illustrative of the thought processes of the source. Presumably, the communicator will have gone through an elaborate thought process before arriving at what he feels is the best solution. The pattern is simply used to present the final results of those thought processes to a receiver or group of receivers.

Like the motivated sequence, a problem-solution pattern is familiar to the receiver. The pattern allows both source and receiver to feel that they have been part of a decision-making process. Both the motivated sequence and the problem-solution patterns of organization are designed for those situations where persuasion is going to be accomplished primarily through an appeal to the emotions. We must note, however, that all the logical patterns of organization can be adapted for motivational patterns of organization. In similar fashion, the motivational patterns can be used with logical materials and classified as rational appeals. We separate them on the basis of their primary use by sources and receivers.

Conclusion

The sources in any communication situation may have little to say about the impact that they will personally have on receivers, i.e., their credibility. The sources frequently cannot pick the receivers in a situation or control the situation itself. But sources can exercise a great deal of control over the messages delivered. We have emphasized in the opening chapters in this book that sources create messages with intent— intent to elicit various types of responses from receivers. The better control sources exercise over their messages, the more likely is it that their intents will be realized.

All messages should be created in a rational fashion. Rationality will allow sources to be assured that the basic decisions they make about evidence, the claims to be made, and the warrants to be followed will be subject to as little distortion as possible. Following these decisions comes the actual construction of the message itself. Here rationality will be assisted and clarity will be improved if the Toulmin elements are utilized in argument construction and presentation. Finally, common patterns of message organization assist the source in final message presentation.

TERMS AND CONCEPTS FOR REVIEW

appeal
assertion
audience analysis
backing
biological drives
claim
clarity
credibility
data (evidence)
deductive
demographic characteristics
direct evidence
indirect evidence
inductive
learned motives
logical patterns
materiality
membership groups

motivated sequence
motivational appeal
negative evidence
problem-solution pattern
proposition (thesis)
qualifier
rational appeal
real evidence
rebuttal
recency
relativity of standards
relevancy
reluctant testimony
tests of evidence
Toulmin model of argument
verbal evidence
warrant

REVIEW QUESTIONS

1. How can persuasive and informative messages be organized?
2. What are the seven principles for evaluating and constructing informative messages?
3. Explain the Toulmin model of argument, applying it to both simple and complex arguments.
4. What are the five general standards for evaluating evidence offered in support of a claim?

REFERENCES

Bettinghaus, E. P. *Persuasive Communication.* New York: Holt, Rinehart & Winston, 1973.

Ehninger, D., and W. Brockriede. *Decision by Debate.* New York: Dodd, Mead, 1963.

Monroe, Alan H. *Principles and Types of Speech.* New York: Scott, Foresman, 1935.

Toulmin Stephen. *The Uses of Argument.* New York: Cambridge University Press, 1958.

Part Two

CONTEXTS OF COMMUNICATION

Chapters 4 through 7 discuss communication in the interpersonal, group, organizational, and mass-communication contexts. The symbolic, transactional process of communication occurs in each of these contexts, but the nature of each of those defining characteristics of communication varies across those settings. Figure 4–1 in chapter 4 is a useful starting point for comparing the contexts.

Of the four contexts, the interpersonal context perhaps best illustrates the transactional nature of communication, for each participant in the usual dyadic encounter has the potential for directly affecting and being affected by the other. Momentary adaptations of messages are common in the interpersonal process as source and receiver gather more information about each other, often on the psychological level, and then try to create messages accordingly. The rules which govern their interaction are usually unstated, yet are negotiated by the pair rather than dictated by external sources to the extent that the dyad goes beyond culturally ritualistic exchanges.

Indeed, all the goals of communication are obtained via interpersonal communication, for dyads often engage in communication to establish human contact, exchange information, and influence or reinforce attitudes and behaviors. However, as described in the developmental view of interpersonal communication, the messages and relationships of people involved in more personal communication are qualitatively different from those of people in less personal communication. For example, instead of merely sharing cliché-level or general information, the more intimately involved communicators will be more likely to discuss opinions, feelings, and attitudes toward the relationship.

The more communicators in an interaction, the more rules they usually need to reach their goal. The rules of a group may come from the culture as well as from the norms of the group. The members are interdependent as they join together to accomplish their purpose, and they may or may not share personal-level information. Thus the communication of group members may be either noninterpersonal (as defined in chapter 4) or interpersonal.

As in interpersonal communication, individuals may develop their self-concepts while interacting in groups. The roles a person plays in a group, the degree to which normative behaviors of the group are internalized by the group member, and the status he or she enjoys in the group all affect the individual's self-concept. The view members have of themselves in the group may carry over into other groups and other settings.

Cooperative systematic work toward a specified goal can also define an organization. However, organizations usually have more people and a more hierarchical structure to control and coordinate the activities of the organization. Compared to norms for behavior in a small group, the rules of an organization are usually more precisely defined and include both procedural and content rules. Thus operations and flow of information via specified communication channels are usually more predictable in an organization than in a group.

Communication in an organization, despite its predictability, is still a symbolic, transactional process. As messages are sent through appropriate or inappropriate channels, they affect and are affected by the communicators involved. Indeed, handling the flow of information in an organization is a key problem, for too much or too little information can greatly hamper the effectiveness, accuracy, and efficiency with which the organization accomplishes its tasks. Because of the great potential for overload or underload, and the difficulties of locating the source of the problem or solving it, communication specialists suggest means of coping with communication load imbalances. In addition, by describing the type of network used and roles filled by individuals in the organization, it is easier to locate potential communication problems.

While certain members of the organization may engage in interpersonal communication and some small groups may create their own norms, most of the communication will be at the cultural and sociological levels. The organizational members will abide by the externally imposed rules for communication and usually will not engage in high levels of self-disclosure, since that is not necessary for the accomplishment of organizational goals. They may gain part of their self-concept through their role and status within the organization. As in small groups, the more central a person is in the organization, the more satisfied he or she is likely to be with its operation.

Mass communication differs greatly from the other contexts of communication, since it is the least transactional on an instantaneous basis. As described in chapter 7, sources of mass communication direct their messages to a much larger, more diverse audience than do sources in any of the other contexts. The predictions made about the receivers of mass messages are based on cultural and, to some extent, sociological data. The symbolic nature of communication also changes in this context, for the receivers are confined to using their senses of hearing and seeing and are often highly influenced by the use of mediatory nonverbal codes (e.g., music, lighting), which complement or augment the verbal and visual messages being sent. Another characteristic of mass communication is the necessity of delayed feedback. In interpersonal, group, and usually organizational communication, immediate feedback enables the source to adapt messages to fit the receivers.

Nonetheless, mass-media communication is a transactional, symbolic process.

The messages created—both visual and verbal—depend upon symbols to convey them. The messages affect receivers directly and indirectly, on the cognitive, affective, and behavioral levels; and the audience's acceptance or rejection of the messages affect the way in which mass communicators design future presentations.

To consider the differences and similarities among communication in these four contexts, the reader is advised to analyze a communication model in terms of how the source, message, channel, receiver, feedback, levels of predictions, and transactional nature of communication changes from context to context.

Situational View of Interpersonal Communication

SITUATIONAL CHARACTERISTICS
Small number of people
Face-to-face contact
Maximum number of communication channels
Immediate feedback

Developmental View of Interpersonal Communication

THE OCCURRENCE OF RELATIONAL CHANGES
Changes in prediction-making data
Changes in rules governing relationships
Changes in levels of knowing
Implications of developmental view

Strategies for Gathering Information

INTERROGATION

SELF-DISCLOSURE

SPECIALIZED STRATEGIES

Trust in Communicative Relationships

MINIMAL CONDITIONS FOR TRUST
Contingency
Predictability
Alternative options

BEHAVIORAL DIMENSION OF TRUST

MOTIVATIONAL DIMENSION OF TRUST

Conflict in Communication Relationships

AVOIDANCE VERSUS MANAGEMENT

WAYS OF MANAGING CONFLICT
Dissolving relationship
Suffering through conflict
Dampening conflict
Resolving conflict

4

Interpersonal Communication

After reading this chapter, you should be able to:

1. Give examples of the situational view of interpersonal communication.
2. Give examples of the developmental view of interpersonal communication.
3. Differentiate between the situational and developmental views of interpersonal communication.
4. List several important ways that relationships may change over time.
5. Describe the strengths and weaknesses of interrogation and self-disclosure to gain information from others.
6. Explain how trust differs in noninterpersonal and interpersonal relationships.
7. Demonstrate rudimentary skills in conflict management.

How long has it been since you conversed with a friend or acquaintance? Talked with a teacher about a term paper? Planned an assignment or a task with another student or co-worker? Sought a date for the movie or football game? Discussed your career plans with your parents or spouse? Negotiated a transaction with a salesperson at a local department store? Chatted with another passenger on a plane? Aired a personal problem to a counselor or minister?

Unless you are virtually a recluse, you have undoubtedly engaged in some or even all of the above communicative activities quite recently. Many people never have the chance to communicate with others through the mass media. While the majority have probably presented some kind of public speech, such opportunities (or nerve-wracking challenges) arise infrequently. Most people's communicative activities consist primarily of face-to-face exchanges with a few other persons in informal social settings; communicative time and effort are primarily devoted to such exchanges. Furthermore, the important decisions and the crucial issues of life are usually made and resolved in this kind of setting. People choose to marry or divorce, to attend college or take a job, to use or abstain from drugs largely on the basis of their personal transactions with family, friends, and acquaintances. Even when the president appears on national television to announce some momentous political decision, he is merely sharing a conclusion reached after hours of consultation with trusted advisors. As political experts remind us repeatedly, the significant business of Congress occurs in the cloakroom, not the hearing room.

Interpersonal communication occurs in this kind of communicative setting. Indeed, some writers argue that interpersonal communication *is* this kind of setting; they define the term "interpersonal communication" by placing it within a particular situational context. While not subscribing fully to this view, we grant that most interpersonal communication takes place in face-to-face informal settings; seldom do persons communicate interpersonally via the mass media or the public platform. Moreover, as we have already stressed, skill at interpersonal communication is an invaluable ally in our attempts to achieve environmental management. Almost without exception, effective interpersonal communicators manage their environments more successfully than ineffective communicators.

This chapter will begin by offering a perspective for thinking about interpersonal communication, one that aims to help you become a more skilled interpersonal communicator. We will then consider some strategies for developing interpersonal communication relationships, for beginning to move from casual acquaintanceship to close friendship. Next, we will deal with the role of *trust* in interpersonal relationships, for while everybody subscribes to the importance of this elusive notion, they often find it difficult to answer the question: What does it mean to trust someone? Finally, we will discuss the place of *conflict* in interpersonal relationships, focusing particularly on ways to manage conflict creatively so it can be used to strengthen, rather than to weaken or destroy, relationships.

The Situational View

The **situational view** of interpersonal communication transactions holds that they can best be distinguished from other exchanges by identifying certain situational characteristics. Although various writers have developed different sets of characteristics, we will center on four: number of communicators, degree of physical proximity, number of sensory channels potentially available for the communicators' use, and immediacy of feedback.

Figure 4–1 shows how these characteristics help to distinguish interpersonal communication from other communicative transactions. As you can see, mass communication involves many communicators, occurs through mediated communication systems under conditions of low physical proximity, permits the use of only one or two sensory channels (e.g., sight, touch, hearing), and usually does not allow immediate feedback. By contrast, interpersonal communication involves a relatively small number of communicators, occurs in a physically proximal, face-to-face context, permits the use of a maximum number of sensory channels, and allows immediate feedback. Small-group, public, and organizational communication fall between the two on the four characteristics; e.g., organizational communication typically involves more communicators than interpersonal or public communication but fewer than mass communication.

According to the situational view, then, all the transactions mentioned at the start of this chapter involve interpersonal communication. If two strangers exchange greetings or briefly pass the time of day on an airline flight, they are communicating interpersonally. By the same token, two close friends or a husband and wife embroiled in a financial dispute are also cast in the role of interpersonal communicators. In short, as long as a transaction conforms to the appropriate situational characteristics, it qualifies as interpersonal communication.

Although it may seem like a reasonable approach, the situational view suffers from several problems. A relatively minor, yet sometimes annoying problem concerns the ambiguity of certain of the characteristics

Figure 4–1
Categories Employed in the Situational Approach to Distinguishing Kinds of Communication

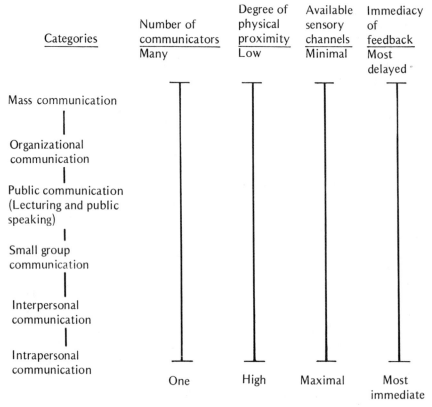

Source: Adapted from G. R. Miller, "The Current Status of Theory and Research in Interpersonal Communication," *Human Communication Research*, 4 (Winter 1978), 164–178.

themselves. For example, what numerical range should be assigned to the characteristic "a relatively small number of communicators"? Surely dyadic, or two-person, communication qualifies, since this is the smallest number who can engage in a transaction. Likewise, three persons seem like a relatively small number, though moving from a dyad to a triad permits the emergence of additional interactive processes not present in two-person transactions. For instance, coalitions can form in a three-person transacton; two communicators can gang up against the other one. Moreover, in a triad each communicator must usually share interaction with the two other participants, rather than focusing on a single individual. This fact partially explains the strains often encountered by marriage partners following the birth of their first child (LeMasters,

1957); what had been undivided attention, of necessity, becomes divided.

Still, most students of communication would agree that three people can communicate interpersonally. But what is an acceptable upper range? Is an eight-person transaction interpersonal? If so, a category labeled "small group" is probably unnecessary, since most small-group communication would also, by definition, be interpersonal. Although such questions may seem trivial, they can easily assume great importance in discussions about human communication. We have witnessed intelligent individuals involved in long, heated arguments about the "proper" number of communicators for an interpersonal transaction. Unfortunately, even if agreement is reached, such disputes yield little or no useful information about communication. Suppose, for instance, everyone were to concur that six is the maximum number of communicators for a transaction to be considered interpersonal. Their conclusion would reveal nothing about the way communication works, nor would it enable anyone to become a more effective interpersonal communicator.

A second, more serious problem with the situational view lies in its *static* conception of interpersonal communication. Throughout this volume we stress the desirability of adopting a process view of communication, of remaining aware of the inevitability of personal and relational change. A process perspective implies that different communicative relationships manifest varying levels, or degrees of "interpersonalness"; e.g., your communication with someone you met five minutes ago is probably not as interpersonal as your communication with a friend you have known for several years. But the situational view does not take account of degrees of interpersonalness; instead, a communicative transaction either *is* or *is not* interpersonal. If it conforms to the appropriate situational characteristics, the exchange is interpersonal, regardless of the relationship between the communicators or the content of their messages; if it does not conform with these characteristics, it is, by definition, not interpersonal.

Stated another way, the situational view does not take account of *qualitative* differences in communicative relationships. Consider these two brief dialogues:

Dialogue 1: (Person A turns to Person B, seated in the adjacent seat on the plane)
A: "Looks like we're in for some rough weather on this flight."
B: "Yeah, I've been getting more than my share of bumpy trips lately."
A: "I know what you mean; seems like the storm fronts love this area."
B: "Well, I just hope we can get down in Cleveland."
(The two passengers lapse into silence)

Dialogue 2: (Phone rings and wife answers)

HUSBAND: "Hi darling, just thought I'd let you know I made it to Cleveland."

WIFE: "I'm glad to hear your voice. How did you know I was thinking about you?"

HUSBAND: "Well, after the spat we had last night, I was feeling bad, and I thought you might be, too."

WIFE: "I sure am, and the more I think about our argument, the sillier it seems."

(A warm, animated conversation ensues)

How does the situational view handle these two communicative exchanges? Interestingly, while the first transaction qualifies as an instance of interpersonal communication, the second does not. By imposing Ma Bell's complicated system of mediated communication between the two conversants, we have removed the wife's and husband's exchange from the realm of the interpersonal, since it does not conform to the situational criterion of face-to-face interaction. This conclusion is bothersome, for the most literal meaning of the term "interpersonal"—"inter" meaning *between* and "personal" meaning having to do with persons— suggests that the second dialogue is certainly as interpersonal as the first, even though it occurs via electronic channels. Moreover, there are marked qualitative differences that place the second dialogue on sounder interpersonal footing. To underscore this point, reflect for a moment on the probable responses of the initiating communicator to these changes in the two dialogues:

(1) A: "Looks like we're in for some rough weather on this flight."
B: "Be quiet, please, I don't feel like talking right now."

(2) HUSBAND: "Hi darling, just thought I'd let you know I made it to Cleveland."
WIFE: "Who cares?" *(Hangs up phone)*

Although the initiating communicator has been rebuffed in both dialogues, the wife's angry termination of the conversation will undoubtedly exert a stronger psychological impact than the seatmate's unwillingness to converse.

Thus we believe the situational view provides an inadequate conceptualization of the interpersonal communication process. While this perspective identifies some *necessary* characteristics for labeling a transaction interpersonal, they are not enough to provide a useful distinction between interpersonal and noninterpersonal communication. What is needed is a view that also takes account of qualitative differences in the relationship. Let us look at such a view.

The Developmental View

The **developmental view** assumes all initial communicative transactions are necessarily noninterpersonal or impersonal. By "impersonal" we mean that the communicators are relating to each other according to their social roles, rather than as persons (Peters, 1974); or, recalling our discussion of communicative contexts in chapter 1, that they are basing predictions about each other's message responses on cultural and sociological, rather than psychological, information (Miller, 1975; Miller and Steinberg, 1975). Moreover, as Charles Berger and Rick Calabrese (1975) have emphasized, unfamiliarity breeds uncertainty, and both communicators in an initial transaction usually settle on a cautious communicative strategy. Thus they tend to exchange commonplace comments and to make informational queries to reduce this uncertainty. Only under the most unusual circumstances are they likely to share intimate self-disclosing messages.

If the communicators choose to continue their relationship, *if* their motivation is strong enough to warrant the effort, and *if* their interpersonal skills are sufficiently honed to permit it, their relationship may undergo certain qualitative changes. When these changes accompany relational development, communicative transactions become increasingly interpersonal. In other words, the developmental view conceives of communication relationships as varying in their *degree* of interpersonalness, depending upon certain qualitative characteristics of the relationship, rather than defines interpersonal communication in terms of situational characteristics. Figure 4–2 depicts the development of three relationships which vary in their degree of interpersonalness.

Two important general comments capture the crux of the developmental view of interpersonal communication. First, as communicative relationships become more interpersonal, the forces guiding the relationship shift from being primarily *extrinsic* to being primarily *intrinsic*. That is, the communicators, not the culture or the society, decide how the relationship is to progress. Recall our example of the employee and his supervisor discussed in chapter 1. Initially their relationship was largely guided by externally imposed sociological rules, or **extrinsic rules**, pertaining to appropriate communication between supervisor and subordinate. As their friendship developed, the two participants agreed on their own **intrinsic rules** to guide their relationship, or at least the social dimension of it: they became the rule makers, rather than allowing the rules to be imposed from outside.

As relationships become more interpersonal, the participants also manifest greater concern for differentiation, for perceiving and responding to each other as individuals. At the outset of a relationship the participants usually label each other as "student," "teacher," "real estate agent," or "politician." If the relationship continues, they may begin to

Figure 4–2
Continuum of Relational Development Showing Several Alternatives

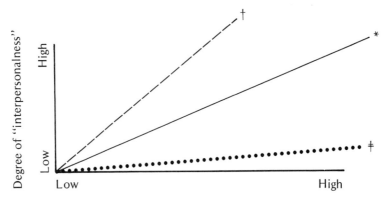

Amount of time spent in relationship

*A slowly escalating relationship which becomes more interpersonal over time.
†A rapidly escalating relationship which becomes more interpersonal over time.
‡A non-escalating relationship which remains relatively noninterpersonal over time.

Source: Adapted from G. R. Miller, "The Current Status of Theory and Research in Interpersonal Communication," *Human Communication Research*, 4 (Winter 1978), 164–178.

differentiate this "politician" from "politicians in general," to identify each other's unique characteristics. The developmental view holds that if certain qualitative changes do not take place, the communication remains "impersonal." We will now examine what some of these changes are.

Changes in Prediction-Making Data

A newspaper cartoon of several years ago depicts a husband and wife entering a used-car lot. The husband turns to his wife and remarks, "Martha, as soon as we get where the salesmen can see us, I'm going to walk up to one of the cars and kick the tires. Then they'll know they can't put anything over on us." The scene shifts to the lot office, where two salesmen are peering out the window. "Hey, Sam," exclaims one to the other delightedly. "Get ready for a big commission. There's another chump out in the lot kicking tires."

The cartoon provides a humorous example of how people make predictions about responses to messages in noninterpersonal relationships. By some process, the prospective car buyer had arrived at a sociological generalization regarding used-car salesmen: if a customer kicks the tires, the salesmen will perceive him as a seasoned veteran of car-lot battles, one who will drive a tough bargain for the best price. Actually, his prediction was dead wrong; instead of earning the salesmen's respect, he was immediately tagged as an easy mark. Of course, the salesmen's prediction about the customer is also based on noninterpersonal sociological data, suggesting that a really shrewd customer might gain the upper hand by kicking the tires and thereby luring the salesmen into a sense of false complacency.

Our car purchasing example underscores the point that *at the outset of a relationship, communicators must rely on cultural and sociological information for making predictions, since this is all the data they have available.* If someone is buying a new car, his or her best initial strategies are the ones that have proved successful in prior negotiations. This fact partially explains why people are particularly vulnerable in certain business transactions. For instance, horror stories abound about the rip-offs perpetrated on customers by funeral directors. Since most people probably deal with funeral directors only once or twice in their lifetimes, they have not accumulated much experience in message strategy selection. Even at the cultural and sociological levels of prediction, funeral shoppers are relative novices. Furthermore, their agitated frame of mind severely curbs their prediction-making skills; their emotional state prevents them from analyzing information rationally and selecting the best available communicative strategies. Thus, whether or not these horror stories are exaggerated is irrelevant. The fact remains that conditions are ripe for consumer exploitation.

As the communicators continue to exchange messages, the opportunity for gathering psychological information presents itself. This is not to say that such information *will* be gathered, only that it *can* be. The communicator(s) must be motivated to ferret out psychological information, for its acquisition often demands considerable energy expenditure. Frequently, the data which permit differentiation consist of subtle nonverbal behaviors—a momentary facial grimace, a telltale muscle twitch, a rapid shifting of the eyes, etc. The task of detecting and interpreting such messages is laborious. Moreover, some individuals lack the necessary communicative skills or attitudinal dispositions to make these discriminations. For instance, Miller and Steinberg (1975) contend that inflexible persons have a hard time employing psychological information in selecting effective message strategies, since their rigidity predisposes them to think in terms of cultural and sociological stereotypes. Archie Bunker and George Jefferson are familiar television characters who display this kind of stereotypic thinking. Both find it impossible to differentiate between members of various ethnic groups, preferring instead to respond to all "Polacks," "Micks," or "Honkies" in the same way. As a result, most of their relationships remain at the noninterpersonal level, with few, if any, predictions about appropriate message strategies being based on psychological information.

Even with these limitations, communicators are sometimes sufficiently motivated to seek psychological information about each other. As they acquire more of this information and begin to use it to make predictions about probable responses to their messages, the communication relationship becomes increasingly interpersonal. Furthermore, accurate prediction making is enhanced by their reliance on psychological information, since they are now beginning to identify ways that their relational partner *differs* from other members of his culture or social group.

Two points about the process of moving from the cultural and sociological levels to the psychological level of prediction merit emphasis. First, since this process usually requires a great deal of effort, it will occur only in relationships deemed sufficiently important by the participants. Obviously, people differ markedly in their personal criteria for assessing importance. For some, economic or social gain may justify the effort required to gather psychological information; two industrial tycoons may take pains to size each other up because each wants to come out on top in an important business merger. For others, personal growth and the development of a few intimate, rewarding relationships may be the chief motivating factors; such individuals are likely to be more concerned about the potential attractiveness of the relationship itself. Whatever the grounds for assessing importance, serious attempts to acquire a large store of psychological information probably occur relatively infrequently.

A second crucial point concerns a needed distinction between *interpersonal communication* and *interpersonal communication relationships.* If one communicator relies heavily on psychological information for making predictions about probable responses to his messages, he is communicating interpersonally; if both (or all) relational participants make extensive use of psychological data, they are involved in an interpersonal communication relationship. Obviously, *mixed-level* relationships (Miller and Steinberg, 1975) sometimes develop; i.e., relationships where one communicator bases predictions primarily on psychological information and the other relies primarily on cultural and sociological information. In such situations, the party who is communicating interpersonally usually has more relational power, since he is in a better position to make accurate predictions about the consequences of various message alternatives. Thus, to return to the example described earlier, if the used-car customer is basing predictions primarily on cultural and sociological information and the car salesman is relying on psychological information, then the former will usually pay a premium price for the car and the latter will probably take home a fat commission. Conversely, if the customer can gain psychological information about the salesman, he will be able to drive a hard bargain for the car. Finally, the more psychological information the two parties have about each other, the more interpersonal their relationship; this is one qualitative change that is in line with the developmental view of interpersonal communication.

Changes in Rules Governing Relationships

We have seen that initially a relationship is governed by rules that are largely prescribed by cultural and sociological constraints. Consider the common social occasion known as the cocktail party. Although neither the guests nor the hosts may give it a second thought, many of their behaviors are guided by commonly accepted rules associated with this social event; i.e., their degree of choice about certain procedures and messages is limited.

Cocktail parties typically start with invitations that specify the time guests should arrive. If the hours of the party are from five to seven, they take pains to arrive during that time. To make an appearance at four-thirty or seven forty-five would be considered rude and would call unfavorable attention to the rule-violating guests. In some cases, the invitation also requests a confirmation of attendance (the time-honored RSVP). If such a request is made, the guests are expected to respond; and should they fail to do so, they would be guilty of a breach of etiquette.

Upon arriving at the party, the guests are expected to greet and to acknowledge the hosts. In addition, they are expected to become acquainted with other guests they have not previously met. Typically, the hosts perform the introductions, though in some cases the guests introduce themselves. After the introductions have been completed, the guests are expected to mingle, to move from guest to guest exchanging a few minutes of polite conversation. The content of these exchanges usually centers on relatively mundane, unthreatening topics: a bit of professional news, some commentary on the weather, plans for a forthcoming trip, tips for effective lawn care. In most cases, the guests are reacting to one another as social-role occupants, rather than unique individuals.

Upon departing, guests must observe appropriate leave-taking rules. They are expected to thank the hosts and to bid them farewell. If the party is small, they should also say goodbye to the other guests, but if it is a large gathering, these exchanges are unnecessary. The guests will usually depart at an appropriate time. If the party is scheduled from five to seven, most if not all of the guests will be gone by seven-thirty.

Lest our example reads like a chapter from Emily Post, we should stress that we are merely trying to illustrate the complex fabric of cultural and sociological rules that underlie cocktail-party relationships. Moreover, such relationships are predominantly communicative in nature; a cocktail party is a communicative event. To be sure, all the rules mentioned are not equally binding on the guests. Although mingling with other guests is desirable, people can sometimes get away with moving to

a corner of the room and talking only to one or two guests. Even here, however, there are differences in who can most safely engage in such reclusive behavior. Higher-status guests are more likely to remain aloof from the "milling" norm and to restrict their conversations to a small number of guests—unless, of course, they are designated as guests of honor, in which case they are expected to circulate.

The communicative transactions described thus far can best be labeled noninterpersonal, at least from the developmental perspective. Imagine, however, that among the party guests are a wife and husband who differ in their attitudes about the social benefits of cocktail parties; whereas she enjoys them immensely, he detests every minute. To accommodate their differing attitudes, the couple may have agreed on a whole set of idiosyncratic cocktail party rules. For instance, they may agree that while she mingles with the guests, he is permitted to retire to a corner and chat with a friend. In return, he must stay at the party a reasonable length of time. They may also have agreed upon some specific nonverbal cues which signal the time for departure. In short, they may carry on an extensive interpersonal conversation within the context of many noninterpersonal cocktail-party transactions.

The negotiation and definition of these idiosyncratic rules confer a sense of intimacy and uniqueness on interpersonal relationships. Parties to the relationship share numerous communicative secrets; they are able to exchange private messages in a roomful of strangers. They are like people who at social gatherings converse in a foreign language that others cannot comprehend (actually, such conversations are more likely to be overheard in restaurants or other public places, since deliberate use of an unfamiliar language at a social gathering would be considered rude and would itself be a violation of social rules). But unlike speakers of a foreign tongue, parties who rely on an idiosyncratic rule structure can communicate without others even being aware of their exchanges.

As is also true with the information used for prediction-making, continuance of a communication relationship does not ensure that the participants will begin to negotiate and define their own relational rules. Undoubtedly, many long-term relationships continue to be guided primarily by externally imposed rules. Most people have numerous casual friends and acquaintances with whom they maintain cordial noninterpersonal relationships. But in instances where societal rules are gradually replaced or supplemented by internally negotiated ones, the developmental view suggests that the relationship becomes increasingly interpersonal.

Changes in Levels of Knowing

People "know" each other in various ways and at differing levels of complexity. Consider the following three statements:

"I know that woman is my sister."

"I know my sister supports the Equal Rights Amendment."

"My sister supports the Equal Rights Amendment because her husband is a domineering male chauvinist."

Each of these three statements concerns knowledge that the speaker has about her sister. But as one group of writers has pointed out (Berger et al., 1976), the three statements reflect differing levels of knowing.

The assertion "I know that woman is my sister" reveals only that the speaker knows her sister at the **descriptive level**. Descriptive knowledge concerns the superficial, surface attributes of a person and permits the knower to discriminate the individual from other persons. Occasionally one encounters a newspaper article describing the reunion of two family members who have been separated for most of their lives. It is easy to imagine one of them saying, "I know that woman is my sister," on the basis of a picture she has been carrying and studying for years. But if this is all she knows about the long-lost sister, the two will have a great deal of catching up to do. By the same token, most people have a number of "speaking acquaintances" whom they know only at the descriptive level. Although they can pick these acquaintances out of a crowd and can carry on a friendly conversation with them, they do not claim to know the acquaintances well.

The assertion "I know my sister supports the Equal Rights Amendment" transcends description and encompasses the **predictive level** of knowledge. To know someone at this level is to be able to make some accurate predictions about the ways he or she believes or behaves. Obviously, people are likely to feel they know others better if they can make predictions about their behavior, rather than being restricted to surface attributes. Furthermore, as Berger and his colleagues (1976) point out:

> [Predictive] knowledge is more difficult to obtain, for while the statement "Mary is tall" can be verified relatively easily by observation, the statement "Mary believes that abortion on demand should be extended to all women" is less subject to direct verification. In the first case, others can determine Mary's "tallness" by unobtrusively observing her. Moreover, it is relatively difficult for Mary to hide her height from view. However, even if others hear Mary assert that she endorses abortion on demand for all women, they cannot be certain that she is telling the truth. In other words, they can never know with complete certainty what Mary "really" thinks (p. 150).

The statement "My sister supports the Equal Rights Amendment because her husband is a domineering male chauvinist" indicates that the speaker believes she possesses some knowledge about the sister on the **explanatory level**. This level goes beyond both descriptive and predictive knowledge, since the knower thinks he is privy to the individual's *reasons* for behaving and believing in certain ways. The predictive level deals with *how* a person will behave in certain situations, while the explanatory level deals with *why* a person behaves that way. Since there are usually many conceivable reasons, or explanations, for an individual's behavior, explanatory knowledge is hard to come by. Moreover, like predictive knowledge, the knower can never be absolutely certain that he has hit upon the right explanation for a particular behavior, since people's reasons for behaving in one way or another are not directly observable; going from behavior to reasons for behavior always requires an inferential leap.

As communicators add to their fund of explanatory knowledge—i.e., as they increase the number of seemingly accurate attributions they can make about the reasons for each other's beliefs and behaviors—their communicative transactions become increasingly interpersonal. Indeed, in many noninterpersonal relationships, explanatory knowledge is largely superfluous. A customer usually deems it sufficient to know that the milkman will deliver fresh dairy products regularly and punctually (predictive level). Seldom does he pause to speculate about the reasons for the milkman's good delivery record; as long as the behavioral prediction remains accurate, the reasons for his behavior are irrelevant. Concern for explanatory knowledge is likely to surface only if the milkman begins to violate predictive expectations; e.g., if deliveries suddenly become irregular or the milk is frequently sour. At this point, the customer may remark, "I wonder why that milkman is late all the time. I thought he was dependable, but I'm beginning to doubt it." This remark reveals two of the customer's concerns: first, he wishes to discover an explanation for the milkman's sudden tardiness; second, he wants to indicate increased uncertainty about the validity of certain predictive knowledge concerning the milkman. The "explanation" implied in the remark rests on the customer's perception of the milkman's "dependability"; whereas the customer used to think the milkman was dependable, he is now beginning to regard him as undependable. Although people often invoke these kinds of attributions (Kelley, 1967; Shaver, 1975) to "explain" others' behaviors, the resulting "explanations" leave much to be desired, for to say that someone is dependable says only that he conforms to our behavioral expectations.

As people establish more intimate relationships, it becomes increasingly important to them to expand their stock of explanatory knowledge about each other. There are several possible reasons for this increased interest in acquiring explanations of behavior. First, individuals in a close relationship are expected to try to find out what makes each other tick. Part of the cultural and sociological mystery surrounding close relationships deals with the importance, to put it in contemporary terminology, of "getting inside the other person's head." Thus acquiring explanatory knowledge becomes a sought-after relational end, a signal that the parties are heavily committed to maintaining and expanding their relationship. Indeed, a comment like "You're the first person who ever really understood me" is certain to be rewarding for the participants.

There are also practical reasons why interpersonal relationships are characterized by a continuing quest for explanatory knowledge. *As participants move from noninterpersonal to increasingly interpersonal relationships, they typically become concerned with more and more areas of each other's behavior.* Recall our example of the noninterpersonal relationship between a customer and a milkman. How many areas of behavior concern the two? Obviously, a limited number: the customer's primary concern is whether the milkman supplies fresh dairy products punctually, while the milkman's major interest is whether the customer pays milk bills promptly. As long as both conform to each other's expectations regarding services and payment for services, they will probably get along well *and* will remain relatively unconcerned about other aspects of each other's behavior. The customer does not worry about the milkman's romantic adventures or financial entanglements, nor does the milkman care whether the customer spends weekends gambling at the track or weeding in the garden. Since both are interested in establishing limited domains of prediction and control of the other's behavior, they need only observe the appropriate behaviors to discover if they conform with expectations.

In intimate relationships, however, the participants frequently seek to establish broad spans of prediction and control, so broad that it becomes impossible to observe all the relevant behaviors. To make inferences about such unobservable behaviors, participants try to understand the *whys* of behavior, the factors that motivate the other parties to behave as they do. Consider the following question and two answers:

Question: Why doesn't Smith flirt with other workers at the office?

Answer 1: Because he is a person of *integrity*, who approaches relationships *honestly*.

Answer 2: Because he is a *clever manipulator*, who flirts only when there is *no danger of being discovered*.

Obviously, if the only issue involved is Smith's lack of flirtatious behavior at the office, his motive for not flirting is of little consequence. But if the important question deals with willingness or unwillingness to flirt, regardless of the surroundings, then his reasons for not flirting at the office are of utmost significance. The first explanation suggests that Smith is not likely to flirt anywhere; the second implies that he will flirt whenever the probability of being discovered is low. If you were involved in a close interpersonal relationship with Smith, would both reasons (explanations) be equally reassuring? Or, to anticipate a topic we will discuss shortly, would you *trust* Smith as much if you thought he was a clever manipulator, rather than a person of integrity? The answer to both questions is clear: one explanation of Smith's behavior is quite rewarding, while the second is potentially punishing.

In summary, then, explanatory knowledge facilitates prediction making, both by expanding the number of situations where predictions are possible and by helping to identify the message strategies most likely to maximize environmental control. When communicators are motivated to move toward a more interpersonal relationship, they attempt to amass explanatory knowledge about their relational partners. By contrast, in most noninterpersonal relationships the communicators are limited to descriptive and predictive knowledge, and in many instances explanatory knowledge is not even relevant to the relationship.

Implications of the Developmental View

Since it stresses qualitative changes that may occur as relationships develop over time, the developmental view conceives of communication as dynamic rather than static. Unlike the situational perspective, which defines interpersonal communication as either present or absent, the developmental view allows for degrees of interpersonalness. Initial transactions are almost invariably noninterpersonal. If the relationship continues, the communicators may be motivated to gather information which results in greater individuation and yields explanatory knowledge concerning the other's beliefs and behaviors. Furthermore, they may define and negotiate a number of idiosyncratic rules to guide their relationship. As these things happen, the relationship becomes increasingly interpersonal.

Due to the costs involved in realizing these relational changes, interpersonal communication occurs relatively infrequently, at least for most people. Nevertheless, it is extremely important, since it is associated with particularly intimate, significant relationships. The developmental view suggests that interpersonal communication most frequently occurs among close friends and lovers. As a result, the communicators themselves choose whether to enter into an interpersonal relationship; they define the limits of the relationship and the degree of energy and commitment they are willing to devote to it. Thus, rather than being an elitist view of interpersonal communication, as some people have suggested, we believe the developmental perspective is democratic in the best sense of that term.

Strategies for Gathering Information

Besides being motivated to accumulate information about other relational participants, effective communicators must also understand the advantages and limitations of various information-gathering strategies. The beginning stages of a relationship can best be characterized as a period of uncertainty reduction (Berger and Calabrese, 1975; Berger et al., 1976). Inadequately armed with cultural and sociological information, the communicators seek to get to know each other better, to acquire additional information that will improve the accuracy of their predictions and provide some clues about the way the relationship should be defined. Certain strategies are frequently used to obtain this information, and we will consider several of these strategies next.

Interrogation

The most direct way to find out something about other persons is through **interrogation**, i.e., by asking them about themselves. When strangers meet, they usually spend some time asking for biographical and personal information about each other. Indeed, this question-and-answer phase seems indispensable in initial transactions, so much so that when communicators are instructed to dispense with it, they are frequently at a loss for something to talk about (Berger, 1973). From the developmental perspective, these exchanges serve an important function: they yield additional cultural and sociological information which bolsters the communicators' confidence in selecting appropriate message strategies. For instance, when first introduced, two people may know only that they are both "college students." By means of mutual questioning, they develop more detailed sociological classifications; e.g., "a physics major from a small town in northern Michigan who belongs to the Young Republicans and who enjoys movies and sports." Each additional item of information improves chances of selecting effective message strategies. Moreover, it permits the parties to form judgments about the potential for relational development: "I'd really like to get to know this person better" as opposed to "What a loser; the sooner I get out of this situation, the better!"

Unless the rules dictate otherwise—e.g., job interviews, oral examinations, or other situations where one of the parties is designated as the questioner—initial questioning is governed by a norm of **reciprocity** (Gouldner, 1960). Simply stated, this norm implies that if you want to ask questions about someone else, you should be prepared to answer similar questions about yourself. Research by Rick Calabrese (1975) reveals that people ask a similar number of questions of each other during initial conversations. Furthermore, when persons request information but refuse to provide the same information when it is requested of them, their attractiveness declines in the eyes of the information giver (Sermat and Smyth, 1973). Thus if a communicator plans to use interrogation as a message-gathering strategy, he must be willing to share similar information with the other person. If he is unwilling to part with the information, then interrogation will be of limited strategic value.

The utility of interrogation is also restricted by the constraints imposed on questioning during initial conversations. Having just met someone, a communicator will be ill-advised to ask questions such as "How often do you cheat on examinations?" or "How do you feel about group sex?" for such queries violate the norms of initial transactions. Consequently, even if two comunicators wanted to know some personal information about each other, they might be reluctant to ask the appropriate questions in a beginning transaction. Calabrese's study does reveal that as the transaction progresses, the participants begin to ask each other to explain their reasons for certain beliefs; hence it appears that communicators do try to gather some explanatory knowledge rather early in the relationship.

Finally, the fruits of interrogation should always be assessed cautiously because of some people's tendency to stretch the truth so as to paint the best possible initial portraits of themselves. Even commonplace queries may be answered untruthfully; to enhance status, a waiter may say he is a *maître d'hôtel*, a wine steward, or a chef. When attempting to heighten their perceived attractiveness, people may inflate their bankbooks or their grade-point averages. And as questions become more personal, the likelihood of deception increases, either because of deliberate attempts to impress or to mislead or because the questions are painful and difficult to answer.

Despite these limitations, interrogation is probably the most frequently used information-gathering strategy during initial transactions. When coupled with other direct and indirect techniques for acquiring information, it can assist communicators in broadening their predictive horizons and in assessing the potential for relational growth and development.

Self-disclosure

One of the most effective ways of eliciting information from others is to disclose information about oneself. As we have mentioned, the norm of reciprocity implies that if one party to a relationship is willing to reveal information about his beliefs, the other party is likely to respond in kind. Thus instead of asking questions of the other communicator, the person in search of information volunteers some "news" about herself on the assumption that the other party will reciprocate.

In the broadest sense, self-disclosure means any statement that reveals previously unknown information about the self. Hence assertions such as "I am twenty-three years old" or "I am from Muscatine, Iowa" would qualify as self-disclosure. For the most part, however, writers (e.g., Culbert, 1967; Gilbert, 1976; Miller and Steinberg, 1975) distinguish between **self-disclosure** and **self-description**, the key to the distinction being the relative privateness of the information:

> Self-disclosure refers to an individual's explicitly communicating to one or more persons information that he believes these others would be unlikely to acquire unless he himself discloses it. . . . Self-description designates self-data that an individual is likely to feel comfortable in revealing to most others (Culbert, 1967, p. 2).

Thus statements about one's age or place of residence would typically be considered self-descriptive items, while assertions about one's economic problems or sexual hangups would qualify as instances of self-disclosure. In other words, self-disclosure involves *personally private information* which the discloser is unlikely to share with many people, since sharing it involves significant risks.

Unfortunately, it is not always easy to discover what kinds of information another individual regards as personally private. This difficulty has led Miller and Steinberg (1975) to distinguish betwen *genuine* and *apparent* self-disclosure. Genuine self-disclosure occurs when individuals reveal information they actually regard as personally private. Apparent self-disclosure, on the other hand, takes place when people reveal information that most members of the society would define as personally private, but which is not, for some reason or another, seen as personally private by the discloser. Unlike genuine self-disclosure, which often yields benefits in terms of mutual understanding, apparent self-disclosure can be a manipulative strategy usually employed to gain information or compliance from another by creating a false sense of frankness or intimacy.

Despite the possible manipulative use of self-disclosure, many persons are inclined to sing its praises uncritically. People who readily engage in self-disclosure are viewed as honest, open, and authentic; while persons who are more cautious about sharing personally private information are seen as dishonest, secretive, and lacking authenticity. We believe such unquestioning allegiance to the virtues of self-disclosure is naive. As we have indicated, genuine self-disclosure entails personal risks for the disclosing party. Consequently, people who disclose personally private information indiscriminately should not be surprised if their frankness sometimes comes back to haunt them. Although it is vital to have a few close relationships that encourage candor and openness, it seems only prudent to assess the dependability of others carefully before divulging highly personal information to them.

Fortunately, the issue of going too far seldom arises in initial conversations. As with interrogation, prevailing norms and expectations limit the intimacy of message exchanges. Indeed, excessive self-disclosure is likely to be viewed negatively, or even suspiciously, by other relational participants. As a result, self-description is more often used than self-disclosure to elicit reciprocal information. If a relative stranger appears to be baring his soul to you, it is wise to respond cautiously, keeping in mind the likelihood that the "disclosure" is more apparent than genuine. Furthermore, should you doubt the authenticity of a disclosure, try to check out the person's communicative transactions with other strangers or casual acquaintances. Often you will discover that what seemed to be a series of startling revelations is actually common communicative currency that the "discloser" shares freely in a variety of relationships.

The virtues of sympathy notwithstanding, several studies (Gilbert, 1976, 1977) have shown that people initially respond more favorably to positive than to negative self-disclosure: generally speaking, it is more effective to reveal little-known praiseworthy tidbits about oneself than to confess indiscretions or to drag out skeletons from one's personal closet. This fact again suggests the possibility of deceit; when conveying information to others, some people may be tempted to stretch the truth a bit to create a favorable impression of themselves. This is another reason early acts of self-disclosure should be viewed somewhat skeptically.

Although limitations and risks are associated with self-disclosure, it remains a useful strategy for accumulating information during initial transactions. Because it is less obtrusive than interrogation, it often conforms more closely to the informal quality of most social transactions. Whereas excessive questioning may cause the conversation to take on the characteristics of a formal interview, self-disclosure retains the declarative tone associated with most communicative exchanges, while at the same time encouraging reciprocity on the part of other relational participants.

Specialized Strategies

While interrogation and self-disclosure are probably the two most frequently used information-gathering strategies, Berger and his colleagues (1976) suggest several other strategies that are sometimes useful for gaining certain kinds of information. Suppose, for example, that a communicator suspects someone of attempting to curry favor, or to *ingratiate* herself with the communicator. Typically, a person who is out only to create a favorable impression will readily agree to opinions expressed, use flattery, or offer favors. By using a strategy called **deception detection**, the communicator may be able to find out if the other person is sincere or not. Suppose the person agrees with an opinion expressed by the communicator. The communicator "clarifies" the opinion so that it now opposes the one originally expressed and watches to see whether the person follows suit and changes her position. If she does, there is good reason to believe that ingratiation is her chief motive.

Environmental structuring can sometimes be used to elicit particular kinds of information. For instance, a couple's first date is often carefully planned to capitalize on a specific type of environment. Dinner at an excellent restaurant, with candlelight, flowers, and a fine wine, provides an excellent opportunity for a person to assess his partner's feelings about their relationship. Of course, it may be hard to separate the information-gathering aspects of this situation from its persuasive attributes; i.e., the individual may hope to *induce* his partner to view their relationship in a certain way.

Finally, skilled communicators sometimes use the strategy of **deviation testing** to obtain information. Deviation testing involves deliberate violation of a relational norm to see how the other person reacts to it. Thus if both parties are addressing each other formally—i.e., using a title plus last name—one of them may depart from the norm and address the other by her first name. If the other party responds in kind, this indicates her willingness to redefine the relationship on less formal grounds. Conversely, if she continues to address the norm-violating communicator formally, it conveys reluctance to assume a more informal relational stance. Of course, deviation testing must be used cautiously, for if communicators depart too radically from accepted norms, they are almost sure to be perceived unfavorably.

Doubtless there are other information-gathering strategies that may be employed in early communicative exchanges. As we have stressed, the purpose of these strategies is to reduce uncertainty and to provide the communicators with a larger fund of information for use in making predictions. Moreover, the results of this early information search probably determine whether the communicators make a concerted effort to move to a more interpersonal relationship or choose instead to maintain the relationship on a noninterpersonal footing.

The Role of Trust in Communicative Relationships

Unquestionably, people attach great importance to the concept of *trust*. Save for the term "love," the word "trust" probably pops up with greatest frequency in conversations about social relationships. Popular songs sing of the joys of trusting lovers, as well as the agonies of not trusting them. Mass media commercials inevitably stress the trustworthiness of the company or manufacturer whose products they are promoting. Political candidates are always "people we can trust." Trust is touted as a cardinal virtue of positive, satisfying relationships, while distrust and suspicion are viewed as absolute evils certain to pollute or even poison the relational waters.

What does it mean to say another person can be trusted? We will provide a tentative answer to this question in the next few pages, and, in addition, we will consider how trust differs in noninterpersonal and interpersonal relationships.

Barnett Pearce (1974) has identified three situational characteristics that must exist for trust to develop. First, there must be what Pearce calls **contingency**, or the likelihood of some continuing relationship between the involved parties. If the persons involved are merely passing like ships in the night, neither risks anything by his behavior—and as in self-disclosure, risk is an essential component of trust. Thus trust is not at issue for the "stranger on the plane" phenomenon; i.e., a situation where people disclose intimate, embarrassing aspects of their lives to strangers with whom they are traveling. Since the communicators remain anonymous and since they are unlikely to see each other again, they can disclose personal information with relative impunity.

Second, the presence of trust entails **predictability**, or some stable assumption about the way the other person is likely to behave. As Pearce points out, lack of predictability is relative rather than absolute, for when individuals lack experience with each other, they base their predictions about each other's trustworthiness on their prior experiences in similar situations. This tendency to rely on prior experience leads to a distinction between **generalized trust**, which is the typical level of trust people manifest across persons and situations, and **person-specific trust**, which is the degree of trust displayed in particular situations and with specific persons. Some individuals may demonstrate a great deal of generalized trust; they may assume trustworthy behaviors on the part of most unfamiliar people. We would expect such individuals also to place considerable trust in many of their friends and acquaintances, to display a high level of person-specific trust. Conversely, other persons are low in generalized trust; given an unfamiliar situation or person, they are likely to proceed cautiously and to avoid risky behavior that hinges on trustworthy responses by the other individual. Nevertheless, their generally suspicious bent would not prevent them from placing considerable trust in people they have learned are trustworthy. The major difference between the two types of people concerns the kind of predictive error they are most prone to make: whereas a person with high generalized trust is more likely to err by trusting someone who is untrustworthy, an individual with low generalized trust may often remain suspicious of someone who merits trust.

A final situational prerequisite for the existence of trust is **alternative options**, or the opportunity for the potentially trusting party to choose other desirable behavioral alternatives. It is not very meaningful to speak of trust in situations involving only Hobson's choice. "When a person has no viable options other than remaining vulnerable, his behavior may be better interpreted as desperate or hopeful rather than trusting" (Pearce, 1974, p. 240). Consider a situation where a prisoner has the options of turning state's evidence, on the promise that the charges against him will be dropped, or of being tried for a serious crime. If he chooses the former alternative, it may be wrong to infer that he trusts the prosecutor to drop the charges. Indeed, he may have considerable doubt about the latter's veracity, but there are no other desirable alternatives available to him. On the other hand, we can think of Charlie Brown's annual autumn placekicking adventure with Lucy as an instance of trust, albeit a misguided one. Charlie has other acceptable alternatives at his disposal; e.g., he could put the ball on a kicking tee, or he could punt rather than placekick. Instead, he always persuades himself that *this time* Lucy will keep her promise and not remove the ball. The fact that she always reneges may mean that Charlie is not very good at sizing up people's trustworthiness or, what is more likely, that it is desperately important for Charlie to think that Lucy can be trusted, since her behavior provides an indicator of her affection and esteem for him.

In summary, Pearce's analysis implies that it is meaningful to speak of trusting behavior only in situations where: (1) there is a likelihood of a continuing relationship; (2) there is some basis for assessing the proba-

bility that the other will or will not behave in a trustworthy way; and (3) the potentially trusting party has recourse to other acceptable behavioral options. Given these three situational characteristics, individuals can be said to *trust* or *not trust* another person, depending upon how they choose to respond.

There are, of course, many ways a person can manifest trust in another. Of particular interest to us are those manifestations of trust involving communicative behavior. Genuine self-disclosure reflects trust, since the discloser makes himself more vulnerable by sharing personal information with the trusted party. At the most odious extreme, misplaced trust could result in blackmail or personal exploitation. More commonly, the discloser risks being held up to scorn or ridicule should the other person treat the information cavalierly. Finally, personally private information can be used in retaliation; i.e., should future relational conflict occur, the information can be thrown back in the discloser's face. Although this latter tactic represents a relatively mild violation of trust, it can be particularly annoying and often causes people to reevaluate the trustworthiness of the offending party.

Secrets are a kind of self-disclosure that depend on trust in another person; indeed, the term "secret" implies that the involved parties can be relied on to treat the information confidentially. Sharing secrets is a frequent communicative activity in close interpersonal relationships, since the confidentiality of the information contributes to a sense of relational uniqueness. Undoubtedly, every pair of close friends and every romantically inclined couple have their stock of secrets, information to

which only the relational parties are privy. Furthermore, strong normative sanctions are associated with breaking vows of secrecy; to be known
as a person who violates confidences inevitably results in social censure.

Finally, individuals demonstrate their level of trust in someone by the
way they choose to interpret ambiguous or unexpected messages origi-
nating from that person. Imagine that someone you know has reputedly
said your communication professor is extending preferential grading
treatment to you—an untruthful statement you would not have expected
from the person. If you doubt the person's trustworthiness, you are likely to interpret the message as evidence of malicious motives on her part
and to respond accordingly. On the other hand, if you have reason to
trust the person, you will probably respond quite differently. You may
question the veracity of the account: "Oh, I can't believe she would say
that; I'll have to check it out with her." Or you may express surprise
about the comment but cling to the belief that the person's reasons or
motives were benevolent: "I can't believe she said that, but if she did,
there must have been a good reason for it." Indeed, people are sometimes so eager to expect the worst of persons they do not trust that they
read sinister or malicious intent into the most innocent communicative
behaviors. Take the case of the lover caught cheating by his romantic
partner. Although he may never cheat again, the betrayed partner often
persists in attributing illicit motives to his behavior. Thus a casual glance
or a brief comment directed at a member of the opposite sex may be interpreted as a romantic invitation, although no such meaning was intended. Even seemingly thoughtful behaviors may be viewed as admis-
sions of guilt or conspiracy; e.g., a gift of flowers or candy may be taken
as an attempt to ease a guilty conscience or to quell suspicion rather
than as a token of love or affection.

The preceding discussion suggests an important distinction between
the way trust functions in noninterpersonal and interpersonal relationships. As Miller and Steinberg (1975) point out, parties to a noninterpersonal relationship usually are primarily interested in the behavioral
aspect of trust: *in such relationships trust means there is a high probability the
person will perform trustworthy behaviors.* The statement "I trust my communication professor to grade me fairly" means the person believes her
grade will represent a good faith judgment based on class performance,
not a reflection of some lurking prejudice the professor has against the
student. If the professor's behavior conforms with the student's expectations, the former's precise motives are irrelevant: he may be assigning
grades fairly because he is a scrupulously ethical person, because he is
afraid the student will file a grievance if given an unfair grade, because
he believes that colleagues will consider it unprofessional to grade un-
fairly, or for yet some other reason.

As relationships become more interpersonal, however, there is a corresponding increase in concern for the motivational aspect of trust: *in interpersonal relationships, it is insufficient for the person to engage in trustworthy behaviors; he or she must also engage in them for the right reasons.* In a sense, the difference is between the predictive and explanatory levels of knowledge discussed earlier. To say, "I trust my wife to remember my birthday," means not only that she will purchase a gift (behavior), but also that the reason for buying the gift stems from her love and affection for her husband, not from a sense of responsibility or a feeling of guilt (motivation). Thus conflicts over the motivational bases of trust are likely to occur more frequently in interpersonal relationships, while conflicts about the behavioral bases of trust will flare up more frequently in non-interpersonal relationships.

Trust is an important ingredient of successful relationships. Furthermore, communication is people's chief tool for forging bonds of trust. Though the experience of trust remains elusive, an understanding of the conditions it requires and how it works from one relationship to another can aid in developing more trusting interpersonal relationships.

Conflict in Communicative Relationships

Avoidance versus Management

For most persons "conflict" is a dirty word, something to be studiously avoided. Until recently, the vast majority of writers have treated the topic of conflict in the same way. The prevailing tendency has been to conceive of conflict as an undesirable deviation from the normal turn of events, a system disturbance which requires rectifying as soon as possible. As a result, the issues most frequently discussed have been how to *avoid* conflict and how to *resolve* it as quickly as possible.

Like some other recent writers (e.g., Coser, 1956; Simons, 1974), we take a radically different view of conflict. First, we believe it is impossible to avoid conflict; it is as inevitable as the proverbial death and taxes. Try to think of any relationship in which you have participated, save for the most fleeting and superficial, where some conflict did not occur. Whenever two or more individuals spend time together, disagreements about means and goals are sure to arise. Greg wants to attend the basketball game Saturday night, but Patricia prefers to go to the movies. Mike wishes to spend a modest inheritance on a new car and some household appliances, but Judy wants to bank the money for a rainy day. Margaret would like to invite Lisa to the picnic, but Kathy can't stand her. Norm hopes to get in an evening of writing at the office, but Ed wants to visit with him. The list of issues that spark relational conflict is almost endless.

In addition to being inevitable, conflict is, or at least can be, beneficial. Without conflict, opportunities for personal and relational growth would be severely restricted. Conflict forces people to sharpen and test their thinking about themselves and their ideas; it introduces alternative viewpoints for them to weigh; and it engenders tolerance for diverse attitudes and life styles. A healthy level of conflict ensures an interesting, challenging life, while its complete absence produces a boring, unrewarding existence.

Still, everyone can point to examples of the destructive consequences of conflict. Relationships are damaged beyond repair; reputations are sullied or destroyed; indeed, as the statistics on crimes of violence grimly remind us, lives are snuffed out: all because relational conflicts have escalated beyond the control of the involved parties. As a result, it would be naive to say that conflict is sure to have beneficial effects on a relationship. Instead, the two faces of conflict emphasize the importance of learning to deal with conflict intelligently and creatively. *Constructive* **conflict management**, *rather than* **conflict avoidance**, *should be the primary goal of effective communicators.*

Ways of Managing Conflict

Whenever conflict arises, the involved parties can respond to it in various ways. Borrowing from an analysis by Miller and Steinberg (1975), we will consider some options available to the conflicting parties and will offer our assessment of their probable effectiveness in strengthening rather than weakening relational bonds.

One way of dealing with conflict is to dissolve the relationship. During the turmoil of the late 1960s, the phrase "giving off bad vibes" gained considerable popularity. People who used this phrase were often advocates of the relational dissolution viewpoint. As long as a relationship was running smoothly and beneficially for them, everything was fine, but let even a glimmer of conflict surface and they immediately threatened to end the association. Their message seemed to be, "As long as we travel the path on my terms, I'll continue the journey, but should you stop dispensing goodies for a moment, look out!" These individuals displayed a self-centered, irresponsible attitude toward relationships, and their prevailing response to problems was to abandon the ship.

We do not endorse this approach to managing conflict. Nor do we support the opposite position, which holds that once people are committed to a relationship, they should maintain it no matter what. Some relationships need to be terminated; the costs involved in continuing them are too high for the involved parties. But dissolution should not become an habitual first response to conflict, for such a "solution" is nothing more than a cop-out. Since some conflict is inevitable in all ongoing relationships, knee-jerk termination dooms the individual to a life of short-lived shallow relationships.

Another way of dealing with conflict is by suffering through it. This

approach is frequently used by persons who see no viable alternatives to the conflictful relationship (Thibaut and Kelley, 1959). You are probably acquainted with people who maintain relationships even though they are fraught with conflict. If they were asked why they persevere, these people would probably reply, "Well, I know ———— and I have a lot of problems in our relationship, but if I didn't have ————, I don't know what I'd do." Although such individuals may endure their situation for a long period of time, they are obviously not managing their conflict very effectively.

Sometimes people try to deal with conflict by dampening it. Dampening can occur in several ways. The relational parties may ignore their conflict; they may attempt to sweep it under their psychic rugs. Unfortunately, a conflict out of sight is seldom, if ever, a conflict out of mind. Although the combatants may be able to sidestep the issue briefly, hostilities are certain to flare up again, frequently more intensely than before the truce was declared. To ignore conflict is merely to postpone the problem.

If one member of the relationship has much more power than the other, conflicts can sometimes be dampened through the imposition of a solution by the more powerful individual. We have witnessed the use of this approach in a dispute that arose between a graduate student and a faculty member over the order of authorship of a journal article. Both persons felt they had made the greater contribution to the article and hence deserved to be the senior author. After a rather lengthy argument, the faculty member finally exclaimed, "Look, I don't want to hear anymore about this! I'll be the senior author, and if you keep complaining, your name won't even be on the paper." Since the faculty member was operating from a position of greater power, the student lapsed into a grudging silence. To say that the student remained angry and resentful, however, would be an understatement. Never again did the relationship assume a note of cordiality; and while there was no further overt conflict about the authorship issue, the two parties did become embroiled in several other disputes over the next few months. The lesson seems clear: dampening conflict in such a unilateral way is, at best, a stopgap measure that leaves the relationship in disarray.

The only effective way to manage conflict, short of dissolving the relationship, is to resolve it. Resolution does not necessarily eliminate the source of the conflict. Conflicts are pesky things which have a way of recurring during a relationship's course. Thus *to resolve a conflict is not to purge it eternally from the relationship, but rather to reach an immediate solution which is perceived as equitable by the conflicting parties.* Suppose that a husband and wife are consistently at odds on how to spend vacations; whereas she enjoys getting out in the woods to backpack and camp, he prefers to stay at a plush resort hotel and to dine at exclusive restaurants. They may resolve their conflict by spending part of their vacation in the wilderness and part of it at a resort. Or they may agree to alternate the location annually, so that each gets his or her preference every other year. Neither of these solutions eliminates the conflict; the husband and wife will continue to disagree on the best way to spend vacations. But as long as they both feel their compromise solutions are fair and equitable, the conflict has been resolved rather than dampened or endured.

When seeking to manage conflict effectively, the parties should observe two communicative rules. First, they should be alert for pseudo-conflicts and should strive to resolve them quickly when they arise. **Pseudoconflict** is a communication problem that occurs because ambiguous messages lead people to believe they are in disagreement when in fact they are not. Consider the following exchange:

CALEB: "I thought I might go over to Harold's for awhile tonight."
JANE: "But you promised me you weren't going to play poker anymore."

If Caleb's purpose for visiting Harold's is to play poker, a genuine conflict may be in the offing. Suppose, however, that while his usual reason for going to Harold's is poker playing, no game is scheduled for this evening. To resolve the budding pseudoconflict, the following message should suffice:

> CALEB: "I'm not going to play poker; I just want to talk to Harold about the fishing at Lake Lansing."

Unfortunately, momentary resentment or hostility may result in the following response:

> CALEB: "I don't know why my playing cards occasionally bugs you so much."

At this point, Jane's erroneous assumption concerning a poker game has been reinforced, and the pseudoconflict is likely to escalate rapidly.

The tone of Caleb's last response leads to the second communicative rule: the parties should keep conflict **issue-centered** rather than **ego-centered**. Conflict becomes particularly nasty when the parties feel their self-concepts are being attacked. Consequently, conflicts can be managed more effectively if messages deal with points of contention instead of personalities. To illustrate, we will continue our hypothetical dialogue:

> JANE: "I guess it bugs me because you're just like your father, and his gambling always kept him broke."
>
> CALEB: "Who are you to criticize my father! The only reason I play poker is to get out of this house and away from your griping."
>
> JANE: "Well, I wish you were half as cheap about your own entertainment as you are about this house. It's been so long since we bought anything new. . . ."

By now, you can probably predict where events are leading Jane and Caleb. The original conflict (in fact, in this case, pseudoconflict) has been lost in a barrage of mutual insults and recriminations. At best, the two antagonists are in for a period of strain in their relationship; at worst, they are inflicting wounds that will never heal completely. Had they focused on the issue, rather than attacking each other's self-concepts, their angry exchange might never have occurred.

Having achieved an interpersonal relationship can be either a blessing or a curse in dealing with conflict. If the parties are serious about their desire to resolve conflict, the ability to make psychological-level predictions and to employ explanatory knowledge about the other can culminate in more sensitive, effective selection of message strategies calculated to speed the conflict toward an amicable resolution. On the other hand, if anger or hostility steer the conflict on an ego-centered course, the combatants are driven to inflict pain and suffering—to transmit just those messages likely to create the greatest psychological turmoil for the other party. Given this fact, it is not surprising that some of the most destructive conflicts emanate from intimate interpersonal relationships. Communicating interpersonally is emotionally advantageous only when the parties are favorably disposed toward each other and their relationship.

Conclusion

Interpersonal relationships require communicative skills and sensitivity. The developmental, as opposed to the situational, view of interpersonal communication would seem to be the most useful approach because it makes qualitative distinctions among relationships. When people meet for the first time, they can use certain strategies—principally interrogation and self-disclosure—to gather information. These strategies reduce uncertainty and provide the means for assessing the potential of the relationship. Trust—when and how it functions—is an important consideration, both in interpersonal and noninterpersonal relationships. Conflict is unavoidable, but if managed effectively, it can be resolved and even enhance the quality of the relationship.

TERMS AND CONCEPTS FOR REVIEW

alternative options	generalized trust
conflict avoidance	interrogation
conflict management	intrinsic rules
contingency	issue-centered conflict
deception detection	person-specific trust
descriptive level of knowledge	predictability
developmental view	predictive level of knowledge
deviation testing	pseudoconflict
ego-centered conflict	reciprocity
environmental structuring	self-description
explanatory level of knowledge	self-disclosure
extrinsic rules	situational view

REVIEW QUESTIONS

1. What is the situational view of interpersonal communication? Explain with examples.

2. What is the developmental view of interpersonal communication? Explain with examples.
3. What is the difference between the situational and developmental views of interpersonal communication?
4. What are several important ways in which relationships may change over time?
5. What are the strengths and weaknesses of interrogation and of self-disclosure to gain information from others?
6. How does trust differ in noninterpersonal and interpersonal relationships?
7. What are some rudimentary ways of managing conflict?

REFERENCES

Berger, C. R. "The Acquaintance Process Revisited." Paper presented at the annual convention of the Speech Communication Association, New York, December 1973.

———, and R. J. Calabrese. "Some Explorations in Initial Interaction and Beyond: Toward a Developmental Theory of Interpersonal Communication." *Human Communication Research*, 1975, 1, 99–112.

———, R. R. Gardner, M. R. Parks, L. Schulman, and G. R. Miller. "Interpersonal Epistemology and Interpersonal Communication." In G. R. Miller (ed.), *Explorations in Interpersonal Communication.* Beverly Hills, Calif.: Sage, 1976, pp. 149–171.

Calabrese, R. J. "The Effects of Privacy and Probability of Future Interaction on Initial Interaction Patterns." Unpublished doctoral dissertation, Department of Communication Studies, Northwestern University, 1975.

Coser, L. A. *The Functions of Social Conflict.* New York: Free Press, 1956.

Culbert, S. A. *Interpersonal Process of Self-Disclosure: It Takes Two to See One.* Washington: N.T.L. Institute for Applied Behavioral Science, 1967.

Gilbert, S. J. "Differential Effects of Unanticipated Self-disclosure on Recipients of Varying Levels of Self-esteem: A Research Note." *Human Communication Research*, 1977, 3, 368–371.

———. "Empirical and Theoretical Extensions of Self-Disclosure." In G. R. Miller (ed.), *Explorations in Interpersonal Communication.* Beverly Hills, Calif.: Sage, 1976, pp. 197–215.

Gouldner, A. W. "The Norm of Reciprocity: A Preliminary Statement." *American Sociological Review*, 1960, 25, 161–178.

Kelley, H. H. "Attribution Theory in Social Psychology." In D. Levine (ed.), *Nebraska Symposium on Motivation, 1967.* Vol. 15. Lincoln, Neb.: University of Nebraska Press, 1967, pp. 192–237.

LeMasters, E. E. "Parenthood as Crisis." *Marriage and Family Living*, 1957, 19, 352–355.

Miller, G. R. "Interpersonal Communication: A Conceptual Perspective." *Communication*, 1975, 2, 93–105.

————. "The Current Status of Theory and Research in Interpersonal Communication." *Human Communication Research*, 1978, 4, 164–178.

————, and M. Steinberg. *Between People: A New Analysis of Interpersonal Communication*. Chicago: Science Research Associates, 1975.

Pearce, W. B. "Trust in Interpersonal Communication." *Speech Monographs*, 1974, 41, 236–244.

Peters, R. S. "Personal Understanding and Personal Relationships." In T. Mischel (ed.), *Understanding Other Persons*. Oxford, England: Basil Blackwell, 1974, pp. 37–65.

Sermat, V., and M. Smyth. "Content Analysis of Verbal Communication in the Development of a Relationship: Conditions Influencing Self-Disclosure." *Journal of Personality and Social Psychology*, 1973, 26, 332–346.

Shaver, K. G. *An Introduction to Attribution Processes*. Cambridge, Mass.: Winthrop Publishers, 1975.

Simons, H. W. "Prologue." In G. R. Miller and H. W. Simons (eds.), *Perspectives on Communication in Social Conflict*. Englewood Cliffs, N.J.: Prentice-Hall, 1974, pp. 1–13.

Thibaut, J. W., and H. H. Kelley. *The Social Psychology of Groups*. New York: John Wiley & Sons, 1959.

What Is a Small Group?

WAYS OF DEFINING SMALL GROUPS
- Common perceptions
- Motivation
- Goal orientation
- Interdependence

CHARACTERISTICS OF GROUP COMMUNICATION
- Systemic
- Complex
- Dynamic

How Are Groups Formed?

REASONS FOR MEMBERSHIP
- To accomplish a task
- To enhance self-concept
- To meet cultural demands

PHASES OF GROUP DEVELOPMENT
- Orientation
- Adaptation
- Integration
- Goal attainment

COALITION FORMATION

How Do Groups Work?

SPATIAL ARRANGEMENTS

COMMUNICATION NETWORKS

SATISFACTION IN GROUPS

The Social Environment of the Group

GROUP COHESIVENESS

STATUS

NORMS
- Obligatory
- Permissive

ROLES
- Made up of norms
- Reciprocal
- Dependent upon task
- Role conflict

SOCIAL POWER
- Attraction
- Reward
- Coercion
- Expert

LEADERSHIP
- Authoritarian
- Democratic

GROUP PRESSURE

The Task Environment of the Group

TYPES OF TASKS

TASK DIFFICULTY

5

Small-Group Communication

After reading this chapter, you should be able to:

1. Identify the ways small groups can be defined.
2. Describe the characteristics of group communication.
3. List the reasons for joining groups.
4. Outline the phases of group development.
5. Discuss the satisfaction level of groups using structured and unstructured communication networks.
6. Explain the effects of cohesiveness, status, norms, roles, social power, leadership, and pressure on a group.

One of the earliest and most profound realizations we have as human beings is that we are not alone in the world. We exist as social beings. We learn very quickly that we are inextricably bound up with others. Parents, family, and friends all play a part in how we see ourselves and what we become.

As a result of our social nature, the transactions we share with others become part of the fabric of our lives. As was pointed out in the first chapter, transactions occurring within the cultural context help us to identify who we are with respect to our society. Transactions within the psychological context help us form our self-concepts. And transactions in the sociological context, i.e., the small groups and organizations in which we participate, have an important impact on our lives as well. The small-group context provides the focus of this chapter.

Although we learn at an early age how to participate in small groups, their value becomes increasingly evident as we progress through adolescence. Consider high-school cliques. Many teen-agers identify strongly with other members of the clique to which they belong, and as a result, the cliques are instrumental in forming their behavior and attitudes. Other situations, such as the discussions young people experience at dinner time, may also serve as a proving ground for their self-concepts. And throughout adulthood, people's participation in small groups affects their values, social lives, and ability to do work.

What exactly is meant by a small group? How are small groups formed and how do they develop? How do small groups work? What social processes determine how group members behave? How do tasks affect interaction? These are the five questions we will address in this chapter.

What Is a Small Group?

We begin our discussion of the ways in which small groups can be defined by imagining an example—a typical high-school clique consisting of three guys, Ed, Don, and John. Since these guys spent a great deal of time together sharing many experiences, they became very interdependent. Over time each member began enacting a fairly specific role based largely on his particular talents. Don was the unchallenged leader; the others would seek his support for any decision they made, including whom they should date and whom they should cultivate as friends. John was the man-about-town with all the right social graces; his way with girls was famous. Ed was the comedian and the social butterfly; the group members looked to him whenever they had to meet with groups from other schools.

How did these people define themselves as a group? In his excellent review of the small-group literature, Marvin Shaw (1976) indicates that small groups can be defined in four ways: through common perceptions, individual motivations, group goals, and interdependence.

The members of the high-school clique would probably agree that they defined themselves as a group because they had a *common set of perceptions* about the world. Smith defines a small social group as "a unit consisting of a plural number of separate organisms or agents who have a collective perception of their unity and who have the ability to act and are acting in a unitary manner toward their environment" (1945, p. 227). The guys in the clique shared a sense of their unity and of their ability to act in concord toward other members of the school, other friends, and even family. The essential feature is that they consistently perceived the existence of the group and maintained that perception as an essential part of themselves.

Small groups can also be defined in terms of *motivation*. Cattell (1951, p. 167) specifies that the essential feature of a small group is the satisfaction of individual needs. People have needs that can be fulfilled through group affiliation. John's need to be known as a social mover, Don's need to be a leader, and Ed's need to gain attention as the comedian were, in part, satisfied by their group participation.

A third way of defining a small group is by its pursuit of group aims. Mills suggests that a small group is a unit "composed of two or more persons who come in contact for a purpose and who consider the contact meaningful" (1967, p. 2). In other words, people join groups to *achieve certain goals*. In the high school clique those goals could range from planning a caper to organizing a car pool.

Similarly, McDavid and Harari define a group as "an organized system of two or more individuals who are interrelated so that the system performs some function as a standard set of role relationships among its members and has a set of norms that regulate the function of the group and each of its members" (1968, p. 237). This is an accurate description of the organizational dimension of our high-school group. Their role relationships became fairly standard over time, and a set of norms governing how they accomplished their goals began to emerge. Those norms also regulated how they communicated with one another and with people outside the group.

Perhaps the essential feature of small groups is suggested by Shaw. He defines a group as "two or more persons who are interacting with one another in such a manner that either person influences and is influenced by each other person" (1976, p. 10). Typically, members of high-school cliques become **interdependent** over time. Cliques are instrumental in forming members' values and goals and in developing their

social skills. Members control and are controlled by one another's behavior. The closer these groups become, the more they demand from
one another in terms of time, favors, advice, etc. Relate this notion of interdependency and the exercise of control and influence to your own interactions within small groups.

Achieving interdependence is accomplished through communication.
Groups are created, maintained, and terminated through communicative transactions, the exchange of messages. Let us look at the essential
characteristics of the group communication process.

Applebaum and his colleagues (1974) identify three characteristics of
the group communication process. First, group communication is **systemic**—it occurs in a system. The components of the system are the situational context, the communicator, the message, the receiver, and the
interaction patterns that emerge as the group communicates. A change
in any dimension tends to result in changes throughout the system.
Thus understanding messages or interaction patterns requires an understanding of the communicators' attitudes, values, and beliefs; the
context within which the group communicates; the cultural and linguistic orientations of the group; and a range of psychological factors as
well. What happens in the absence of such understanding? For example,
what happens if a new student tries to enter a typical high-school clique?
Often such groups develop elaborate jocular rituals to amuse themselves and to reinforce the interdependence of the group. If the new student is unwilling to play these games or cannot understand the members' attitudes, the context of the banter, or the cultural characteristics
of the school, he will have trouble entering the clique.

Second, group communication is **complex**. Applebaum and his associates suggest two reasons why communication in a group is complex.
First, the systemic dimensions affecting group communication are operating simultaneously. When we communicate in groups, our culture, the
situation, and our psychological makeup all interact to contribute to the
discussion. Second, the influence of these factors changes while we interact. One moment our attitudes may be uppermost in determining the
flow of communication; the next, the context or some cultural tradition
or ritual dominates our interaction.

Third, group communication is **dynamic**. It is important to remember
that communication in groups occurs over time. Our ability to be interdependent depends on the continual exchange of messages. We say
things and others respond to them. Through this feedback we learn
about other people's feelings toward our values and attitudes.

In summary, small groups can be defined in terms of common perceptions, motivation, and goal attainment. However, the essential feature of
all groups is interdependence. Members affect and are affected by one

another; they also exert a degree of control over one another. Without at least minimal interdependence a collection of individuals cannot be defined as a small group.

How Are Groups Formed?

Reasons for Membership

To illustrate why people join groups, consider Ed, the comedian in our high-school clique, now grown up to be a college freshman. Of course, one of the first things young men do in college is search for action. Ed, being typical in that regard, thought he would see what fraternities had to offer. He visited one and found a party in progress—oddly enough, a party designed to attract new members. Ed decided to pledge the fraternity because it looked like fun and seemed a good way to meet college coeds.

As a member of the pledge class—the group of new fraternity recruits—Ed became fairly close to the other pledges during the initiation period. They performed many interesting activities together. They organized scholarship dinners for professors, conducted fund-raising events, and serenaded local sororities. They also pulled various pranks on the fraternity house from time to time. (These activities are illustrative only and not intended to be representative of the kinds of activities performed by all fraternities or Greek-letter organizations.) Unfortunately, these pranks often got Ed and his gang in trouble with the fraternity members, who made them do various chores. But as a result, Ed and his fellow pledges became even closer. Such initiation periods often draw out the common set of values and perceptions that the recruits share about the fraternity and about other facets of campus life.

In addition to his desire to have fun and meet girls, Ed probably had other reasons for joining the fraternity. He had not been a great social success in high school, and he probably thought that by joining a fraternity he could become a big man on campus. He might also have been attracted to the way the fraternity people dressed, partied, and aided various civic groups.

Other people have similar reasons for joining groups. In general, we join a group to achieve some physical, economic, or social reward. We compare what we have to what we would like to have and become members of a group that we think might help us achieve our goals.

Within the general goal of achieving some reward, there are three specific reasons why people join groups. The first is *to accomplish some task*, one that could not be achieved independently. There are two kinds of tasks that we can accomplish in a group: personal and organizational. A personal task might be that of meeting people. Ed felt that he needed to join the fraternity to meet people in other parts of the university. Perhaps he also wanted to help the university community in any way he could—another personal task. An organizational goal might be to learn how to organize dinners and fund-raising drives. Ed will probably attend many fraternity meetings to decide how much money and time to spend for which civic events or scholastic awards. He may become involved in establishing appropriate rules for living in the fraternity house. And he will undoubtedly spend time evaluating new members. These are examples of ways in which groups accomplish organizational goals.

We also join groups to *enhance our self-concepts*. This was a main reason Ed joined the fraternity. Generally, when we join a group to enhance our self-concept, we assume that the group will perform various functions for us, such as making us more attractive. Ed may have felt that his association with the house would make him a more interesting, well-rounded person. Further, people assume that the group will tend to reinforce their values. This is usually a safe assumption, since most members of a group are generally from similar educational and cultural backgrounds and share common political and philosophical ideas. This is another way of saying that we often join groups in which people are perceived to be similar to ourselves.

The third basic reason why people join groups is to *meet cultural demands*. One of the major ways culture influences our group membership is through rituals. We attend various meetings because we wish to conform to cultural expectations. More specifically, we become interdependent (a little or a lot, depending on the event) as a group to accomplish some goal or activity that the culture has been doing for some time. We gather together to witness the marriage of people, to express our bereavement for the loss of a loved one, to initiate people into churches and fraternities, etc. Observing religious holidays, meeting people in bars, and attending large family dinners all may have standard communication patterns that have remained the same for as long as you can remember. If you examine your group behavior carefully, you may find that much of the group communication in which you participate is ritualistic.

People often join groups for a combination of reasons. Ed joined the fraternity to learn how to better organize people and activities. At the same time, he met new people, gained some new values while reinforcing some old ones, and generally improved his opinion of himself. Also, he was able to participate in a number of fraternity rituals that were fun and interesting. And Ed's reasons for joining the fraternity were not necessarily the same as his fraternity brothers. Each individual is likely to have a complex set of reasons for participating in groups.

Phases of Group Development

Understanding people's motivations and intentions for joining groups can help make participation in groups more satisfying. For example, if you organize a group of friends to discuss an important issue and one of the members joins for social reasons, he may disrupt the group and its attainment of the goal. Thus it is often wise to clarify the purpose of a group discussion from the start. However, knowing the best way to start a group discussion does not guarantee it will work. You should also know how groups typically develop, that is, what phases they go through. For example, if you knew what phase a group was entering, you could avoid introducing the wrong information at the wrong time. Fortunately, a great deal of work has been done on phases of group development, which you can use to enhance the timing of your comments in group discussions. In an excellent summary of these studies, Edward Mabry (1975) found that most researchers agree that groups develop in four phases.

The first phase of group development is **orientation**. This is the starting point of group formation when group members attempt to find out about one another and the situation. During this phase they do a great deal of information gathering, trying to sort out the relevant facts. There is little self-disclosure at this point, because people are primarily conerned about getting the facts. They are still making sure they understand the rules of appropriate behavior. This suggests that during the orientation phase people try to determine the status and power positions of other members of the group.

The second stage of group development is **adaptation**. Adaptation emerges out of the tension created in the first phase by competing points of view and attempts to achieve status in the group. During the adaptation phase the group generally demonstrates a desire to work toward the goal. Typically, it searches for ideas and directions to adapt to the requirements of the task at hand. A large number of messages are shared concerning individual member's wants and needs in relation to the task.

The third phase is the **integration** of group discussion. Generally the end of an adaptation stage produces some conflict. Since members know each other better, they express their points of view more freely. During the integration phase conflicts may be heightened. As loyalties form over the proposals raised in the adaptation phase, people come into opposition with one another. Thus integrating people's ideas involves an intense evaluation of others' proposals. Often this evaluation can be interpreted as personal attack resulting in group conflict.

The fourth phase of group discussion is **goal attainment**. During this phase people often become impatient that they are not achieving their original goal. Individuals try to shift their communication away from the conflict and back to the task at hand. Struggles for leadership also become less intense. A great deal of compromising may occur during this phase as people try to work toward a solution.

Group discussion does not always go through these four phases. Some groups may go through only one or two. The number of phases a group goes through depends on how much time it spends together, leadership in the group, past experiences of the participants, and the nature of the task. A group that spends a great deal of time together is likely to experience all four phases. A group that has a powerful leader may skip the integration phase since the leader will be able to control the conflict in the group. The kinds and number of phases a group goes through is hence difficult to predict.

Consider once again Ed's pledge class. It is likely that it went through all four phases. Interaction began in the orientation phase. The pledges probably shared many facts about one another and the fraternity when they first got together. Armed with this information, the members of the class may have begun to search for ways to cope with the trials of pledging. At this point the interaction would have entered the second phase of group discussion, adaptation, with each member openly expressing his preferences about how they ought to approach the active members of the house. Since this expression of individual choice often leads to the third phase of group discussion, integration, the pledge class might then have experienced a great deal of conflict. Chances are that some of them began to take sides about ways of approaching various situations.

This generally leads to an evaluation of one another's ideas. Finally, toward the end of the pledge period, they probably developed techniques to reduce the importance of the loyalties they had formed and worked to redirect their efforts toward becoming active members of the house.

Think about these four phases in relation to various group discussions you've experienced. Could you have made your discussions more productive if you had been aware of the phase your group was entering? For example, could you have saved some time avoiding conflict if you had known that the potential for conflict was high at a certain point? Such an awareness would have been helpful for Ed at many fraternity meetings.

Coalition Formation

As we have just suggested, members of groups often take sides concerning the way things ought to be done. They may believe that by joining forces they have a better chance of achieving their goals. When two or more people ally themselves against another it is called a **coalition**. Coalitions have a tendency to form for four basic reasons. First, they form when group members have inconsistent goals. When two members in a group discussion agree with one another and disagree with a third member, there is something to be gained by forming a coalition against the third member. Second, coalitions form when few resources, such as time, money, or materials, are available. Coalitions are often perceived as a way of increasing one's chances of winning those resources. Third, the group simply may encourage people to form coalitions to accomplish goals. When some groups have meetings, it is expected that on certain issues cliques will form. Fourth, coalitions are sometimes formed as a last resort to accomplish goals. For example, members of a jury may form coalitions to persuade indecisive jurors to make a decision and put an end to lengthy deliberations.

To summarize, people join groups for three reasons: to accomplish tasks they could not do alone; to enhance their self-concepts; and to comply with cultural rituals or expectations. The groups that we join tend to develop in certain phases, from orientation, to adaptation, to integration, and finally to goal attainment. Finally, as group members continue to communicate, they may take sides and form coalitions to achieve their goals. Based on these principles, what advice about group communication could you give someone who was a leader in a group?

How Do Groups Work?

Our description of how groups work begins with a case study. Several years ago a woman named Audrey went to work for a small slide-show production company as a script writer. The company consisted of twelve people and prided itself on being "one happy family." However, the company had previously consisted of only four people, and when Audrey began to work there, the owner was having difficulty dealing with twelve individuals at one time. As a result, he had become very strict and watched over people nearly every minute. This made the employees nervous, and productivity began to slump.

Often the employees would have group meetings, both informal and formal. Informal meetings occurred during the lunch hour or, less frequently, at other times during the day. Formal meetings were held about every two weeks to discuss business and to set company policies. Since the company was growing, the boss felt he needed input from his staff concerning benefits and salary increases. However, most of the employees believed that he was not genuinely interested in their opinions, but only wanted them to feel as if their opinions were important. The boss tended to dominate the meetings he attended and was generally successful at gaining people's agreement on important issues. In addition, most of the employees were young, inexperienced, and afraid to confront the boss. When one employee conformed to the boss's requests, others would follow suit. "Don't make waves" became the group's slogan.

Many of you have experienced situations like the one described here. Learning how groups work can help us function better in them. Let us start with the effects of the physical environment on group processes.

Spatial Arrangements

Spatial arrangement is the way individuals are placed physically around the room in which the discussion takes place. Seating position is one variable that communicates status to other group members. People who perceive themselves to have high status or power generally choose to seat themselves in a central position. This may be conscious or unconscious, but it gives the high-status person greater access to other persons in the group. This was the case with Audrey's boss. As soon as he came into the room, he would take a chair at either the head of the table or at another central location in the room.

In his review of relevant research, Shaw (1976) found that when seated at a round table, group members tend to communicate with persons across the table rather than with those adjacent or next to them. In general, these people are easier to watch, or pay attention to, since attending to someone on one's immediate right or left can often be physically uncomfortable. Thus the arrangement of people may have an effect on the flow of communication in a group. If a person wants to facilitate communication among certain individuals in a group, he should place them across from one another to increase the likelihood they would communicate with one another.

Communication Networks

Seating arrangements may also affect the type of communication network the group develops (Shaw, 1976). A **communication network** is the pattern of communication flow in a group. Networks vary according to the amount of structure in the group: the less structured a group is, the more freedom it has to communicate. Five basic types of networks are illustrated in Figure 5–1. The most unstructured communication network is the **com-con** (completely connected) **network.** In this arrangement, each person in the group is linked to each other person in the group. There is no centralization of message flow, that is, no one person controls the flow of messages. Control is shared equally.

The second type of communication pattern is called the **circle network**. This network is more structured because everyone does not talk to everyone else. But no one person or coalition controls the interaction; there is simply less contact among group participants than in the com-con network.

The two most structured networks are the wheel and the chain. In the **wheel network** everyone interacts with person *A*. This puts person *A* in a position of power because he has contact with everyone and can control the information the others use to guide their actions. The person in this position often becomes the leader. In the **chain network**, person *C* is central because he has to go through only one other person at the

Figure 5–1
Four Types of Communicative Networks

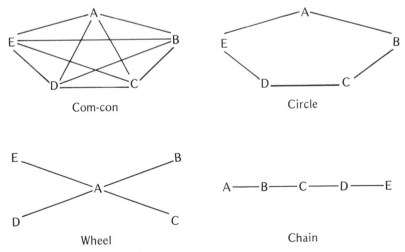

Note: Each link indicates a two-way flow of communication.

most to reach any group member and thus has more access to the other members of the group. Once again, this superior access increases the possibility that person C will become the leader in the group.

The wheel model comes close to describing the organization where Audrey worked. In meetings, the boss attempted to maintain control over most of the information. Usually people would direct their comments toward him and he would talk back to them. The employees did not usually talk to one another about business matters. They took such concerns up with the boss, because he generally insisted on evaluating what people did. Audrey's scripts, or someone else's photography, had to be approved by the boss. Peer evaluations meant little.

Satisfaction in Groups

Research has demonstrated that people who are in the center of the group generally derive more satisfaction from the group interaction. Greater satisfaction results from the ability to vent frustrations, present opinions, and generally maintain greater freedom to meet self-concept, task, or cultural needs. According to Shaw (1976), group members engaged in the com-con network are generally more satisfied with their interaction than people in the wheel or chain networks, because the com-con pattern allows them to talk to more people about their problems.

The freedom to communicate, however, may get in the way of accomplishing certain tasks. People may spend too much time talking and not enough time doing. Structured groups are generally found to be best at solving simple problems with a clear answer, such as a puzzle. The reason is that it is easier for one person to coordinate information and come up with the correct answer. Unstructured groups are best at solving complex problems with no right or wrong answer, such as policy decisions. Complex problems require many new ideas, and the best way to get them is to provide an open environment that encourages people to freely express their views.

Unfortunately, Audrey's boss did not seem to be aware of this principle. Most of the problems on which the employees worked were fairly complex. Probably one of the main reasons productivity slipped was that communication was too structured. People would go only to the boss to figure out how to solve their problems, and he did not always have the answers. When the employees suggested making communication less structured, he was unreceptive; he felt a more unstructured group would give him less information and reduce his control over his staff.

These physical variables affecting group interaction are significant indeed. But social factors must also be considered when discussing how groups work. In fact, many of the social processes that determine group communication behavior probably grow from physical restraints on the

group. But the social environment the group itself creates needs to be understood. Let's take a closer look at some of these social processes.

The Social Environment of the Group

Group Cohesiveness

Group cohesiveness is the result of all the forces acting upon members to remain in the group. Aside from money, important characteristics determine the extent to which group members will stick together. For example, according to Shaw (1976), members of highly cohesive groups express strong attraction to the group and thus are resistant to leaving it. This attraction produces greater motivation to participate in group activities, permitting the group to work fairly well together. Members of more cohesive groups may thus come to depend on one another more for rewards, suggesting that the group maintains a great deal of potential control over individual members.

Audrey's work group was not particularly cohesive. The employees were not strongly attracted to one another, nor were they highly motivated to participate in meetings. This may be another reason for their declining productivity. In talking with others at the company, Audrey probably discovered that the group exercised little control over individual members, an indication of its lack of cohesiveness.

When the group is cohesive and the potential control over individuals is great, it exerts pressure on members to conform to group norms and standards. For example, Ed's pledge class was a fairly cohesive group. When anyone did something that was not perceived as appropriate to the goals of the group, members put pressure on him to get back into line. This kind of pressure can become intense and often results in people going along with the crowd even though they do not want to do so.

Cohesiveness can also affect the productivity of the group. Members of cohesive groups feel freer to communicate with one another; hence they can generally coordinate their behaviors more quickly and they can produce a greater pool of ideas. As a result, they are probably better at solving complex tasks. Their high motivation and interaction also increases the chances that members will be satisfied with their group participation.

Status

Several variables structure the group's social environment. One of these is status. **Status** is the importance of an individual's position in the group. Generally speaking, there are two kinds of status: ascribed and achieved status. **Ascribed status** is that which is attributed to the individual by the group. The individual may not have any special qualifications, but for one reason or another, the group thinks the individual merits an important position. For example, Audrey often traveled to consult with clients of the company she represented. Simply because she was from out of town, she was perceived by the clients to be important. This is commonly called the "out-of-town" effect.

Achieved status is usually derived from an individual's performance within the group. Often members of groups can distinguish themselves by having a certain unique qualifiation that enables them to do a good job. Achieved status is likely to be more durable than ascribed status, since achieved status is earned and based on the group's perception of the individual's accomplishments over time.

What are some of the characteristics of high-status people? First, they tend to be more central and more involved in the communication network. They generally receive more information from the other group members. Second, high-status people tend to receive more information from low-status individuals. This is because low-status people usually try to enhance their position by interacting with higher-status people. Third, high-status people generally are allowed to deviate more from group norms. Because of their credibility in the group, high-status people are not questioned as often about their motives for straying from group norms. Others in the group tend to feel that the high-status person is probably deviating for a good reason. However, the high-status person, who finds group interaction rewarding, generally conforms to group norms in an effort to maintain the status quo. Low-status people are more likely to deviate from group norms because the interaction is less satisfying to them. They are also more likely to seek a wider range of other group memberships that will help them accomplish their goals.

Basically, status gets translated into power and control in group communication. This power and control results in greater satisfaction for the high-status person. Looking back on Audrey's work situation, it is clear that her boss maintained most of the status in the group. He was central in the network, he received a great deal of information from lower-status people, and he had control over the members of the group. However, there were times when this status got in the way of getting the job done.

Norms

A great deal of an individual's status is governed by group norms. **Group norms** are standardized generalizations concerning expected behavior in matters of importance to the group. As we have seen in our discussions of cohesiveness and status, norms can exert a great deal of power over group interaction. Norms are standards that members use to judge the appropriateness of another's behavior and to figure out how they themselves should act.

Some norms have more power to control interaction than others. Group norms that are strong and rigid are called **obligatory norms**; individuals are expected to adhere to these norms without exception. Norms that are more flexible are called **permissive norms**. They allow more freedom of choice for the individual since the group does not enforce them as often as obligatory norms.

According to Cushman and Pearce (1977), obligatory norms exert greater control over the individual, reducing the amount of choice the individual has in acting on his own. The individual is expected to act more in line with accepted group standards. Also, obligatory norms tend to make groups do things in a routine manner. Consider Audrey's production meetings. Participants would talk about client relationships, production schedules, and equipment needs, in that order. Discussing other topics, making jokes, or engaging in small talk was not tolerated when business affairs were being discussed.

Groups with an obligatory norm structure are usually more efficient in accomplishing simple tasks. They will generally spend less time talking about how to get the job done and more time doing it.

Permissive norms have different effects on groups. Permissive standards of behavior operate only sometimes, depending largely upon the requirements of the situation. As a result, permissive norms exert less control over individual behavior, producing greater deviation from standard ways of doing things and allowing for greater creativity within the group. Permissive norms operate most frequently in new situations, when a group has not had the time to set up standard ways of operating. Also, when the group is new, it is not likely that a dominant leader has emerged. Dominant leaders tend to set up rather rigid norms as a way of controlling the group. Thus the extent to which the norms control the group has a lot to do with the amount of time people spend in that group.

Norms, particularly obligatory norms, encourage conformity. As networks become more structured, the norms become more obligatory and ways of doing things become more standardized or more routine. An excellent example of highly structured group interaction is the cocktail party given for a candidate who is being interviewed for a specific position. Several obligatory norms serve to structure the guests' communication with one another. One of those norms is that the conversation is kept at a fairly superficial level. Another is that the language and jokes that are told should avoid profanity. Such norms tend to produce routine conversations about the weather, activities on the job, and so on.

Norms also exert a great deal of influence on the roles individuals perform in groups. We now turn to a discussion of roles and their relationship to norms.

Roles

Roles are behaviors that are expected of the occupant of a position in a group. For example, parents are expected to perform certain behaviors in the family. The father or mother is usually expected to make the decisions, indicate what is right and wrong to the children, and manage the family budget. Certain roles in certain groups are complex and diverse. In some groups, roles can become specialized, such as the role of a gossip in a fraternity house. The fraternity members do not have a wide range of expectations for the gossip's behavior. Typically, they do not ask the gossip to help them with their problems. The gossip is simply expected to fill everyone in on the latest rumors.

Roles demonstrate a number of important characteristics. First, *roles organize norms.* People in a certain position are expected to have certain standards for their behavior. The father, the mother, and the sons and daughters all have standards expected of them. This whole group of standards is organized into roles. When an individual is given a role in a group, a whole set of expectations or standards goes along with that role. Typical examples are the roles of leader and follower. These two labels simply summarize the expectations the other group members have for the behavior of those individuals.

Second, *roles are reciprocal.* A mother necessitates children; a winner necessitates a loser; a leader necessitates a follower. We enact roles in relationship to other roles. We assume that when we act as leaders, others will be acting as followers; when we act as teachers, others will be acting as students. Thus acting out roles is a give-and-take process between the members of the relationship.

Third, *roles are dependent upon the task* being performed by the group. We can have different expectations about an individual's role based on the function of the group. In one situation we assume one role, in another we assume a different role. When someone is teaching students, he or she enacts the role of teacher; at a party that same person may enact the role of entertainer.

Fourth, *role conflict can develop* in groups. **Role conflict** occurs when a person performs a task in front of two groups who have different expectations for that individual's behavior. You have probably attended parties in which employees and the employees' bosses have been present. The employees expect the boss to act like a boss, and the boss expects other bosses to act like colleagues or friends. Under those conditions, the boss may have to be careful how he or she behaves to avoid violating the expectations of either group. In a work situation, role conflict can result in low productivity, confusion, and a decrease in satisfaction and in the group's ability to meet its needs. If possible, it is best to get this conflict out in the open by discussing it with the groups involved. If the discussion is successful, the role expectations of both groups will be adjusted so that the two sets of expectations are more compatible.

People may have roles that provide them with greater power than others in the group. The roles of leader, parent, and teacher generally carry considerable power. It is desirable, therefore, to examine the phenomenon of social power as it operates on group interaction.

Social Power

In addition to norms and roles, a group's social structure also depends upon how social power is distributed. We can define **social power** as control over others through the use of rewards and punishments. People who maintain a great deal of social power are often more self-confident and more satisfied with themselves than those with less power. They are also most often the targets of communication, because they are seen as capable of helping or hurting others in achieving their goals.

From a communication point of view it is useful to study how power is used to affect group interaction. In other words, what strategies do people use to gain power or to implement the power they already have? French and Raven (1959) have identified five main types, or strategies, of social power. The first is the power of **attraction**. When others are attracted to or like an individual for some reason, then the individual has more control over the others. Your friends have more control over you than strangers do because of the attraction between you and your friends. The second is **reward** power. When individuals give physical rewards, such as money, or social rewards, such as flattery, to a person, they are implementing reward power. The third is the power of **coercion**. When one person tries to take away another's power by interrupting or threatening him, that person is using coercion. The fourth is **legitimate** power. Legitimate power results from one's formal position in an organization. An employer has legitimate power over his employees. The last is **expert** power. This power derives from a person's having greater skills or competencies than others.

Recently a review of a case being argued by two lawyers appeared in a local newspaper. The lawyers were negotiating a civil-suit case out of court. The first lawyer tried to use a reward-power strategy by complimenting the second lawyer for the way he had handled a recent case in court. Similarly, the second lawyer gave some initial concessions to the first lawyer in an attempt to implement a reward-power strategy. The concessions were also meant to demonstrate good will and increase the first lawyer's attraction to the second lawyer. Later in the negotiation the lawyers began to argue intensely, interrupting and threatening each other. Each was using coercive tactics in an attempt to take away some of the other's ability to control the interaction. Since both had equal status, neither had legitimate power over the other. However, the second lawyer demonstrated some expert power because he knew more about the case and the issue they were negotiating. As a result, the second lawyer was able to reach a much better settlement than he had anticipated initially.

Social power is often related to status in group interaction. The higher one's status is, the greater is one's ability to control the outcome of the interaction. Status and power are not necessarily the same thing; rather, an increase in one generally leads to an increase in the other.

The relationship between social power and problem-solving efficiency merits consideration. Our discussion of social power suggests that there are certain times when it is productive to use power strategies and certain times when it is not. Whether or not a power strategy works depends upon several variables. First, it depends upon what the members of the group perceive the powerful person's intentions to be. If they trust the powerful person, they might respond positively to a power play by that person. But, if they mistrust the powerful person's intentions, they might disrupt the task by trying to use their own power strategies. Second, the effects of power on productivity depend upon the group's perceived alternatives. If the powerful person is able to limit alternatives, then the members of the group are likely to comply because they have few choices. If the group members have a range of alternatives, the person in power will be less able to control their behavior. Shaw (1976) supports the conclusion that productivity is greater when the members of the group trust the intentions of the powerful person and when that person is successful in limiting the number of alternatives open to the group.

Leadership

Power and status are closely related to leadership. According to Rosenfeld and Plax (1975), leadership is a consequence of a combination of personal and social influences. These writers found that leadership can be predicted with some regularity according to the following variables: self-confidence, self-assurance, lack of nervousness, dominance, empathy, and intelligence. In addition, leaders are likely to be the center of attention, receive more communication, and exercise more influence over the group's decision.

In Ed's high school clique, Don was the person enjoying the leadership role. He was a smooth communicator, always confident, quick with a joke. In addition, he was physically attractive. The elected leader of the fraternity pledge class probably had many of the same characteristics.

One characteristic of leadership, intelligence, is meant in two ways. There is the intelligence a person is born with and there is situational intelligence. In some situations a person might emerge as the leader of the group, and in other situations involving the same people that person might not be a leader. Nevertheless, most of the research suggests that leaders demonstrate many of the characteristics named above across situations.

Leadership styles generally fall into two categories: authoritarian and democratic (Rosenfeld and Plax, 1975). An **authoritarian leader** tends to be anxious, cautious, unsympathetic, unaffectionate, unfriendly, unresponsive to people, skillful, and a recognized authority. Such leaders tend to have gained their leadership role because of the special skills they demonstrate in certain situations. The key characteristics of an authoritarian leader is that the person is object-oriented rather than person-oriented. He or she is typically more interested in getting the task done and is less interested in peoples' feelings. Audrey's boss is an obvious example of an authoritarian leader.

The **democratic leader** is the opposite of the authoritarian leader. While usually less forceful, democratic leaders are more relaxed, farsighted, friendly, affectionate, and introspective (in that they monitor their own behavior frequently). They try to help others succeed, are low on aggression, and are not interested in seeking revenge. They are person-oriented, i.e., interested in people's feelings.

In some situations the authoritarian leader may be more effective than a democratic leader. When the group has a simple task to perform and little time in which to do it, the authoritarian leader may be more successful in getting the group to finish the job on time. People may be more irritated at the end, but the task will be done. The democratic leader is probably a better person to select for complex tasks that take more time. This person will try to promote cohesiveness among group members, making them feel freer to express their ideas and generate alternative ways of solving the problem.

Most people find that in a new situation it is generally best to start with a democratic leadership style. Since new situations are often confusing and ambiguous, leaders find that by taking advantage of what people have to offer they can learn how to cope with the situation in relation to individual needs and desires. Then if the group needs to be disciplined, or time grows short and getting the job done is important, the leader can switch to an authoritarian style.

Group Pressure

Previously it was stated that when cohesiveness is high, the group has a great deal of control over individual behavior. Under these conditions the individual invests more of himself or herself in the group. Groups also exert pressure to conform in making decisions toward accomplishing some task. Several studies have found that individuals within a large group of strangers tend to go against their own beliefs and go along with the opinion of the group. In one group of studies, Asch (1951) placed a naive person in a group of confederates who were in on the experiment. When the confederates put pressure on the person to conform to beliefs that were contrary to his own, the naive person gave way an overwhelming number of times.

Another example of the ways in which a group affects an individual's behavior is the **"risky shift" phenomenon** (Shaw, 1976). Originally it was thought that individuals were more likely to make risky decisions than groups. The assumption was that individuals often acted as mavericks and were far less conservative than groups. However, researchers found that this was not true. They discovered that when the group reaches a consensus on matters of risk, it generally makes riskier decisions than would be made by individuals working alone. The best explanation of this phenomenon is that individuals may feel they have less personal responsiblity for a decision made by the whole group. Therefore, there is less overall risk to one person. This explanation seems to be supported by mob behavior. Mobs are considerably more willing to take risks than individuals working alone. Demonstrations in the 1960s and 1970s showed that when people get together in large mobs, the pressure starts building and people start doing things they wouldn't do by themselves. In short, there is support in numbers with relatively little individual responsibility at stake.

The Task Environment of the Group

A **task** is the set of activities a group must complete to accomplish its goals. When all group goals are accomplished, or considered unimportant, the group ceases to exist. Of course, group members and the group as a whole can have many complex goals, so that some groups may stay together for reasons outsiders cannot determine.

Types of Tasks

It is possible to identify three kinds of tasks. First, there are **discussion tasks** in which people participate to resolve some issue by reaching a consensus. Discussion tasks are issue-centered. Teen-agers who are trying to resolve important issues with their parents, such as who they can go out with and when it is appropriate to take the car, engage in discussion tasks.

The second type of task is the **production task**. Production tasks are designed to create products of one kind or another. These tasks are probably the most frequently cited reasons for engaging in group activity. Planning parties, negotiating work schedules, and developing procedures are production tasks.

Problem-solving tasks are the third type. These tasks deal with a problem by evaluating how things were done in the past. The procedure is to gather information, assess it, and solve the problem based on the information. Marriage counselors often handle problem-solving tasks. They gather information about a couple, then work out alternative ways the couple can satisfactorily live together. In tasks of this type, the ability to solve the problem depends largely on the quality of information.

It is important to know what kind of task a group is tackling so that the right people can be matched to the right task. For example, if you have people who want to engage in an issue discussion, and you want to solve a problem, you may look for people who are more interested in problem-solving tasks. But matching people to tasks involves other considerations, such as task difficulty.

Task Difficulty

According to Shaw (1976), difficult tasks (highly complex, time-consuming, or beyond the group's ability) tend to decrease the quality of performance in a group. The group makes more errors and takes more time to get the tasks done. Further, there is a greater struggle for leadership as members get frustrated and lose confidence in the leader. To reduce the frustration, people feel the need to communicate more frequently. By contrast, when the task is easy and things are going well, members are more reluctant to express dissatisfaction. There is less struggle for leadership because what the leader is doing must be right. In addition, the group is probably happy with the quality of performance since fewer errors are made and less time is taken.

Difficult tasks become easier if people are encouraged to express their frustrations. This may lead them to generate new ideas that will help the group get the job done. Another way of making difficult tasks easier is to clarify the group's goals at the start. When goals are clear, people are more highly motivated and the group's progress is more efficient. If goals are vague or confusing, motivation will decrease, conflict will increase, and the job is less likely to be accomplished. A common example of a group with an ambiguous goal is the class project. Professors hear students say they are frustrated because they don't know what they are doing. Often, these groups do not sit down in advance and determine exactly what they are trying to achieve. They just set out to do talking about "it," whatever "it" is.

The best recommendations for matching people to tasks are (1) keep the task simple if accuracy and time are big considerations; and (2) if you have a difficult task to perform, and you need it done quickly and accurately, pick a strong, but not necessarily authoritarian, leader who takes the time to define group goals.

Conclusion

Perhaps the best way to conclude this chapter is to provide a set of recommendations for organizing and participating in groups. In informal group discussions, being a skillful participant will help you understand others' positions more accurately and keep the discussion from having negative effects on individual members. In more formal settings (such as school presentations or work groups) you may be called upon to set up a group discussion to solve some important problem. In either case you'll need strategies to guide your plans.

1. Remember that people join groups to accomplish tasks in organizations, enhance their self-concepts, or conform to cultural expectations. Whatever members' goals, group discussion will probably go through four phases. First, they will sort out the information; second, search for ideas; third, engage in conflict over evaluating proposals; and fourth, focus on getting the task done. If your goals are task-related but others' goals are something else, you may spend more time in conflict than in constructive activity. Thus recommendation one is to determine people's goals before you get them together to get things done.

2. After identifying people's goals, consider the physical arrangement of the room. Central positions are usually viewed as more controlling. Select a central place to sit if you wish to influence the group's direction.
3. If you have a complex problem to solve with no clear-cut answer, give it to an unstructured group. Ideas will be more plentiful.
4. Choose or develop a group that is cohesive. Members of cohesive groups tend to be more highly motivated, more open, and better at solving complex problems.
5. When interacting in a group, try to identify and make contact with individuals in high-status positions. These persons are often central to getting things done. Identify the low-status persons so you can help integrate them into the group.
6. Select a group governed by more permissive norms if you plan on deviating from acceptable group practices. Permissive norms offer greater freedom and encourage more flexible behavior.
7. Try to avoid situations where people have vastly different expectations about what you ought to be doing. Any control you may enjoy from group cohesiveness may be compromised if roles conflict.
8. When implementing power strategies, make sure the group trusts your intentions. Otherwise, they'll fight you all the way. Try not to use coercion or legitimate power at first. These can irritate people. Instead, use reward, attraction, or expert power. They may take longer, but trust can emerge and people will feel better about helping you.
9. Unless group members need to be disciplined to get the job done, select a democratic type of leader who tends to be person-oriented. This individual will probably be better at enhancing genuine cohesiveness among members. But remember that leadership style should be matched to the task.
10. Be aware of the amount of group pressure operating in your group to get the task done. Otherwise, you may do things you might regret later. Make decisions based on facts, and avoid making decisions based solely on your emotional response to group pressure.
11. Keep the task simple enough for the group to handle. Difficult tasks threaten group structure and are harder to perform accurately and efficiently. However, if getting people to talk a great deal is your main goal, give them a difficult task. Just be aware of your purposes.

These recommendations are designed to help you control the group communication situation so as to achieve your goals. They are not comprehensive, but a good way to start improving your effectiveness in groups.

TERMS AND CONCEPTS FOR REVIEW

achieved status
adaption phase
ascribed status
attraction power
authoritarian leadership
chain network
characteristics of group
  communication (Applebaum)
circle network
coalition
coercion power
com-con network
communication network
complex
democratic leadership
discussion tasks
dynamic
expert power
goal-attainment phase

group cohesiveness
group norms
integration phase
interdependent
legitimate power
obligatory norms
orientation phase
permissive norms
problem-solving tasks
production tasks
reward power
"risky shift" phenomenon
role conflict
social power
spatial arrangement
status
systemic
task
wheel network

REVIEW QUESTIONS

1. Give several definitions of a small group.
2. What are the characteristics of group communication?
3. What are several reasons for joining groups?
4. What are the phases of group development?
5. What is a communication network? Discuss the satisfaction level of groups using structured and unstructured communication networks.
6. What effects do cohesiveness, status, norms, roles, social power, leadership, and pressure have on a group?

REFERENCES

Asch, S. E. "Effects of Group Pressure upon the Modification and Distortion of Judgments." In H. Guetzkow (ed.), *Group Leadership and Men.* Pittsburgh: Carnegie Press, 1951, pp. 177–190.

Applebaum, R. L., E. M. Bodaken, K. K. Sereno, and W. E. Anatol. *The Process of Group Communication.* Chicago: Science Research Associates, 1974.

Cattell, R. B. "New Concepts for Measuring Leadership in Terms of Group Syntality." *Human Relations,* 1951, 4, 161–184.

Cushman, D. P., and W. B. Pearce. "Generality and Necessity in Three Types of Human Communication Theory: Special Attention to Rules Theory." In B.

Ruben (ed.), *Communication Yearbook I.* New Brunswick, N.J.: Transaction Books, 1977, pp. 173–183.

French, J. R. P., Jr., and B. Raven. "The Bases of Social Power." In D. Cartwright (ed.), *Studies in Social Power.* Ann Arbor, Mich.: Institute for Social Research, 1959, pp. 150–167.

McDavid, J. W., and H. Harari. *Social Psychology: Individuals, Groups, Societies.* New York: Harper & Row, 1968.

Mabry, E. A. "Exploratory Analysis of a Developmental Model for Task-Oriented Small Groups." *Human Communication Research*, 2, 1, 1975, 66–75.

Mills, J. M. *The Sociology of Small Groups.* Englewood Cliffs, N. J.: Prentice-Hall, 1967.

Rosenfeld, L. B., and T. G. Plax, "Personality Determinants of Autocratic and Democratic Leadership." *Speech Monographs*, 42, 3, 1975, 203-209.

Shaw, M. E. *Group Dynamics.* New York: McGraw-Hill, 1976.

Smith, M. "Social Situation, Social Behavior, Social Group." *Psychological Review*, 1945, 52, 224–229.

Definition of an Organization

Functions of Organizational Communication
CONTROL
COORDINATION

Information Processing
LOCATION IN NETWORK OF INFORMATION FLOW
INFORMATION OVERLOAD AND UNDERLOAD
JOB INTERDEPENDENCY
TIME PRESSURE
INFORMATION-LOAD ANALYSIS

Communication Rules
PROCEDURAL RULES
CONTENT RULES
FORMAL RULES
INFORMAL RULES

Communication Flows
DOWNWARD
UPWARD
HORIZONTAL

Organizational Communication Networks
FORMAL
KINSHIP
OLD-BOY
PRODUCTION
INNOVATION
MAINTENANCE
NETWORK ANALYSIS

The Organization as a Form of Culture

6

Organizational Communication

After reading this chapter, you should be able to:

1. Identify features in modern organizations that can be traced to the first recorded large organizations.
2. Define the major attributes of organizations and explain how they differ from small groups.
3. Relate "control and coordination" to the discussion in chapter 1.
4. Define information load, overload, underload, and describe strategies for coping with load problems.
5. Define communication rules (procedural and content, formal and informal), and explain how they help an organization to function.
6. Describe various types of communication networks in organizations and explain the purposes they serve.
7. Describe some of the problems involved in incorporating new members into established organizations.

Several thousand years ago the first groups of hunters and foragers began to settle along the outlets of some of the world's major rivers. There are records of emerging civilizations that go back some seven thousand years in the great Nile River Delta basin. At sites like this one the foundations of modern organizations were first laid, and some of the features that are still useful in understanding today's organizations were first reported.

These early communities are thought to have developed largely due to some peculiar characteristics of the rivers themselves. Each spring the waters would rise and flood the surrounding lowlands. Rich silt would be deposited as the river levels subsided. The silt provided fertile land for growing crops. Abundant crops made it possible to shift life styles from hunting for game and searching for edibles to a concentrated productive use of the rich soil for growing food.

As this transition took place, new social arrangements emerged. First, individuals could grow enough food to support themselves and their immediate family and kin and still have a surplus to feed other people. The efforts of the others could be spent on different tasks. Second, for the agricultural system to work efficiently, it soon became obvious that large-scale cooperative efforts among individual farmers were needed. This cooperation was a distinct contrast to the individual efforts of the hunter-forager.

Why was cooperation needed? Although the spring floods did enrich and renew the soil each year, the floods were unpredictable and often created considerable damage—ruined dwellings, injuries and deaths, and other uncontrolled destruction. Consequently, in many of the early communities, groups organized to construct dams, channels, and dikes that would help bring the yearly floods under control.

Third, surplus food enabled membership in religious systems to flourish. Religious beliefs demanded offerings of worship and devotion to the gods as another way to help control the environment. Over time, these offerings became increasingly elaborate and complex and had to be looked after by specified members of the community.

In the most ancient of recorded civilizations, then, we already find evidence of some features of organizations that have carried through to the present day. A system of **hierarchy** evolved, in which individuals took positions of leadership. The leaders directed and controlled the behavior of those under them, their subordinates. In turn, leaders looked to higher-level leaders for overall guidance and direction. Gradually the first hierarchical chain of command became long and complex.

The new organizations required the creation of new jobs that had not been needed in the hunter-forager days. Administrators, or managers, were needed to see that the right materials, goods, and information were moved to the proper locations at the correct times. Administrators were not directly involved with actual production; instead, they tried to make the work of individuals more efficient than it could have been without any coordination or guidance.

As larger and more complicated organizations began to function, records became necessary. One reason for the rise of written language was to preserve vast amounts of complicated information: details of trade, the law, construction, religion, weather, etc. It soon became clear that no individual or group could memorize all of the information that was required to operate the city. This problem led to the first forms of writing. The typical forms of early written messages discovered by archaeologists are long lists of supply requests, ship cargoes, names of workers, transactions, and the like. Different media were used to store information. Among those that remain today are such things as stone engravings, bronze or other metal tablets, and wax cuttings.

Another feature of early organizations was an increase in the **impersonality** of membership. Larger numbers of people became involved and tasks became more specialized. There were priests, teachers, governors, soldiers, traders, and farmers. Each person had to learn how his or her work fit in with that of their co-workers. But few people could fully grasp the entire organizational process in which they were involved, in the way people had done when they lived in hunting bands.

Whenever impersonal relationships characterize an organization, the behavior of individuals will often be influenced, if not controlled, by others they may never see or know. This sense of isolation, and in many cases, frustration, can be injurious to a person's psychological and physical well-being, depending on how others act in the organization. Consequently, one of the problems that any organization must face is how to integrate or link its members into the overall structure. This process takes the time and attention of many managers. It requires a concentrated effort from all members of an organization if it is to be successful. The cost of failing to integrate new members into an organization can range from poor morale or low satisfaction to nonproductivity.

In the years that have passed since the formation of the first large organizations, there have been countless organizations formed to accomplish many different goals. Most have flourished for awhile and then died away. But a few organizations existing today have survived for several thousand years. The Catholic church is about two thousand years old. Military organizations, while they have had shorter life spans, have used essentially the same organizational form for thousands of years. However, the life span of most organizations still tends to be relatively short. Recent estimates suggest that approximately three-fourths of all the newly-founded small businesses in the United States will no longer exist five years from the date they first open their doors to the public. So while organizations flourish and grow more abundant in modern society, there is still much turnover and alteration in their form and their purpose for existence.

Definition of an Organization

An **organization** can be defined as (1) some number of individuals who (2) desire to achieve some set of goals, (3) recognize that goal achievement is best attained by cooperation rather than independent action, (4) gather whatever materials and information are needed from the environment, (5) process materials and information, and (6) return the modified materials and information to the environment with the intent of obtaining sufficient rewards so that the goals of the various members can be met (Farace, Monge, and Russell, 1977).

This definition of an organization is not restricted to the large corporations one most frequently hears about. Families, small groups (ranging from rock bands to prison work forces), communes, volunteer organizations (such as the "CB radio" groups), small businesses, state and federal bureaucracies, large profit-making organizations, multinational corporations—all of these labels identify different types of organizations. What is the difference, then, between organizations and small groups as discussed in chapter 5? Organizations, in general, are typically *larger* than groups (organizations are sometimes called "groups of groups"), have a much more extensive *hierarchy* (to control and coordinate their members), and have much greater *specialization* and *differentiation* (so that their members can perform a wide range of tasks). Finally, organizations develop a subculture of their own into which new members must fit. So while groups and organizations have a number of similarities, these issues, when looked at from the larger perspective of an organization, can take on different meaning and result in different outcomes, which will be discussed in the remainder of this chapter.

Functions of Organizational Communication

Communication is one of the central concepts in the study of organizations. Communication refers here to (1) the *control* processes that govern the operation of the organization's members, and (2) the *coordination* of the activities of the members of the organization.

As in chapter 1 "control" means the use of messages to achieve desired outcomes. Unfortunately, control has a negative connotation. Communication is used as a form of control in organizations primarily to direct the activity of a member so that it fits into the overall scheme of the organization. While some management styles (to be discussed later) treat control in a highly directive and one-way fashion, in many modern organizations the process of control and decision making that goes on between a manager and subordinate is much more transactional than it is mandatory. Thus while control is a key purpose of communication activities in an organization, it is typically not meant to be used in a negative, punishing, or demeaning sense.

"Coordination" refers to the need to direct the flow of materials and information from place to place in an organization. Further, the flow has to be timed so that each person can perform his or her work assignments as efficiently as possible. Thus communication serves to integrate the various parts of an organization into a harmoniously working whole. Poor coordination can cause many kinds of breakdowns, from the failure to assemble a car with all the proper parts to the exclusion of a key individual from a meeting at which important decisions are to be made.

As an individual, you function under the influence of a variety of organizations: family, peer groups, social and legal organizations, and, not the least, the college or university in which your education is taking place. Each one has its own distinct culture, that is, a shared, unique set of behaviors, expectations, procedures, and sanctions that, when taken together, allow one to describe the organization. It is important to understand the concept of an organization as a "culture." Only as you gain insight into how a particular organizational culture operates can you learn how to operate effectively in it. Individuals who are unaware of, uninformed about, or simply indifferent to the organizational cultures in which they exist are frequently destined for trouble.

Four key features of organizations seem especially important for "survival" purposes: (1) the *information-processing* procedures in the organization, (2) the communication *rules* of the organization, (3) the *flow of information* upward, downward, and horizontally in the organization, and (4) the *communication networks* that enable the individual to be fitted into the larger set of organizational processes that are taking place.

Information Processing

Information processing refers to the tasks that every individual engages in, on a day-to-day basis, in an attempt to deal with the torrent (or drought) of messages that arrive from many sources. In organizations, this means the specific activities that each member is expected to do as part of his or her job. A person's responsibilities include (1) finding out exactly what work to do each day, (2) identifying the other members of the organization who should receive completed work, and (3) specifying the tasks (writing, summarizing, reporting, presenting) that the individual is responsible for completing. Information processing in the organization, then, is a complex series of tasks which every member must perform reasonably well. It reflects the individual's contribution to the organization's adequate functioning.

Position in Information Flow

Many factors influence how much information processing any individual member does, that is, the person's **information load**. One is the person's location in the organization's network of information flows. Some individuals are more central than others to the flow of information and consequently have more information to process. Highly central individuals have to process and digest a great deal of information from many people and have to see to it that this information gets circulated in a timely, accurate, and complete fashion. Obviously, such central individuals have to be highly skilled in handling information. If people are required to process more information than they can handle, then they have an **overload**.

Jobs with a high information load are found in many parts of organizations and are not restricted to the managerial levels. The men and women who work behind the counters of busy coffee shops must deal with large numbers of people, each making different requests. A receptionist in a busy office is often under heavy pressure to process information both from people who come to the desk and from other members of the organization. This can often be a tricky business. Sometimes delicate issues have to be balanced, such as, for example, where someone "really is" as opposed to where the receptionist is supposed to *say* where the individual is.

If the information load typically falls well below the level that a person can process, then **underload** results. Underload is reported by many college students who take part-time jobs on factory assembly lines, by secretarial-clerical personnel whose capabilities are underutilized, and by sales personnel during a business slump. And being underloaded, like being overloaded, can be an unpleasant experience.

There are many techniques for coping with overloads and underloads. The basic goal of each technique is to give the person who is overloaded or underloaded more *control* over his or her information environment. We will describe some representative techniques for handling each situation; see Farace, Monge, and Russell (1977) or Johnson (1977) for further examples.

One way of dealing with an overload is to assign *priorities* to tasks and do the most important ones first. In addition, similar tasks can be put into common groups, a strategy called **chunking**; the individual tasks in each chunk can then be handled in much the same fashion, while minor differences between them can be ignored. Finally, it will usually be found that some tasks are unimportant and can be *omitted* entirely.

Underload can be coped with also. Some people bring reading material to work, for use when times are boring. Social conversation can occupy time as well. Daydreaming or speculating about future events is another way of treating underload.

All methods for solving overload or underload carry both positive and negative aspects. A strategy that helps you—called **adaptive coping**—may be detrimental to the organization, for whom it would represent **maladaptive coping**. For example, the priorities you assign to task completion may interfere with the completion of something desperately needed elsewhere in the organization. Or, reading on the job may get you fired if you are caught. The key to success is to analyze the situation first and then select an appropriate strategy.

Job Interdependency

A second factor which affects the amount of information load on an individual is **job interdependency**, that is, the amount of linkage between the person's job and other jobs in the organization. For example, if someone's work entails a steady stream of inputs which must be dealt with and sent on to other members of the organization, then there is a high degree of job interdependency. This is in contrast to the situation where an individual is relatively free to proceed at his or her own pace in the completion of any work.

The original models for high interdependency jobs came from the late 1800s and early 1900s, when mass production first appeared. Prior to that time, all phases of a production task were done largely by single individuals, e.g., a seamstress made a garment, or a carpenter built a house, from start to finish. This type of relatively self-contained work is often called a cottage industry.

The shift from cottage-industry work to mass manufacturing came about in recognition of some simple laws of efficiency. If labor is divided among many workers, with each one concentrating on only one operation of an entire production process, goods can be manufactured faster and more economically. Consequently, a flow of work is generated, beginning with the initial raw materials and moving step by step to the finished product. The automotive assembly line is the classic example of mechanized work. Obviously, jobs are highly interdependent in such situations. To control and coordinate highly interdependent jobs, a considerable amount of information flow must accompany the work

flow. If the information flow fails, the rate and quality of production will suffer. Failure can occur in control, coordination, or both.

Other kinds of organizations in today's world also have highly interdependent jobs. However, since they do not produce tangible goods (cars, appliances, etc.), their interdependence is less obvious. For example, the "product" of many governmental organizations is information, and the "manufacturing" process consists of printed data and messages, face-to-face discussion, group meetings, and other forms of information exchange. Insurance companies and banks are other examples of "manufacturing" that is primarily information processing. In such cases, information is not only the major product, but it also requires an accompanying, separate flow of information for control and coordination to function properly.

Certainly, even in the busiest of organizations, not every individual is highly centralized and involved in the information flow process. Many members find themselves at the periphery of the flow and can become organizational **isolates**. These are the people who often say that they "never know what's going on around here" or "I'm never told anything about important changes that take place." Isolates represent a genuine problem to the management of an organization since, by definition, they are not involved in an ongoing work-flow process and consequently can contribute relatively little to it. At the same time, they are consumers of the organization's resources, in the form of salaries, space, benefits, etc.

Time Pressure

Thus far we have suggested two factors—a person's position in an organization's information flow and job interdependency—that help determine how much time and effort will go into information processing. A third factor is the *time pressure* under which work takes place in an organization. Time pressure refers to the interval allowed for the completion of certain tasks. Obviously, there are situations in which an individual has a relatively unlimited amount of time to complete a task. However, in most organizational situations, tasks must be done quickly. The greater the time pressures that are placed on individuals, the larger their information load will be. Correspondingly, the greater the time pressures that are placed on the organization, the larger the information load that the organization itself has to bear.

When an organization has a high information load, the opportunity for overload and hence communication breakdowns is significant. Mistakes are more commonly made and often have more serious consequences, since there may be less time to recuperate from them. On the other hand, a very low information load (as is sometimes found in organizations that suddenly lose major contracts, or which exist without a clear job description in federal or state governments), can also have negative consequences for the organization. People become bored in extended underload conditions and seek things to do. They may read paperbacks, play cards, or form football pools to pass the time. Of course, short-term underload can be beneficial if it provides much needed rest and recuperation. The important point, however, is that both overload and underload can have adverse effects on an organization.

Information-Load Analysis

As a member of an organization, how do you assess your information-load situation? Perhaps the first step you should take is to analyze your information processing requirements. What kinds of information input, output, and processing requirements are expected of you? Who should supply you with information, where is it to come from, what are you supposed to do with it, and to whom are you to send it?

The next thing to determine is how much of the information flows relevant to you come under your influence. For example, if you work in the library at the check-out desk, where all the demands for information processing come from individuals over whom you have little control, you need to identify this aspect of your job. You may not be able to influence your load level immediately, but you at least know where the problem lies and may work to solve it. If, however, you are in a position to speed up or slow down the rate of information input to you, you can adjust your information work load and make it more predictable.

Next, you should estimate the length of time and the amount of effort you require to complete the different kinds of information processing tasks that affect you. If you find that your "output speed" is too slow, for example, that you're unable to write fast enough and cannot type or dictate, then your problem might be solved by learning new skills, such as typing or using a tape recorder or dictating machine.

You may also find that your procedures for processing information are not very efficient and that there are ways in which you could do the job more swiftly and thoroughly. For example, rather than "queue-ing"—processing each information request as it comes to you—it may be more efficient to sort the requests into similar groups and then handle each group as if its members were identical. Earlier, this strategy was called "chunking."

The kinds of information you produce, your output, should also be analyzed. Where are you supposed to send different types of information? What form is the information to take (short written summaries, long reports, illustrated reports, personal memos)? When should each type of information reach its destination? How can you establish feedback procedures so that you can determine whether your efforts have been worthwhile? The reason for including output activities in your analysis is to specify the linkage of your information behaviors with those of the rest of the members of the organization. In effect, this is how you see where you fit into the organization.

Once you have completed your information-processing analysis, you can see whether your problems are occurring in the input, processing, or output stages of your activities. Some of the problems you encounter may not be easily resolved, if at all and you will have to adapt to the situation as best you can. But in many instances, you can make changes in your behavior or the behavior of others, so that both you and the others are able to perform more efficiently. Such a result is the true benefit of the analysis we have just described.

Communication Rules

After years of dealing with people of all ages involved in organizational settings, it seems clear to us that the term "rules" is uniformly disliked by almost everybody. The reason is that, in our younger days, we learn (perhaps when our parents first try to curb our television viewing) that rules are generally things to be avoided. Rules are often seen as forms of punishment, as negative aspects of our life, and are "meant to be bent if not broken." In the organizational context, rules are used in a somewhat different and considerably more positive sense (Johnson, 1977).

Rules are most generally defined as patterns of expected or typical (normative) behavior which individual members of an organization follow. Rules describe the fundamental way an organization is structured, whether the organization happens to be a "do-your-own-thing commune" or a militaristic counterintelligence agency. Individuals who are contemplating forming some type of organization have basically two choices to follow. First, they can decide to impose *no* constraints on the behaviors of individual members, with the hope that if each member shares the same goals, all the various tasks in the organization will somehow get completed on time and properly. This view has often been expressed in attempts to develop communal organizations which lay down few, if any, rules.

The second choice is to formulate an initial set of agreements or understandings (rules) that are accepted by the members of the organization-to-be. These understandings form the basic structure under which the behavior of members is regulated. If the rules are adequate, they make it possible to accomplish the tasks the organization needs to get done. Obviously, the complexity and number of rules developed depend on how complicated the organization tasks are.

In some situations, such as a mini-organization which will exist only temporarily, relatively few rules are necessary. For example, if a group of individuals have decided to organize themselves to attend a rock concert, they need to reach only a few simple understandings—who will collect money for tickets and buy them, when they will go, how they will get there, where they will go afterwards, etc. Other situations will require more formal and enduring rule systems.

One way to evaluate the rule system of an organization, particularly in the early stages of the organization's development, is to determine the degree of efficiency that can occur if the rule is adopted. Rules can make things run more smoothly for all members of the organization because they provide a measure of *predictability* to the behaviors and expectations of members. The rules are one form of the sociological and cultural information discussed in chapter 1.

At a university, for example, an extensive rule system regulates each term's registration process. It is conceivable that students could be registered in the absence of an elaborate rule system. The cost of this, both to the students and to the university, however, would be staggering. All cases of registration would have to be treated as unique, and each would require a unique solution. Unique solutions are far more costly than standardized ones. Moreover, if there were no rules, there would be no attempt to provide fair access to registration facilities. There would be no uniform sets of cards or documents to use in completing the registration. There would be no simple way of getting money back if a course were selected but then dropped. At least in principle, the rule systems of an organization are designed to raise the predictability of the behavior of the organization's members. This in turn reduces the amount of time, effort, frustration, and energy they must spend completing their tasks. A similar increase in efficiency occurs for all the other aspects of organizational life, from paychecks to work flow to vacations.

Thus far we have discussed rules in general; we now turn to communication rules in particular. **Communication rules** refer to the procedures for interacting or communicating in the organization and to the types of content (message content or topics of interaction) that are appropriate and expected in the organization. Just as general rules help the organization function more efficiently, so communication rules allow communication processes to take place more efficiently and effectively than would be the case if no such rules existed.

Procedural and Content Rules

Communication scholars generally divide these rules into two categories: procedural rules and content rules. **Procedural rules** deal with the *how* of interaction. For example, how does one go about making an initial contact with a manager, another organizational member, or a person outside the organization? Procedural rules define the appropriate channels by which such problems are handled. They tell one when it is proper to just drop in, sit down, and chat with someone; when to telephone versus when to write a memo about something; when to start a conversation on one's own rather than wait for another person to start it; and, in general, how to proceed in dealing with people.

The procedural communication rules operating in a classroom have been built up over many years of prior school experience. In many classrooms, students raise their hands to indicate a desire to make a statement. Similarly, rather than just dropping by a faculty member's office, it is customary to arrange a meeting time in advance. Usually class members and the instructor take turns in speaking, to avoid "talking over" and obliterating one another's comments.

Content rules deal with the *what* of interaction. These rules refer to the kinds of topics or issues which are appropriate for discussion in an organization. Content rules include the "in-house" language system that goes with almost any organization. This language system includes such things as key abbreviations (e.g., ATL may refer to American Thought and Language in one setting, to Alpha Tau Lambda in another, or the American Tax League elsewhere). In the early 1960s it was not considered an appropriate communication content rule to use sexual terms during classroom conversations; however, the rule shifted in the late 1960s and early 1970s. Interestingly, it has moved closer to its original position in recent years.

Other instances of content rules are found in the interaction between faculty members and students. Often both parties feel constrained about the kinds of issues they will discuss. For example, the faculty member may not deem it appropriate to probe into the personal life of the student. The student may feel the same compunction in his or her interaction with the faculty member.

Formal and Informal Rules

Procedural and content rules are either formal or informal. **Formal rules** are those that have been agreed to and accepted by the majority of the organization, in particular the managerial hierarchy. These rules often appear in the form of published documents or guides which specify the appropriate procedures and content areas for interaction. For example, a document describing the "Rights and Responsibilities of Undergraduates" indicates the step-by-step communication procedures that are to be followed if a student has a grievance against a faculty member concerning a grade or some other matter. The document may also contain content rules indicating what information is appropriate to introduce into the discussion over the disputed grade. The content rules may change depending on whether the grade is being reviewed at the department level or at a higher level. Consequently, formal communication rules are often found in larger, complex organizations. These rules are one of the first things a new member must learn.

Informal rules are those that cover all topics not included under the formal rule system. They are more numerous and more diverse than the formal rules. Furthermore, many organizational observers will argue that the informal rules are as important as, if not more important than, the formal rules. In many cases, the informal rules arise to resolve the difficulties that may be inherent in the informal rules themselves. While formal rules are often management's statement of how procedures should operate, the informal rules indicate "how things really are."

Informal procedural rules vary tremendously from organization to organization. On a university campus, informal procedural rules may indicate such things as who one should seek for counseling about a drug or pregnancy problem. The counselors most often sought may not be those specified by the formal rules. Informal procedural rules may also indicate who key people are in other departments (particularly among the clerical staff) who might provide special favors for the resolution of problems in ways that differ from the formal rules.

A parallel set of informal rules will be found for the content issues. While formal content rules may prohibit students from discussing personal matters with faculty members, the informal system may indicate that certain faculty members can be easily approached because they will provide a sympathetic response and are often competent in giving assistance. Other informal content rules may indicate conditions under which it is appropriate to swear, or to bring up a sensitive topic (such as department politics) which would normally be prohibited on a formal basis.

New entrants to an organization are often first exposed to the formal communication rules system. It may take the form of documents or pamphlets which specify the appropriate procedural and content rules to be followed. Members of organizations may be urged, "If you have a problem, see your supervisor," in an attempt to discourage people from seeking assistance from a higher-level supervisor or from going elsewhere in the organization. However, it may turn out that one's supervisor is precisely the *wrong* person to go to under certain circumstances. Consequently, the new entrant may experience disorientation and confusion before the informal rules structure is learned. Often co-workers quickly help to fill in a new member's knowledge of the informal rules either by example or by direct commentary about what is "safe" or "appropriate."

As your experience in the organization increases, a key test to use to appraise your competence as a member is the extent to which you understand both the formal and informal communication rules system. You should know the formal procedures, ranging from how to find out about your benefits to how to investigate alternative jobs in the organization, because there can be significant penalties for breaking the formal rule structure. Your knowledge of the informal communication rules and your ability to use them provide you with the additional understanding and leverage required to function effectively in the organization. Knowing the rules helps you advance your career, protect yourself from the sanctions of the organization, and improve your standing.

Communication Flows

Understanding the flows and patterns of information in general in the organization has an important bearing on the communication conduct of each member (Farace, Monge, and Russell, 1977).

Communication scholars generally distinguish three types of communication flows in an organization. First, **downward communication flows** are the instructions, orders, and other direction-giving information that typically originate from upper management and are sent to subordinates so that specific tasks will be completed. This process occurs in all hierarchical organizations (and we have earlier argued that all organizations become inherently hierarchical, in spite of any intentions of their organizers to maintain an egalitarian structure).

Second, **upward communication flows** are the reports, replies, and feedback that the lower levels of an organization send back in response to upper-level directives. Third, **horizontal communication flows** refer to communication among co-workers or peers in an organization.

Downward communication presents a number of problems to managers. Even the simplest of statements—such as one announcing a change in tuition—often runs into formidable communication problems. First, the message must be stated differently for each hierarchical level. Lower-level administrators, faculty members, graduate and undergraduate students all want to know what the change means for them. The message should also be stated in language that is appropriate to each level. This type of communication problem is, unfortunately, not often clearly recognized by managers, who may believe that once something is committed to paper, it is by definition clear to all who read it. This is simply not the case.

Another problem in downward communication is that not all messages are equally applicable to all individuals. Consequently, many organizations spend a large amount of money and effort trying to identify the key transmittal paths for each type of message. To the extent that individuals are included or excluded erroneously, the effectiveness of the original message is going to be blunted if not eliminated. What is required is a careful assessment of who the relevant audiences are for each message and then the identification of the most efficient route to these audiences. In some situations a printed message may be less suitable than a video cassette presentation, a tape recording, or some other communication medium.

While downward communication is, therefore, biased to some extent, upward communication is even more biased. There are several reasons. The first is the sheer quantity of information that could be sent from lower levels to higher levels. If each member of a ten-thousand-person organization had only two pieces of information to send to the top of the organization, then some twenty thousand pieces of information would deluge that individual. Clearly, some condensing and filtering of information is necessary.

Communication problems arise when the condensing and filtering that takes place is done on a subjective basis. That is, individuals at each level of the hierarchy are prone to select only that information which they feel is important or suitable for the next level up to hear; negative information is often modified or omitted entirely. Consequently, the information that the top-level person receives is often a highly distorted version of the initial message.

The second major problem faced by upward communication is that even if selective distortion is not introduced, the need to condense and eliminate extraneous information results in a large reduction in total information transmitted. Figure 6–1 illustrates how this process could affect the flow of information in a five-level organization. If we decide that only 90 percent of the information received on each level can be passed on to the next level, then only a fraction—about two-thirds—of the original information reaches the top. In most circumstances, a far smaller percentage reaches the top. This of course leaves high-level managers severely underinformed, although if an attempt were made to fully inform them, then information overload would no doubt take place.

Horizontal information differs from downward and upward information not only in the direction of its flow but also in its content. Instead of being highly work-related (as in the other two types of communication), horizontal information is much more socially oriented. It is apt to deal with sports, gossip, leisure activities, family matters, and other everyday topics of conversation. As such, it adds spice to the routines of work and affords a respite from the basic work-flow information. Horizontal com-

Figure 6–1
A Five-Level Organization, with Amount of Upward Flow of Information Reduced by 90 Percent at Each Level, Resulting in 66 Percent Reaching the Top Level

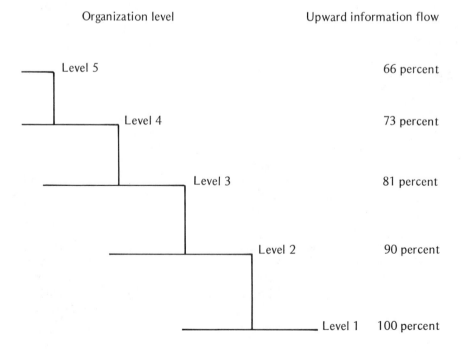

Organization level	Upward information flow
Level 5	66 percent
Level 4	73 percent
Level 3	81 percent
Level 2	90 percent
Level 1	100 percent

munication typically accounts for about half of the total amount of information exchange taking place.

Organizational Communication Networks

Formal Network

One of the first things you notice when you walk into almost any office building is a directory of the names, titles, and office locations of the people who work there. Typically, these lists will reveal the majority of the *formal* hierarchical rank distinctions that are made in the organization. For example, they will identify the president (or other head), the various executive vice presidents, senior vice presidents, assistant vice presidents, and finally the persons who work at managerial levels below them.

As noted earlier in this chapter, authority, or hierarchy, plays a central role in the control and coordination of any organization. In most of today's large corporations, authority provides the central focus around which communication networks are arranged. The authority network, often called the formal network of the organization because it is the one spelled out in organization charts, indicates who is intended to supervise, control, coordinate, direct, and receive reports from other members at every level of the organization. Many persons give a great deal of attention (and perhaps respect) to the formal network. However, the formal network is only one of many organizational networks. Other networks often exert as much if not more influence on the way work takes place in the organization, and these need to be recognized and understood.

Kinship Network

One of these is the **kinship network**. It consists of people in the same organization who have ties, by blood or by marriage, and who endeavor to provide special benefits to one another. These can include "leaking information," giving advice on how to deal with particular problems, and forewarning of major organizational changes. While kinship networks are not necessarily widespread (at least in American organizations) or even ever dominant in a given organization, they do exist and can have significant consequences for the organization.

Old-Boy Network

Another type of network is called the **old-boy network**. This term originally referred to individuals who had gone to school together and then later went into the same organization for employment. Today it is used in a broader sense. Old-boy networks can develop around previous work experience elsewhere or as a result of a long association in various parts of the same organization. They can arise from any circumstances in which a set of people identify closely with and help one another on the basis of similar backgrounds and experiences. The old-boy network becomes particularly important in a later discussion of the way in which new organizational members (particularly women and minority groups) become integrated into the overall organizational hierarchy.

Networks for Special Communication Purposes

There is a variety of networks for particular communication needs in the organization. We have already mentioned one of these, i.e., the particular pathways that messages must take from one level of an organization to another so that they reach the appropriate individuals. This is called the **production communication network**. For example, directives typically flow down the formal authority network, and reports of compliance move upward. Two other networks are also important to communication in an organization. One, the **innovation network**, has to do with the movement of messages about new ideas and practices. The other, the **maintenance network**, refers to the movement of information about social relationships, learning "the ropes," and other forms of interpersonal information.

The innovation network in any organization is critical to its functioning. The production network, while it enables the day-to-day work of the organization to get completed, is typically insensitive to change either inside or outside the organization. The purpose of the innovation network, therefore, is to provide this sensitivity. In other words, the innovation network serves as a means of transmitting information about important changes in the internal or external conditions that may affect the operation of the organization.

For example, some writers have attributed the rise in student protests on university campuses in the late 1960s and early 1970s to the increased feeling among students that they were cut off from effective communication with the central power structure, namely the university administration. Consequently, by engaging in violent and disruptive acts, the students attempted to form communication linkages with the administration. A more ordinary example of an internal innovation network is the "suggestion system," in which members of an organization are asked to write out their problems and observations about the way the organization is operating and forward them (usually anonymously) to higher-level management. The university ombudsman provides one means among several of allowing information about changes needed in the internal operation of the university to reach higher-level administrators.

Innovation communication networks designed to gather information about changes *outside* the organization vary from the use of press clipping services (who collect all published articles making reference to the organization), to special research and development units (marketing or advertising units) or other analytical groups. Often lobbyists are hired to work with state and federal regulatory and legislative bodies to provide additional input to the organization.

Both internal and external innovation networks are necessary for the long-term survival of an organization. The internal networks have to detect potentially disruptive changes occurring within the organization. If serious morale problems, for example, go unnoticed, irreparable damage may occur in the relationships between the work force and management. Such a problem occurred in the Lordstown, Ohio, Chevrolet plant in the early 1970s, when workers rebelled against stepped-up automation procedures designed to increase production. The externally oriented innovation networks must recognize and report changes in the environment such as shifts in consumer preferences or in legislative allocations of funds. Managers can use such information to change their manner of operating and the goods or services they produce.

The final type of communication network—maintenance communication—relates to the organizational member as an individual. The maintenance network becomes important the moment a person first enters the organization. A host of questions need answering, from "When do I get paid?" to "Who's really safe to trust around here?" The maintenance network provides information regarding behavior and dress codes, procedures for handling different kinds of problems (regardless of whether there are "formal" procedures for handling them), as well as the latest gossip and the ins and outs of office politics.

Maintenance communication humanizes the organization. It allows each individual to obtain a perspective of himself or herself in relationship to others and to gain an insight into the character and temperament of managers, of other divisions, of clients, and of co-workers. It is through the maintenance network that people also learn about the quality of their performance—whether "a good job has been done" or "the team really messed up that last task." This feedback allows them to adjust their perceptions of how they are doing their work and how they are relating to other members of the organization.

Network Analysis

The study of communication networks in organizations has received an increasing amount of attention in recent years. It has been found that the formal authority network (the most well-known network) is a poor predictor of many communication events and relationships that take place in almost every type of organization, whether it is a strict "command and control" organization or an open "research and development" organization. Consequently, a series of research techniques have been developed to allow communication scholars to study the relationships between networks and other types of organizational behavior.

Network analysis can assist managers in understanding communication in their organization in a variety of areas. For example, many organizations are interested in the degree to which there exists some kind of innovation communication network and who participates in it. Managers realize the importance of both internal and external communication networks as a means of helping the organization to prosper (if not survive) in a changing world. What are some of the things that a network analysis can indicate to a manager? (A diagram of a network is shown in Figure 6–2.)

First, a typical network analysis reveals the various *groups* of individuals in each network. (For different networks, members may combine in different ways.) A **group** is defined as a set of individuals who share more than half their communication contacts with one another. This information is obtained by asking all the members of the organization to

Figure 6–2
Diagram of a Communication Network. I's Are Isolates (No Links to Others). B's Are Bridges (Group Members with Contacts in Another Group). L Is a Liaison (Links Three Groups but Does *Not* Have a Majority of Contacts in Any One Group). All Others Are Group Members Only.

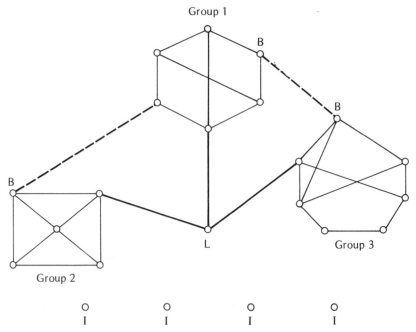

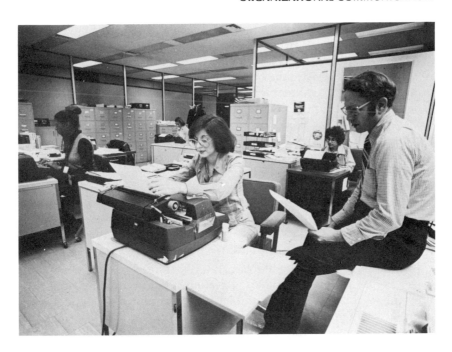

indicate whom they communicate with (in this case, about matters related to innovation), and then the results are computer-analyzed to isolate the groups of people who meet this criterion.

A second product of network analysis is a list of the linkages *between* the various groups that have just been identified, i.e., the individuals within each group who also have contacts with one or more other groups. These individuals, called **bridges**, serve as direct means of contact from one group to another. Other individuals, called **liaisons**, while not having a majority of their communication with any one group, also serve to link two or more groups.

Finally, a typical network analysis locates the isolates in the organization. Isolates, as noted earlier, are individuals who have relatively few, if any, contacts with other members of the organization. It may sound strange to say that isolates can exist in organizations (since theoretically everyone reports to at least someone and should come in contact with that person), but in fact there are organizations in which a relatively high percentage of members (perhaps 5 to 15 percent or more) report that they communicate little with anyone else. Their co-workers, in turn, indicate that they do not communicate with these isolates.

How can the findings of a network analysis benefit the organization? First, by examining the membership of each of the groups in the innovation network, it is possible to determine whether all important parts of the organization are included in the network. If a major portion is left out, it may not become aware of important changes that affect it. For example, a unit may not know about a profitable new technology, without which it will be unable to meet its own expected profit levels. It may be necessary to designate individuals to transmit innovation information to isolated units to increase the organization's overall ability to acquire and process innovation communication.

Second, by examining the organizational members who act as bridges or liaisons between groups, managers can determine how well they are serving this function. It is possible that there are isolated groups, i.e., groups that do not link with any other groups and hence do not participate outside of their own membership in the receipt and transmission of innovation communication. If a person is responsible for passing new ideas back and forth to other parts of the organization, and if it turns out that the person is not fulfilling this function, then it is necessary either to redefine his job description, revise the work he actually does, or perhaps replace him with someone who will be effective in the linking role.

In addition, once linking individuals are identified, they can be treated as **key communicators** in the organization. They are usually already influential in their capacity as information transmitters. Consequently, since most organizations have limited resources to use in disseminating information, or in conducting training programs, these individuals can be brought together for special training and then returned to their work groups. The assumption here is that by expending the available communication resources on the key communicators, it will be possible for them to have a **multiplier effect** when they return to their units. They should introduce new information into the innovation communication network much more efficiently and probably more accurately than if a more general approach to information distribution were taken.

The isolates in the organization may also receive special management attention. By scrutinizing these persons, managers should be able to find out the reasons for their isolation. Often better communication and dissemination programs are necessary for isolates to become integrated into the main flow of information. The cost of continuing to ignore these individuals can be high, since they are drawing upon the organization's resources, yet their work receives relatively little coordination or control. Isolates are unlikely to contribute productively to the organization. Consequently, it is usually wise to try to reduce their number.

The Organization as a Form of Culture

To understand organizations from a communication point of view, it is necessary to realize that all organizations have a "mini-culture" of their own. The term "culture," as noted earlier, is typically used to describe some set of common beliefs, attitudes, and behavioral norms and practices that are subscribed to by the members of that culture. There is an extensive literature on different kinds of cultures, from primitive societies to urban street gangs, from rural farm cultures and communes to artistic-intellectual "elites" and Westernized versions of Eastern philosophies. Each of these cultures is operationalized in the form of some type of organization, and this organization develops its own common set of beliefs, norms, values, and attitudes which makes it coherent and distinctive from its environment.

All organizations, then, represent some type of cultural coherence. This is as true for an individual family as it is for a giant military-industrial complex. To be a member of any organization, you must be able to fit into its established operating procedures. In many ways, you have been participating in the cultures in formal organizations all your life, beginning with your family and then going on to school, church, scout, sports, friendship, work, and other groups. This process will continue throughout your career, and to the extent that you understand the communication principles involved, you will find it easier to enter and to leave any given organization.

Let's look at the individual in relationship to an existing organization with a thriving membership. From the point of view of the organization, a great deal of time and effort has already gone into developing rules and procedures for dressing, working, behaving, and even thinking. These rules and procedures are generally accepted and felt to be of considerable value to the performance and survival of the organization. While we do not want to treat organizations as if they are "living organisms," they can be seen as often large collections of individuals who share common perceptions concerning what the organization is all about. Consequently, when a new member comes along, he or she represents a potential threat to the established order of business in that organization.

How does an organization react, then, to new members? It attempts to socialize them into thinking and behaving the way most people in the organization think and behave. Thus new members are given training programs to acquaint them with some of the fundamental operations of the organization. These can range from dress codes to an explanation of how to apply for various kinds of benefits. In addition, an older member of the organization may be appointed to help entrants learn their way around as quickly as possible. This will include learning how to process information, learning the communication and other rules, and learning how the organizational groups and networks operate.

In the beginning of this chapter, we noted that one of the purposes of organizing is to reduce unnecessary variability in the behavior of the organization's members. This reduction, which makes it possible to

achieve maximum performance, output, satisfaction, and other measures of organizational productivity, is accomplished largely during the
socialization of new members. The process is aimed at curbing the tendency of any new member to behave in a sufficiently deviant way from
the other members of the organization so as to disrupt or interfere with
its operations.

Another name for the process we have been discussing is "learning
the system." Much of the time of college students is spent in learning
the system so as to achieve their goals—from graduating with honors to
just graduating, while enjoying life in both academic and nonacademic
areas. "Beating the system" may take priority once the workings of the
university are understood. "Falling victim" to the system is something
that happens to students who fail to learn some procedure of the university (for example, how to add or drop a course late in the term). All
three processes—learning the system, manipulating the system, or falling victim to the system—depend largely on the use or misuse of communication procedures.

The concept of organizations as cultural entities is especially important for those who do not find themselves members of the "majority" of
an organization. For example, a young person who moves from a rural
community to an inner-city area will find his or her cultural background
widely different from that of an urban street gang. Being accepted by
that urban street gang will not be easy. Similarly, a person from a middle-class socioeconomic background will have difficulty integrating himself into an organization of lower-class construction workers. Thus the
degree of difficulty an individual experiences in becoming a central
member of an organization is correlated to the degree of difference between the backgrounds of the person and of the majority of members.

In our society a high percentage of jobs are in private and governmental organizations that are predominantly managed by white males. Typically, the educational levels found among younger managers (under
thirty-five or forty) are higher than those of older managers (forty and
over).

Many of these managers have worked in their organizations, or in
similar organizations, for many years. From all that we know about communication, and the effects of continual interaction on values and beliefs, it is safe to assume that these individuals exhibit a reasonably homogeneous viewpoint about the world and the way in which it should
operate. They are likely to have a similarly common view of how their
organizations should be managed and how the members of these organizations should act. In other words, today's managers are to a large extent part of a fairly widespread old-boy network based on common sets
of experiences, expectations, and aspirations. Their cohesiveness is not
particularly active or conscious; rather, it is an outgrowth of the similar
courses their lives have taken.

What does this mean for an individual attempting to begin work in an organization? The most obvious point is that to the degree one's own background is different in any major way from that of the middle- and upper-level managers, behavioral changes will have to occur if the person is to be accepted by them. If the individual is female, her sex will set her apart, since the majority of the authority figures she will deal with will typically be white males. If the person is black or a member of some other minority group, the problem may be compounded by a set of values, expectations, and beliefs that differ from that of the predominant managerial hierarchy.

Women and the Culture of Organizations

Let's look specifically at the case of the entrance of women into management (Hennig and Jardin, 1977). A large proportion of women in this country work, but only a very small proportion of them occupy higher-level managerial positions. Research by communication scholars and others has only recently begun to probe some of the reasons for the absence of women in high managerial levels. This research has taken two general directions. Some of it deals with issues related to early childhood socialization, interpretations of the psychological state of women as they mature and enter the work force, etc. Other research deals with communication issues—for example, what are the communication skills and deficiencies of women insofar as they contribute to the managerial success or failure of women? While no firm conclusions have been reached in either of these research areas, some interesting findings are beginning to emerge.

First, women in organizations appear to be less likely to form their own networks for social support and information exchange. Lacking these networks, they are often among the isolates in organizations. This puts them at an obvious disadvantage, because each one is required to start from scratch in terms of what it takes to succeed in the organization. This type of communication failure is obviously one that can be remedied through training and through assertive cooperation on the part of groups of women within the organization.

Another tentative communication finding concerns the ability to accept criticism from others. From their youth on, males are more likely than females to be members of teams (whether organized to play football or to build a new skyscraper), in which a good deal of criticism is often leveled at members. Long-term exposure to critical discussion makes a person less sensitive to criticism and better able to distinguish between criticism of an idea and criticism directed toward the person. The research on the subject suggests that women have less experience in making this distinction and tend to react to criticism on a more personal basis than men. To the extent that this is true (and, in fact, it does not matter whether one is male or female—what matters is how one operates under such a handicap), women will be less likely to fare well in the managerial world.

A third communication problem that women or others may face has to do with the "inside language" of the predominant managerial group. For example, consider a group of people discussing a problem. Suppose the discussion has been a frustrating one, and the individuals are not at all sure which of several possible solutions to choose. One member pipes up and says, "Oh, hell, let's punt!" To the person not familiar with the mysteries of football, this expression will convey little meaning. Furthermore, if one shows ignorance of this sort of thing, one's position as a credible participant in the discussion will probably be damaged. Unfamiliarity with inside language can thus act as a barrier to acceptance by the group and, in turn, to advancement in the organization.

In summary, key communication elements that help people fit into an organizational culture more efficiently include (1) identifying the important background differences between the individual and the managerial hierarchy and anticipating the differences in language, values, dress, etc. that might cause problems; (2) building informal social-support and information-exchange networks with other organizational members; (3) being able to cope with criticism, especially in distinguishing personal from professional criticism; and (4) learning the special language of the organization so as to be able to communicate more precisely and comfortably with other members.

Conclusion

Methods of controlling and coordinating the work of organizations were first developed thousands of years ago. Today one of organizations' major challenges is the processing of information. Having either an overload or an underload of information presents problems, which members of organizations need to know how to handle. Communication rules help guide the flow of information. These include procedural rules, content rules, and formal and informal rules. Communication flows in three main directions: upward, downward, and horizontal; and communication networks play a crucial role in aiding the flow, in providing information about changes within and without the organization, and in humanizing the work. The individual who wants to succeed in an organization must become acquainted with its culture, particularly the ways in which its managers think and behave.

TERMS AND CONCEPTS FOR REVIEW

adaptive coping
bridges
chunking
communication rules
content rules
downward communication flows
formal and informal rules
groups
hierarchy
horizontal communication flows
impersonality
information load
information processing
innovation network
isolates

job interdependency
key communicators
kinship network
liaisons
maintenance network
maladaptive coping
multiplier effect
old-boy network
organization
overload
procedural rules
production network
underload
upward communication flows

REVIEW QUESTIONS

1. What features in modern organizations can be traced to the first recorded large organizations?
2. What are the major attributes of organizations? How do organizations differ from small groups?
3. How does "control and coordination" relate to the discussion in chapter 1?
4. What is an information load? Overload? Underload? What strategy can be adopted for dealing with load problems?
5. What are communication rules (procedural and content, formal and informal)? How do they help an organization to function?
6. What are the types of communication networks found in organizations? What purpose does each serve?
7. What are some of the problems involved in incorporating new members into established organizatons?

REFERENCES

Farace, Richard V., Peter R. Monge, and Hamish M. Russell. *Communicating and Organizing.* Reading, Mass.: Addison-Wesley, 1977.

Johnson, Bonnie McDaniel. *Communication: The Process of Organizing.* Boston: Allyn & Bacon, 1977.

Hennig, Margaret, and Anne Jardin. *The Managerial Woman*, Garden City, N.Y.: Anchor Press/Doubleday, 1977.

The Mass-Communication Process
SOURCE, MESSAGE, CHANNEL, RECEIVER FACTORS

PROCESS OF EXPOSURE AND EFFECT

Audience-Exposure Patterns
TELEVISION, RADIO, NEWSPAPER, AND MAGAZINE CONSUMPTION

OVERALL LEISURE-TIME ALLOCATION

EXPOSURE AMONG DIFFERENT DEMOGRAPHIC SUBGROUPS

FUTURE EXPOSURE PATTERNS

Dimensions of Audience Effects
DEFINITION OF EFFECT

TYPOLOGY OF MEDIA EFFECTS

METHODS FOR STUDYING EFFECTS

DIRECT INTENDED EFFECTS VERSUS INDIRECT SIDE EFFECTS

Effects of Informational Content
IMPACT OF NEWSPAPER AND TELEVISION NEWS

LEARNING OF HARD AND SOFT NEWS CONTENT

STATUS-CONFERRAL AND AGENDA-SETTING EFFECTS

INDIRECT INFLUENCE ON ATTITUDES

Impact of Persuasive Content
FACTORS LIMITING IMPACT ON ATTITUDE CHANGE

ADVERTISING INFLUENCE

Situational View of Interpersonal Communication
SITUATIONAL CHARACTERISTICS

Developmental View of Interpersonal Communication
THE OCCURRENCE OF RELATIONAL CHANGES

IMPLICATIONS OF DEVELOPMENTAL VIEW

Strategies for Gathering Information
INTERROGATION

SELF-DISCLOSURE

SPECIALIZED STRATEGIES

Impact of Entertainment Content
MOTIVATIONS AND FUNCTIONS OF ENTERTAINMENT EXPOSURE

SOCIAL LEARNING THEORY

RESEARCH IN THREE TV CONTENT AREAS

7

Effects of the Mass Media

After reading this chapter, you should be able to:

1. Recognize the various ways in which the media affect a person's thinking and behavior at the conscious level.
2. Explain the broad range of subtle and unintended effects that may be produced by the media on individuals.
3. Discuss the key research conclusions regarding social issues such as the impact of TV violence or political advertising on media users.
4. Predict how the audience will respond to certain types of mass-media content, and identify effective techniques of mass communication.

The mass-communication media play a pervasive role in modern society, although the precise dimensions of their impact are still being documented. This chapter provides an overview of some important types of effects, examining how individuals respond to various messages presented through television, newspapers, radio, and magazines.

Most readers will already hold some notions about how much the media affect themselves and others. In this chapter the scientific theories and research will serve as the basis for understanding the influence of the mass media. The mass-communication process will be described and differentiated from the interpersonal process. Evidence on audience-exposure patterns will then be considered, followed by a theoretical discussion of media effects. A summary of research findings regarding the actual impact of news, persuasion, and entertainment constitutes the largest section of the chapter.

Why study the theoretical perspectives and empirical evidence regarding mass-media effects? A main reason is that research often demonstrates counter-intuitive or complex or unexpected types of effects. Try your own judgment in deciding whether the following conclusions are true or not. (Correct answers are at the end of the chapter.)

T F 1. The average American spends about five or six hours a day watching TV, and this level is increasing as cable TV spreads.

T F 2. Shortly after watching a televised newscast, the typical viewer can remember about half of the twenty stories presented.

T F 3. When a major news story breaks, at least 90 percent of the public gains its first awareness from mass media rather than interpersonal sources.

T F 4. Individuals who are less familiar with a news topic tend to learn the most from mass-media news reports.

T F 5. If the news media devote extensive coverage to a social movement or political leader, the public tends to think the movement or leader is more important and significant.

T F 6. Brief political commercials have a greater informational and persuasive effect than half-hour televised speeches by a candidate.

T F 7. The individual's psychological defenses against attitude change are so strong that persuasive media messages seldom have influence.

T F 8. Both children and adults usually believe that characters and situations on fictional TV programs are realistic.

T F 9. Television has caused a drop in IQ scores, and rock music has increased sexual promiscuity among teen-agers.

T F 10. If parents sit and watch highly violent programs with children, the impact on aggressive behavior is reduced.

T F 11. Television portrayals of positive social behavior are imitated by children.

If you didn't get a perfect score on this quiz, read on and learn more about the effects of the mass media. But first, a preliminary framework.

The Mass-Communication Process

What is mass communication, and how does it differ from dyadic, or two-person, communication? In chapter 1 we emphasized the process-oriented and transactional nature of communication, which applies most appropriately to the interpersonal setting. Although conceptualizations of mass communication may pay lip service to reciprocal sharing between the medium and those with whom it communicates, most approaches focus on the static one-way flow from an active source to an audience of receivers who are influenced by the message.

We define mass communication as a process of *mediated* communication between an *institutional source* and a large, diverse, dispersed *audience* via a mechanical device. Each of the components of the communication model becomes more complex and formal in the mass-communication context:

Source. In the dyadic setting, the source is often an ordinary person who is informally communicating back and forth with a friend or acquaintance; indeed, as we saw in chapter 1, the source and receiver often exchange roles as Communicator 1 and Communicator 2. The source in mass communication is a professional communicator or commercial organization (e.g., Johnny Carson or the *Time* magazine staff), whose livelihood depends on successful communication with large anonymous audiences. As such, the source is likely to have greater technical communication skills but be less persuasive than a personal source can be in a dyadic setting.

Receiver. The receiver in a dyadic situation is typically a single individual in direct contact with the source. In the mass-communication model, the receiver role is played by a large and diverse audience in many locales (ranging from several hundred local readers of a weekly newspaper to 40 million nationwide viewers of a popular TV show). These distant and anonymous receivers have much greater freedom to select which messages to heed than do dyadic receivers who may feel obliged to listen. In ignoring and avoiding messages, mass-communication receivers exercise such selective control that the vast majority of media messages never reach large segments of the target audience.

Message. In catering to the various needs and tastes of a broad range of receivers, mass-communication messages tend to feature general-interest content presented in a mass-appeal format. Unlike face-to-face communication, where a message can be specifically tailored for a receiver, the style and substance of mass-media messages are not so precisely pertinent to specific individuals in the audience. This factor may hamper persuasive effectiveness, but extensive entertainment and informational effects can still occur.

Channel. The large number of geographically dispersed receivers requires that messages be disseminated across time and space through mediated channels via some mechanical device (i.e., a printing press producing words on paper, or a broadcasting transmitter sending signals to home TV sets). Instead of face-to-face exchanges using multiple sense modalities and full feedback, mass communication is characterized by unidirectional flow with limited and delayed feedback involving only one or two senses. This restricts the capacity of some mediated channels to convey meaning (e.g., the nonverbal code system described in chapter 2 is limited for magazine articles and radio programs), although producers have developed shorthand mediatory codes to compensate for this limitation. The source's opportunity to adjust messages as the communication event unfolds is also restricted (e.g., a newscaster cannot repeat or clarify material when receivers do not understand). Reciprocity between the communication parties is quite restricted.

Process. There are several key operations and phases in the process of mass communication. The essential origin occurs when a source organization produces a message and mechanically transmits it through a mediated channel; the source, message, and channel blend together to form a stimulus package (e.g., a televised news report by CBS's Walter Cronkite, or a printed editorial in the *New York Times*). Some individuals in the potential audience approach the stimulus and select the offering while many more do not attend to it. The receivers exhibit widely varying responses to the material and display distinctly diverse learning patterns in the way they take in the content (i.e., some persons in the radio audience enjoy a song while others are repelled; some magazine article readers gain no knowledge while others store the information for later use). It is important to recognize that the receiver is an active agent in this process, not just a sitting duck knocked over by the all-powerful stimulus. As noted earlier, there are some limited feedback loops in this process. After messages are transmitted, media organizations monitor the level of audience exposure and approval with constant research efforts (e.g., TV program ratings, magazine sales figures, and surveys of reader attitudes toward various parts of a newspaper). Occasionally, receivers make a more active response by sending comments to the media. These forms of feedback shape subsequent media output, as when programs are cancelled or newspaper design is modified.

The pattern of consumption by the receiver varies across media. The next section delineates the mass-media exposure in contemporary American society.

Audience-Exposure Patterns

Take away my air conditioner, take away my dishwasher, and take away my garbage disposal, but don't take away my television set. Take away my newspaper, my radio, and my subscriptions to *Reader's Digest* and *Playboy*, but don't take away my television set.

That placement of such high value on television and what it brings into the American home characterizes the massive consumption of that medium. Recent surveys attest to the priority that Americans place on access to and persistent use of television. In fact, the daily usage of the several mass media far exceeds all other activities for adult Americans, except for the amount of time spent sleeping and working. By choice, we turn to mass media as our primary leisure-time activity.

Virtually every home has a television set, and the majority of homes have more than one. The typical adult spends an average of three hours each day watching commercial television programs from the three major networks. Time spent with public television is a barely countable fraction of our TV time. Television is watched with varying degrees of concentration. We tend to focus our attention on a program at its beginning, again when the action picks up, and for the close. In between we may drift off or engage in other activities.

Radio listening gives us far more choices, and we choose to listen about two hours a day. From a dozen or more local stations, in most sections of the country, we can typically find one that specializes in our preferred content. However, listening to the radio is generally a secondary activity, one performed while driving, say, or studying, and not one around which we organize large time blocks.

The newspaper requires more rigorous attention than the broadcast media. It is most difficult to read and play cards, for example. Daily newspapers reach about 80 percent of the population. About a half-hour is spent with the newspaper each day, reading its news, features, and advertisements. Over the past few years, newspaper readership has been dropping, particularly among younger people, who are opting for alternative news sources.

The magazine has become an increasingly specialized medium. Until

the mid-1960s the large general-circulation magazines such as *Life* and *Saturday Evening Post* were the staples of the magazine industry. They were designed to appeal to the broadest possible reader groups. Now, magazines are effectively targeted to specific interests of subgroups of the population. Whatever one's hobby is, there are probably several magazines devoted to it. For example, there were no less than eight different monthly magazines for fans of soap operas in 1977. Typically, adults spend fifteen to thirty minutes a day thumbing through one or more magazines.

These are the major media. Adults supplement their use by going to the movies once a month, by spending five to ten minutes a day reading books (other than textbooks), and by turning on the stereo perhaps fifteen minutes a day.

The compilation of all these media experiences helps explain the widespread interest in possible media impacts. For the typical adult, the daily pattern of behavior includes seven to eight hours spent at work (in or out of the house), another seven to eight hours spent asleep, and the third equivalent block of time allocated to other primary activities. Eating, personal care, commuting, and caring for others is about a two-hour daily chunk. So the disposable time, which the adult can use for activities of his or her choice, is about six hours. A majority of that time, about four hours of it, goes directly to the media.

Averages, of course, can be deceiving. There is a good deal of variability in how different subgroups of people in this country allocate their media time. Certain subgroups watch TV considerably more than others. Research indicates that the greatest fans of television are young children, old people in their retirement years, less educated people, racial minority groups, and homebound women. But the nonviewer is a rare, if not extinct, animal. Print media are typically consumed in larger doses by those who are more educated, who have higher incomes, and who are older. Radio is broadly popular, with the greatest popularity among rock-oriented teen-agers and homebound adults.

These differential consumption patterns may be explained in part by markedly different content emphases across the media. Commercial television devotes more than 90 percent of its programming to entertainment. Radio consists increasingly of specialized offerings. Most stations offer a single strain of music, such as country-western or Top 40; a few offer round-the-clock news. Newspapers, generally oriented to news and editorial content, can now be found to contain an increasing number of special features, columns, and other assorted incentives for readers. The favorite sections of the newspaper include Ann Landers, Art Buchwald, "Peanuts," and the ads, rather than particular news or editorial sections.

Future Exposure Patterns

New media technologies are likely to alter media usage patterns in the future. The most important of the new technologies is that of cable television. Essentially, cable television is bringing even more television offerings to an increasingly large number of American cities and towns. The cable brings in more channels from distant commercial stations. But it also provides a large number of channels for local usage—for government affairs, such as city council meetings; for educational purposes, such as adult education courses, and for public access, so that almost any group in a community can gain access to a television outlet. Further, the abundant cable channels are now making available twenty-four-hour news channels with constant up-to-the-minute coverage of national and local events, sports, weather, and the stock market. Thus the print media may have to find new functions in order to maintain their audiences. Early research returns indicate that television usage increases when a home acquires the cable system.

The advent of cable television in its current format is only the beginning. Without making extravagant claims for the future of this system, which is expensive and has not yet encompassed a majority of the country, it is clear that two-way or interactive television is likely to have a strong impact on our media behaviors. Two-way television will enable home users to make responses to certain programming received. These responses will most likely take the form of our pressing buttons attached to the home set which signal our answers to questions asked of us. For example, we might be responding to public opinion surveys, to formal testing situations, to requests for donations, and to the purchase of goods through an interactive cable system.

These exposure quantities and patterns might suggest an American addiction to the media. At the least, there is a vast consumption of a variety of media and content. Viewing and reading patterns are not random, but selective. Users become habituated in their content choices; they choose similar content in a variety of media, but typically do some sampling from multiple content types. Does all this go in one ear and out the other? We think not. The remaining sections of this chapter will center on the variety of impacts that the mass media can and do produce.

Dimensions of Audience Effects

A great deal of interest and concern has focused on the actual impact of mass-communication stimuli on receivers. As noted in chapter 1, all messages are designed to have an effect. A vexing problem facing scholars involves the identification of significant effects. Is it a noteworthy effect when a comedy film merely causes a viewer to laugh, or must the film produce a change in the receiver's stereotypes about groups portrayed in the film? What if a political commercial only intensifies a previously held attitude rather than converts the receiver to the opposing point of view?

Here is a liberal definition of **audience effect**: an outcome of the mass-communication process involving change in a person's state of orientation, either temporary or persisting. **Orientation** is a broad term that covers moods and knowledge as well as opinions and actions. **Change** can mean minor increases or decreases in degree of orientation (i.e., smoking several more cigarettes a day or a small reduction in boredom); complete conversion from one end of the continuum to the other (i.e., from a feeling of depression to elation, or from a pro-Carter to an anti-Carter attitude); or creation of a new orientation (i.e., gaining new knowledge about Chinese acupuncture or forming an opinion about a new Hollywood celebrity). Following from the discussion of reinforcement in chapter 3, there is also a special case where no apparent change can be considered an effect: when a stimulus serves to maintain a current state of orientation that would otherwise undergo change (i.e., Nixon's TV speeches maintaining political support in the face of eroding counterinfluences, or Crest toothpaste preserving its share of the market with magazine ads that combat persuasive efforts by competing brands). These consequences of mass communication may occur immediately or after hundreds of exposures. The individual receiver is usually selected as the unit of analysis; impact is assessed at the personal level rather than by examining changes in dyads, organizations, or society as a whole. Of course, the aggregate changes across many individuals will amass into large-scale group or societal change.

Unlike transactional dyadic communication, effects are usually judged in terms of the mass communicator's goals rather than the objectives of audience members. "Successful" communication occurs when the source exercises control by attaining closer correspondence between desired and obtained outcomes.

This description of effects in the mass-communication situation corresponds closely to our discussion in chapter 1 of the means by which individuals manage their environments. We stipulated that this was done largely through reinforcement and change in the attitudes and behaviors of others, and by information exchange. Given this parallelism in conception, the emphasis here will be on examining some critical types of effects.

A Typology of Media Effects

Two key dimensions of effects can be combined into a typology that serves to organize the diverse varieties of impact. The first dimension is the temporal locus of effect, which can be divided into **transitory change** during exposure (often called "gratification") versus **persisting change** (termed "learning"). The second dimension is the level of effect, which is divided into **cognitive** (thinking and knowing), **affective** (feeling and evaluating), and **behavioral** (acting) components. The six-celled chart in Table 7–1 identifies some of the specific consequences for the receiver's orientations.

This typology is an elaborated version of the range of responses identified in chapter 3. The most widely recognized type of persisting effect is attitude change, in which receivers alter their evaluation of persons or issues after attending to a mass-media message. However, cognitive learning occurs much more frequently, as receivers gain new pieces of knowledge; over time, these pieces blend together to form images and beliefs about the various aspects of the world portrayed by the media (e.g., perceptions of characteristics of minority groups or national leaders). Several classes of behavior have been prominently studied, such as aggression, voting, and product purchases.

A temporary outcome on the cognitive level is that receivers become mentally occupied while processing media stimuli; they derive something new to think about. At the affective level, the media arouse emotions, change moods, and provide a break from pressing problems. Be-

Table 7–1
Typology of Mass-Media Effects on Receiver Orientations

	Transitory Gratifications	Persistent Learning
Cognitive	Mental stimulation	Knowledge
		Images of reality
		Beliefs
Affective	Emotional arousal	Attitudes
	Escape	Interests
	Respite	Values
Behavioral	Physical relaxation	Social
	Conversation	Political
	Excitation to action	Consumer

haviorally, some receivers relax during exposure and others become agitated; they also talk about the incoming messages with companions.

Methods for Studying Effects

Mass-communication scholars have adopted the methodology of the social sciences for obtaining evidence on the impact of the mass media. Since people spend so much of their time with the media, many introspect about their own responses and the apparent reactions of others; thus it is tempting to rely on nonscientific methods in assessing effects. Consider the question of whether television violence affects children. One approach to resolving this issue is to use common sense or intuition; it is logical to assert that impressionable young people might imitate certain successful antisocial acts viewed on TV, such as lying, cheating, or hitting. Another avenue is to use conventional wisdom; there is a widely held view in society that the family and school are the primary molders of children, so TV makes little difference. Still another approach is to cite authorities familiar with the problem; various psychiatrists, philosophers, and network officials can provide contrasting testimony as to the harmful, nonexistent, or beneficial consequences of televised violence. Finally, informal observation is another source; a mother who gains insight from watching her child might conclude that cartoons serve to drain off aggressive impulses.

More substantial conclusions can be reached through scientific research methods that provide verifiable and objective evidence. This approach combines some elements of other approaches, namely the intuitive or authority-based construction of testable hypotheses of what effects might occur, and the use of observation of effects on real people. The observational procedures are far more systematic and controlled, involving representative sampling of audience members and careful measurement of their behavior. The two basic methods are field surveys (where people are interviewed or fill out questionnaires) and laboratory experiments (where equivalent groups are given different stimuli and their responses are observed). As data accumulate from such studies, conclusions about the impact of the media can be more confidently drawn.

Linking Media Stimuli to the Effects Typology

Perhaps the most efficient approach to organizing the discussion of mass-communication impact is to divide media content into three categories: entertainment, information, and persuasion. These groupings are parallel to the three functions of communication described in chapter 1: to establish contact, to exchange information, and to reinforce or change attitudes.

The messages transmitted by the media can be classified according to the *direct effects* intended by the source: **informational content** (e.g., news, public-service campaigns) is designed to achieve cognitive change, both transitory and persistent; **persuasive content** (e.g., advertising, editorials) aims to produce affective and behavioral change; **entertainment content** (e.g., TV situation comedies, magazine fiction) is intended to provide transitory gratifications at all levels. Some of the most interesting outcomes are not overtly intended, however. *Indirect side effects* are not uncommon. These occur when a message aimed at one effect level is utilized by the receiver on another impact level. For example, a newspaper report may impart knowledge (cognitive level) about a presidential policy that the receiver disagrees with, leading to negative attitude change (affective level) toward the president. Or a violence-prone criminal learns new kidnapping techniques (cognitive level) from a news show and then commits a similar act (behavioral level). Side effects are unintended consequences that are a byproduct of the primary effect and influence a separate category of orientation.

Effects of Informational Content

News is the most pervasive type of information in the mass media. Each day the typical TV station broadcasts two or more hours of news reports, and the newspaper contains dozens of stories. What is the result of exposure to this content?

Most individuals in the audience derive transitory satisfactions while consuming news, particularly from the visually attractive television formats. These reports provide something new and interesting to stimulate the mind, if not on a particularly elevated level, and many stories contain emotionally arousing components. Furthermore, people can physically relax with the evening news, wake up to the morning news, and converse about the news with others during the day.

While the public learns a considerable amount of information from the news media, knowledge gain is limited in certain respects. Referring back to one of our opening true-false questions, viewers of the network newscast can seldom remember more than three or four stories, or approximately 20 percent, just an hour after seeing the news (Booth, 1970–71). Much of the content is apparently treated as transitory mental stimulation. Furthermore, few people acquire a full awareness and understanding of "serious" topics such as international relations, government activities, and scientific developments. Survey researchers who measure the state of public knowledge consistently find low levels of public-affairs information, despite heavy coverage in the media (Hyman and Sheatsley, 1971; Robinson, 1972). A typical survey might find that less than half the population can name their congressperson, only 10 percent can identify the prime minister of Britain or Israel, and just 20 percent can define "detente" with Russia.

Even though the public displays a paltry level of sophistication about current events, the little they do know can be traced primarily to the news media—especially television and newspapers. When asked to pinpoint their primary source of general information about "what's going on in the world," 96 percent of the people questioned cited the media and 4 percent interpersonal sources or direct experience (Roper, 1977); when asked how they learned about specific recent events such as a presidential action or an international crisis, those who were aware credited the media rather than interpersonal sources about 90 percent of the time (Deutschmann and Danielson, 1960). The single exception to this basic finding occurs when big news stories break, such as an assassination or a spectacular disaster; on such occasions, up to half the population finds out interpersonally because the word spreads before many people come in contact with the media (Greenberg, 1964). Even among those who find out from other people, the media usually serve as the original source in a **two-step flow** of information (i.e., first from the media to some individuals, and then from these persons to others). Another kind of evidence comes from research studies that compare knowledge scores of those who are heavily versus lightly exposed to the news media; these investigations find a moderate tendency for frequent newspaper readers or TV news viewers to score higher than occasional readers or viewers (Robinson, 1972; Atkin, Galloway, and Nayman, 1976).

Hard and Soft News

When the effects of news media are broadened from the focus on "hard" public-affairs news to consider "soft" news about crime, sex, accidents, sports, weather, or celebrities, a much greater impact can be detected. While few people learn the names of the president's cabinet members, almost everyone learns the names of his family members. Similarly, many more people acquire knowledge about a plane crash in Brazil than the results of a Brazilian election, and a congressional leader is more likely to become a household word if he is involved in a scandal than if he has performed a significant legislative feat. This type of information is aptly termed "human interest" news—and humans do tend to learn about people and events that are of personal interest to them. Thus the **interest value** that receivers ascribe to the subject is a key factor that facilitates learning. Some other factors that seem to be important are the **entertainment value** of the presentation (a lively and visually attractive story will be learned more often than a dull verbal rendition), the **relevance** of the news to the receiver's personal life (events happening close to home rather than distant developments, economic changes that may affect buying power, and weather forecasts), the perceived **credibility** of the news source (if people trust a newscaster or wire service, the news is more often believed and learned), the **attitudinal consistency** of the news story with the receiver's values and ideology (a reader who opposes abortion will more readily learn about a Supreme Court decision limiting access to abortions), and **familiarity** with the topic (those who know more about space exploration or African politics will learn the most from stories on these subjects).

Over time, individuals integrate the bits of knowledge into images and beliefs about their environment. For instance, daily exposure to news reports about local muggings, break-ins, and murders tends to combine into a composite perception that there is high crime in the city. Stories of occasional bribe-taking and sexual promiscuity of government officials leads to the belief that political leaders are immoral. The isolated incidents that are given play in the news may or may not be an accurate reflection of the real world, but receivers who have few other inputs base their perceptions on the "second-hand reality" presented in the news (Lippman, 1971). The most controversial cases involve image formation that deviates from reality. Thus when major corporations showing a large increase in profits are prominently treated by news reporters while minor profit margins are ignored, the public inaccurately concludes that most businesses are highly profitable. During the Vietnam War, televised coverage shifted dramatically during the 1968 Tet offensive; after having portrayed American troops on the initiative for several years, scenes depicted the enemy attacking Saigon and United States forces under seige. Although military experts argued that the enemy offensive was technically a failure, it scored a psychological success as Americans came to believe that they were not winning the war (Epstein, 1973). As a rule, the less the receiver is able to rely on previous experience or interpersonal contact regarding a subject, the greater is the impact of the media portrayals on images. Thus when televised stories from China were first broadcast during Nixon's 1972 trip, there were major shifts in perceptions toward seeing the Chinese people as industrious, disciplined, regimented, and friendly (Chu, Atwood, and Whitlow, 1972). Similarly, images of contemporary American Indians were rapidly created and altered during their staging of a protest at Wounded Knee.

Priority Effects

One special effect on the audience concerns their perceptions of the importance of various persons, institutions, social problems, movements, and events. Given the large number of cognitions that a person acquires, some criteria must be used to sort them out and rank them in order of significance. The news media play a role in setting the agenda for the issues of the day, making some issues salient while relegating others to a lower ranking. If the newscasts and newspapers consistently give emphasis to an issue such as Watergate or civil rights or crime, it will tend to become of greater concern to the public. Stories placed on the upper front page or at the beginning of the newscast tend to be judged as important and worth thinking about. This increase in perceived importance of events, ideas, or causes is called **agenda setting** (Shaw and McCombs, 1977). A similar process operates for persons in the news; the media have a **status-conferral** effect in making certain public figures seem important (Lazarsfeld and Merton, 1971). This comes from the sheer amount of attention—of time or space—given to such persons. These priority effects are distinct from any positive or negative reactions to the issues or leaders. While the media may help focus attention and confer status on a consumer advocate such as Ralph Nader, entirely divergent attitudes may be formed by various receivers.

Indirect Effects

The impact of news content on opinions and attitudes involves a complex and indirect process. Unlike cognitive impact where the receiver either displays a bit of added learning or none at all, the affective impact may be positive, nonexistent, or negative, depending heavily on the pre-existing orientations of the receiver. The individual's value system and sociopolitical ideology serve as a filter that transforms the news content into attitudes. After gaining knowledge, the receiver reacts to it according to his or her evaluation of the information (i.e., if the president speaks out in favor of more foreign aid to Israel, acquisition of this fact will result in favorable attitude change toward the president for one segment of the audience and negative change for another; this primarily depends on prior orientations toward the Israelis).

Conservatives and liberals react very differently to most news stories about political leaders and issues. Thus news coverage of controversial social movements tends to produce contrasting effects. Right-wing receivers who oppose the extension of civil rights to disenfranchised groups in society tend to react negatively to the gay-rights or Indian-rights causes that are publicized in the news; after seeing reports in the media, they dislike the group and favor repression of their movement. Left-wingers seeing the same stories move to a more positive viewpoint toward gays or Indians and support the goals they are seeking. Similar contrasts occurred during the early phases of the Watergate exposé: Republicans tended to maintain support for Nixon and accept his explanations, while Democrats became more favorably inclined toward impeachment. When crime news is emphasized, some receivers respond by calling for more police enforcement, while others feel that more social programs are needed.

On topics where the audience holds similar values, most receivers shift their views in the same direction. Thus learning about congressional scandals contributes to generally low public esteem for Congress, since most people react negatively to immorality. The vast majority of the public also shares negative values toward high business profits, unsafe products, sharp rises in prices, and pollution of the environment—the very subjects featured most often in business news stories. The consequence of this is an unfavorable attitude toward business institutions among those exposed to such unflattering news.

Finally, there are important behavioral implications. As the perception of the crime rate rises, receivers tend to take more precautions at home, travel less in the dangerous neighborhoods, and even move to safer suburbs. After news coverage of major airplane crashes, a small percentage of travelers cancel their plans for air trips. Many people took to the streets to protest the Vietnam war—partly due to their belief and attitude changes and partly as a result of social contagion after seeing televised street marches in other cities.

Impact of Persuasive Content

Although the mass media are often considered persuasion-oriented, very few of the noncommercial stimuli are overtly aimed at influencing attitudes and behavior. Only a handful of editorials and commentaries appear in the major media each day, although the tempo accelerates during election campaigns. There are occasional religious programs and broadcast speeches by government leaders. Advertising represents the most ubiquitous stimuli advocating attitudinal positions or behavioral enactment, but these messages are seldom studied by academic researchers.

The earliest theories of mass communication posited extensive and pervasive direct effects of stimuli on receivers. The "hypodermic needle" or "magic bullet" perspectives viewed the mass media as all-powerful and the audience members as helpless victims who could be injected with propaganda by skillful mass communicators. There was a naive belief that mass-media messages would almost uniformly achieve the goals set by the creators of those messages. After all, Hitler manipulated the media to achieve power and activate a war effort, and Roosevelt relied on radio messages to get elected four times.

Factors Limiting Persuasive Impact

When researchers in the 1940s and 1950s took a closer look at the media situation, they identified many factors that can limit the persuasive impact of mediated messages. These include *competing messages* in the mass media and interpersonal environment, *psychological defenses* of receivers, and the *stability* of deeply rooted attitudes and action patterns (Klapper, 1960; Weiss, 1969). In short, the mass-media stimuli were resisted by an **obstinate audience** (Bauer, 1971). As a result, current thinking has moved back to a point between the all-powerful and null-effects perspectives. Researchers appreciate the barriers to change but have identified specific conditions when impact is likely to occur. Let's examine the factors that limit persuasiveness and discuss how each might be overcome.

Competing messages. The mass media and interpersonal environment experienced by the receiver may contain many messages that run counter to a particular persuasive appeal. While Chevrolet is promoting the Chevette in hourly TV ads, Ford may be running an equal number of Fiesta ads, and Volkswagen may compete with full-page magazine ads. Furthermore, family, friends, or co-workers may refute advertising claims or simply advise against the Chevette. Political campaigning, the other major type of persuasive content, also involves media competition between the contending parties and generates considerable social discussion of candidates and issues.

Most of the time, however, a persuasive appeal in the mass media does not run up against a solid wall of competing messages that serves to restrict impact. While it is possible that interpersonal sources may uniformly contradict a commercial or a political speech, the more typical situation is an absence of social influence on any particular topic. To avoid conflict, people tend to spend little time debating controversial issues or discussing commercial products. If conversations do occur, it is possible that some people of significance to the receiver will support the position advocated in the mass media and others of equal significance will oppose it. If both support and opposition occur for the same persuasive message, the receiver might be under "cross pressure," with family members promoting one viewpoint while friends argue for the other side. When social inputs on an issue are absent, contradictory, or supportive, the individual is much more susceptible to media effects.

Similarly, there is not always competition from other media stimuli. On many topics, the vast majority of messages appearing in the mass media consistently advocate one underlying point of view. For instance, most content dealing with Christianity, capitalism, materialism, democracy, marriage, beer drinking, fluoridation, and higher education is uniformly favorable—even though the best possible "brand" of Christian religion, beer, or democratic government may be closely contended by opposing parties. The monopolization of political, social, commercial, or religious perspectives is even stronger in other nations where the power structure seeks to propagate its ideology and suppress opposing ideas.

Even when contending political parties or companies are each presenting persuasive appeals, they seldom achieve parity in message dissemination. Conservative newspaper owners dominate the editorial pages, and evangelical religious organizations preempt the Sunday airwaves. Ford may advertise slightly more than Chevrolet and buy much more space and time than Volvo. Indeed, the primary mass-communication strategy for overcoming competing stimuli is to increase one's own messages to achieve a higher rate of exposure than the competition.

Thus there are many situations where the competing stimuli are inoperative or overwhelmed, and in many instances other messages may serve to enhance the effect of the media persuasion. The totality of the persuasive environment must be assessed before likely effects can be calculated.

Psychological defenses. Receivers erect a series of protective devices to maintain prior attitudes and behavior patterns. These devices affect the processing and disposition of incoming persuasive stimuli and are primarily based on needs to preserve consistency and avoid dissonance. The first line of defense is **selective exposure**: people tend to select messages that are congruent with predispositions and ignore discrepant material. For instance, probably three-quarters of those who view a candidate's TV speech or read his newspaper advertisement will be supporters, thus limiting the chance for conversion. If an alien stimulus somehow hurdles this barrier, it is then subject to **selective perception**: receivers tend to twist and misinterpret the intended meaning of the message to fit in with their existing viewpoint. For instance, some racially prejudiced individuals will distort a satirical editorial cartoon that attacks racism by failing to understand the implications or misperceiving the satire to be a literal statement. The third line of defense is **selective retention**: even if a discrepant message is attended to and perceived correctly, it might simply be relegated to the recesses of the mind's storage system so that it doesn't come into play when an attitude is later elicited.

Just as people remember the good times, they tend to recall mass-media inputs that support their outlook and forget items considered inconsistent.

These guardians are not necessarily operative, however. If predispositions are weak or nonsalient, the individual is unlikely to be so protective. Furthermore, certain persuasive strategies can overcome even vigilant defenses. Selective exposure can be dented with obtrusive or frequent message placement (e.g., a presidential address on all three networks, or daily radio advertising) or with an entertaining presentation appeal (e.g., ads that use comedy or beautiful models). Messages that feature clear-cut, unambiguous content reduce the possibility of selective perception (e.g., the flat statement that "cigarette smoking causes death"). Selectivity in retaining material can be attacked by constantly repeating the message over time. Finally, rejection of claims can be minimized by reference to highly credible sources (e.g., government certification of gas mileage, or shampoo endorsement by Farrah Fawcett) or a well-designed message appeal (e.g., advertising that compares the merits of competing brands, or arguments based on irrefutable evidence).

Stability of orientation. People develop certain attitudes and patterns of action over the years after extensive experience and reception of numerous stimuli. By definition, an attitude is a relatively stable disposition that should be resistant to change from any source—especially an impersonal media message.

It is true that some attitudes are well established and strongly held. A single stimulus is no more than a "drop in the bucket" in such cases; for example, a magazine article criticizing President Carter is relatively inconsequential compared to the thousands of previously amassed inputs about him, or a single TV commercial for a new soft drink won't produce a perceptible change among Coke fanciers.

Nevertheless, many orientations are held with weaker intensity, and in some cases no dispositions have been formed toward an issue at all. There is much more opportunity for movement under these circumstances. For example, when Carter was a new political figure in 1975, much shifting occurred with each television appearance; and new soft drinks such as Mr. Pibb have been introduced to "neutral" audiences. Thus mass-communication stimuli can be quite influential in creating attitudes, and somewhat effective where weak dispositions exist. Since some of the people in the audience (especially young people) have yet to form attitudes, and most people have some irresolute attitudes, the potential for impact is considerable.

Even for established orientations there are effective strategies. The most successful approach involves repeated presentation of high-quality stimuli (credible source, effective appeals, optimum organization of content, appropriate channel, etc.) over a long period. Changing people's feelings about Jimmy Carter or their rate of cigarette smoking may require years of persuasion. A persistent barrage of stimuli can result in gradual, cumulative change and eventual conversion.

When predispositions are operative, the most likely outcome of persuasive mass communication is **reinforcement**, that is, a strengthening of existing attitudes. For example, TV commercials for Post Grape Nuts may move a person from lukewarm liking to moderate liking for the product, or rekindle a latent positive predisposition that had faded in prominence. While reinforcement may not seem to produce significant changes, it is important for two reasons: as the attitude is strengthened, the rate of behavior tends to increase and the attitude becomes more resistant to counterpersuasion. This can be critical to the sender of the persuasive message; the candidate will turn out more supporters, and the advertiser will stimulate more frequent brand purchasing, resulting in thousands of votes or millions of sales dollars. Such outcomes may occur even though the actual proportion of the audience with a favorable attitude of behavioral disposition does not increase. Accomplishing an increase in the proportion of supporters is termed **conversion.** Moving attitudes from one side to the other is comparatively rare when predispositions are well established. Although a single message or brief campaign may convert only an unimpressively small percentage of the audience, the payoff may be pragmatically significant when the popularity of a candidate improves from 49 percent to 52 percent or the share of a market increases from 22 percent to 24 percent. And when such modest conversion can be achieved consistently with each new campaign, the cumulative impact can be very impressive over several campaign or marketing efforts.

The Influence of Advertising

One indicator of the potency of mass-media persuasion can be seen by the increased reliance that professional persuaders place on the media. More than $37 billion were spent by advertisers in 1977, a 40 percent increase over 1972. Newspapers attract the most advertising, followed by television (which is limited by the amount of available time; the networks have "sold out" every prime-time minute). Typical effects, in order of incidence, are maintenance of current share of market (e.g., Hertz Rent-A-Car), increased rate of purchasing through reinforcement of loyal users (e.g., McDonald's Restaurants), creation of new demand by repositioning old products or introducing new ones with appropriate media fanfare (e.g., Miller Lite Beer), and conversion of those who prefer a competing brand (e.g., the Un-cola campaign).

Television and radio are being used extensively by religious movements; evangelists such as Rex Humbard, Oral Roberts, Reverend Ike, and Billy Graham spend and receive $100 million per year on TV. The predominant impact is reinforcement of the faithful, although the use of entertainment program formats and spot advertising campaigns (e.g., "I found it") has achieved some converts.

As an example of mass persuasion, let's look at televised political advertising (Atkin and Heald, 1976). Candidates are increasingly relying on brief commercials to reach the electorate. They have determined that few of the unconvinced voters, their primary targets, pay attention to longer political messages, such as TV speeches, telethons, or documentary-style programs. On the other hand, ads are viewed by more than nine-tenths of the voters, most of whom see many ads.

At the cognitive learning level, political advertising imparts a substantial amount of information about candidate qualifications and issue positions. Since advertisements repeatedly present simplified and entertaining claims about the candidate, unsophisticated and disinterested voters are able to learn most efficiently from this type of stimulus.

Ads also influence the ordering of attributes that the voters consider when evaluating the candidates. If ads focus on several personal characteristics, such as integrity or experience, or issues, such as abortion or foreign policy, voters will tend to give these factors more weight in their assessment of the candidate. This can be highly significant if favorable aspects can be emphasized and unflattering attributes downplayed. Attitudes toward each candidate can be shaped in several ways: where voters have low involvement in a particular contest, the sheer number of exposures to candidate advertising stimuli lead to name and face familiarity that usually results in positive affect; where voters are attempting to make a rational and responsible judgment in key races, effects are indirect and contrasting. Voters apply personal values and ideology to the evaluation of informational inputs about a candidate and move toward a more positive attitude if they are impressed by the candidate's attributes or agree with the stands on issues. If a presidential candidate promises to reduce military spending, voters who support strong national defense will react negatively while antimilitary segments of the electorate will view the person more favorably. If a contender affirms deep religious convictions, they may be valued by most voters but turn off others. Thus while commercials may be highly successful in informing the receivers, they do not necessarily result in positive attitude change. Counterproductive boomerang effects are common. However, since candidates usually promote those personal characteristics that are universally valued and often rely on public opinion polls before taking sides on issues, most ads tend to produce favorable change. The less well the candidate is known by the electorate, the more change is likely to occur, and vice versa.

The behavioral effect is also critical. Less than half of the potential voters actually go to the polls in most elections, so ads are designed to stimulate turnout. Commercials tend to increase the rate of voting since they usually heighten interest in the campaign, intensify attitudes, and remind people of their duty to vote. Advertisements are more effective than conventional campaign stimuli in reaching voters who have the lowest initial levels of awareness, interest, and attitudinal strength.

Impact of Entertainment Content

The largest chunks of media content are designed to be entertaining, to provide some lengthy time stretches of relaxation and enjoyment. Even the creators of hard news and public-affairs programming would admit to wanting their content to be entertaining, at least to the extent required to attract substantial audiences. However, it would be difficult to arrive at a common definition of what is entertaining. For the present discussion, it is sufficient to focus on that portion of media content which is fictional, such as adventure stories, situation comedies, and comic strips. What are the likely reasons that Americans feast on such content? What does such consumption lead to?

Reasons for the Appeal of Entertainment

There are several lengthy lists of possible motives for the seeking of entertainment content. These lists have been compiled by various researchers interested in the functions media entertainment serves and the gratifications it offers. Several motives appear consistently throughout the research (Greenberg, 1974). It is interesting that the major gratifications sought from the media can be paired in almost contradictory couplings.

First, people look to entertainment content for **relaxation** and **excitement**. Those approaching the media after a particularly hard day—hard physically or psychologically—are likely to want to relax. Those approaching the media after a series of humdrum activities report that they want to be aroused, to have some excitement, even if it is only vicarious.

Another prominent pair of motivations are **escapism** and **companionship**. For the first of these, imagine an individual who has just had a set of argumentative encounters at school or at work. Once at home, the person wants to get away from it all, and the media provide an accessible noncombative refuge. Now consider a second individual whose workday

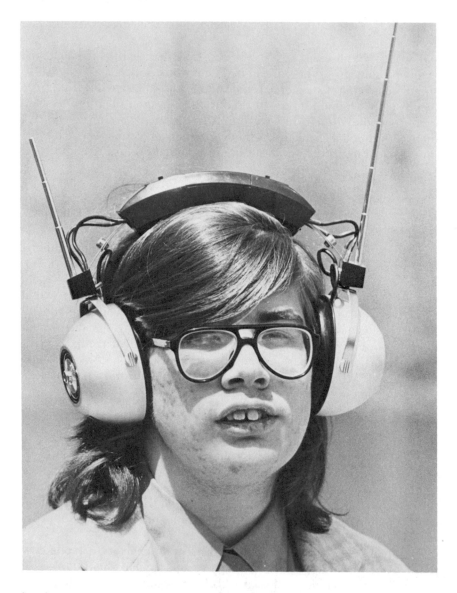

has been on the assembly line at a local factory, where there was little opportunity to talk with others. This person will arrive home eager for companionship. Both people can seek the special gratifications they need from the same medium, perhaps even from the same program.

A paramount reason for using the media is for **learning**. To learn what's going on in the world, the media consumer turns to information-al programs, newspapers, and news magazines. But learning is sought through fictional entertainment programs as well. There one can learn how to deal with personal problems, to handle oneself in social situations—in other words, learn about life. People seek models of human conduct from entertainment programs. Among both young people and adults, but particularly the former, there is extensive belief that the television characterizations and situations are true-to-life, representative, and often isomorphic with reality. Further, the more specific the TV fictional content, the more real it is judged to be by viewers. That is, specific characters, such as the Fonz, are seen as more real than TV teenagers in general. But the seeking of fictional content for information on how to cope with real-life situations is perhaps more impressive than whether people say it is or is not realistic.

Although we have paired some of these motives to point up their seemingly contradictory nature, they should rather be viewed as "different strokes for different folks" and different motives at different times for the same folks. An entertainment program that one person may use for relaxation may be used by someone else for excitement. A shoot-'em-up show may provide escape for one viewer and a vicariously enjoyed adventure for another. Entertainment content thus is a means of satisfying our needs at a particular time in a particular situation. However, no one has yet demonstrated the degree to which different kinds of content, or different media, actually do satisfy specific needs.

Many of our needs are transitory; they come and go frequently and with ease. We often use the media to obtain temporary relief, much as we might take a popular headache remedy. But ailments which are temporary for some people may be chronic for others. For example, if you've just had a fight with a boyfriend or a girlfriend, you may seek temporary escape by turning on the television set—at the same time waiting for the telephone to ring so you can make up. Some people, however, may consistently have unsatisfactory social relationships; others may find themselves generally bored with their everyday existence; still others may be tired early every evening. For these people, turning to entertainment content more properly describes a general pattern of seeking gratifications. How satisfactory consistent use of fiction is as a method of coping with such problems remains unresolved.

Learning Effects

We now turn to a more general concern regarding the effects of entertainment content. What do people "learn" from watching fictional television programs? The focus of the question has typically been on young people. There is widespread public concern that young people are learning socially improper things from their media experiences—primarily from television and films and to some extent from popular music.

The theoretic orientation which has guided much of the research in this area is social learning theory (Bandura, 1977). This theory stipulates that vicarious observation of models, such as those on television, may under certain conditions induce certain important behaviors. These behaviors may result from the *facilitation* of behaviors already in the individual's repertoire or the *disinhibition* of behaviors usually proscribed to the individual, or they may represent the *acquisition* of new behaviors. Media portrayals may also affect an individual's beliefs, expectations, and aspirations.

In order for such social learning to occur from exposure to the media, certain prior conditions must exist.

First, of course, the content must be there. If one is to learn how the police operate, there must be programs that show how law enforcement works.

Second, the content must be presented frequently and consistently. For any particular content area to be a basis for learning, it must be found often in the wide mix of available programming. Further, the subject must be portrayed in a uniform manner. If women are invariably shown as dependent, submissive beings, social learning of this conception is more likely to occur than if women are portrayed as aggressive, independent leaders with equal frequency.

Third, there must be exposure to the content. Given multiple offerings, the viewer must choose content portraying certain characteristics time and again.

Fourth, when the other agents of socialization, such as family and peer groups, do not yield messages within a given content area, then the media can be expected to have optimal influence. If, for example, these other sources do not provide information about minority groups, and if the media provide consistent and persistent negative images about some minority group, then social learning will occur from the media.

Fifth, if there are few personal experiences that are inconsistent with media portrayals, again the media information should predominate. Younger media users of course have had fewer experiences in a variety of the areas presented in fictional material. In fact, young people may turn to the media for behavioral information, as indicated in our discussion of motives. Similarly, some women turn to soap operas for largely unavailable information about health, marital, and personal problems.

In recent years, the media have become a scapegoat for a variety of society's ailments. Television in particular has been blamed for a drop in national achievement test scores, poor reading and writing abilities in school children, a rise in civil violence, and a rise in immorality. There is little empirical evidence to support such accusations, however.

In recent years, three areas of social learning have attracted the interest of researchers. The learning of violence from television programs is the most well known, because of congressional attention and subsequent media reports regarding the impact of televised violence. The two other areas are the effects of prosocial TV content and the portrayal of women on television. The three will be jointly discussed here.

First, there is much entertainment content available for each of these phenomena. Content analyses done over many years document a large quantity of television violence; more recent analyses demonstrate at least an equal amount of such prosocial behaviors as helping others, showing affection, and explaining one's feelings; and analyses of men and women on television indicate that men outnumber women about two to one on prime-time television, suggesting that male characters play a more prominent role in prime-time programs (Greenberg, et al., 1979). The average commercial hour of television has more than forty acts of antisocial behaviors in it, including physical violence, verbal aggression, and theft; it also has more than forty acts of prosocial behaviors. And in these same shows men and women are frequently interacting in a stereotyped manner.

Second, within each of these content areas, there appear to be not only a heavy frequency of models to observe, but some strong consistency in the portrayals. The most common method of solving problems in action-adventure TV series is the use of some form of violence, not once but several times during a program; the incidence of violence is particularly high in the several hours of Saturday morning shows for children. Prosocial behaviors are also observed extensively and generally are reinforced when they occur. Men are typically seen as dominant, physically and verbally aggressive, lending support to others, and making plans for others to carry out; females with these attributes appear far less often. Instead, women are usually shown as tending to need and seek support, and following the directives of others. In commercials, they remain the dutiful housewife, with good information on floor scrubbing.

Next, there is ample evidence that there is exposure, and a good amount of it, to all three of these exemplar areas. The three to four hours a day given to television consists of heavy doses of fictional content. Within fictional content, young people are strongly attracted to action-adventure programs, where a good deal of physical aggression occurs. Prosocial exposures occur to some extent in the same programs, but also throughout the situation comedies, which comprise the bulk of television's offerings. Further, those in their preteens watch even more fictional content than post-teen-agers, and it is expected that the former are more likely to be impressed by the portrayals they observe.

Recalling what social learning theory would suggest, the frequent observation of antisocial behaviors which are successful and rewarding to the heroes (and heroines) would be expected to lead to a disinhibition of antisocial behaviors in the observer. Frequent exposure to prosocial behaviors should result in the facilitation of those positive behaviors. And if a young person is picking up anything from observing the portrayals of men and women on television programs, then it is reasonable to expect certain beliefs and expectations to be forming regarding the roles of the sexes.

Before we briefly examine the evidence regarding these propositions, one further distinction needs to be made regarding levels of impact of entertainment content. It is important to differentiate among *the acquisition of mental skills* to commit a certain behavior, *the acquisition of attitudes and motivations* to engage in a behavior, and the actual *performance* of a behavior. Clearly, the media can provide us with information about a variety of skills if we attend closely to the content. We can "learn" what TV people are doing and how they are doing it. But whether the media alter our attitudes or overt behaviors in significant ways is arguable. Let us now review the evidence (Comstock and Fisher, 1975; Leibert, Neale, and Davidson, 1973).

Several million dollars of research on the impact of TV violence permit these conclusions:

1. There is a modest but consistent relationship between exposure to violence on television and predispositions to commit aggressive behavioral acts. These predispositions include more positive attitudes toward the use of violence, belief in the success of aggression to solve problems, and a willingness to use aggression for problem solving.
2. Field surveys demonstrate a relationship of similar magnitude between watching violence on television and actual commission of antisocial acts.
3. Laboratory experiments demonstrate an increase in aggression after deliberate exposure to video segments of violence.

More recent research has focused on those conditions which could mediate or reduce the impact of televised violence. Most prominent is evidence which suggests that parents can serve a mediating function. That is, if parents watch high-violence programming with their youngsters and offer counterviolence messages, the impact of the program content may be lessened.

Much less research has been done with prosocial effects as the central interest. What we do have indicates effects comparable to those obtained for antisocial content but in the opposite direction. Young people who are deliberately exposed to, or choose to watch, such programs as "Mister Rogers" or "The Waltons" are more likely to perform the prosocial behaviors emphasized on those programs (Atkin and Greenberg, 1977).

Finally, research on sex-role learning from media content is in its infancy as this chapter is being prepared. Nevertheless, experiments which

have presented counterstereotyped portrayals of women have demonstrated that exposure to such portrayals leads to greater acceptance of women in those roles (Miller and Reeves, 1976).

Thus for all three content areas the research evidence supports the theoretic argument that persistent exposure to consistent portrayals of social roles and social behaviors in the media is likely to result in social learning and subsequent modeling.

Before closing this chapter, it may be useful to identify some content areas that future research may focus on and wherein the hypotheses could now be fairly straightforwardly created.

Much fictional content in the media deals with medical situations, ranging from the typical hospital story of soap operas to the emergency teams assigned to deal with crisis incidents. To what extent do these presentations create unrealistic attitudes toward doctors, the treatment of physical ailments, or health maintenance in general? How does the emphasis on pill taking in commercials contribute to an affinity for pill taking?

There is concern over what is described by some as sexual permissiveness in films and television. Are sexual innuendoes understood by young viewers, or are more graphic presentations required? Does such content alter attitudes toward sex or toward the opposite sex? Could one expect greater promiscuity as the behavioral consequence?

Such issues as these are frequently raised by scientific, government, and public groups. Perhaps it is to be expected. So much of our leisure time is given to the media that they comprise a preeminent portion of our lives. As such the mass media serve as fair game for a variety of questions. The questions we have focused on in this section have to do with incidental social learning. The messages contained in media presentations are not created for the purpose of teaching us how to be violent or sexist. They are part of a story, and part of the formula writing, perhaps, that goes into it. Nevertheless, children use entertainment as a source of guidance as well as amusement, and the consequences can be significant and persistent. These indirect and unintended lessons derived from fictional materials require much further research before the exact impact is determined.

Conclusion

The mass media have a variety of direct and subtle effects on individuals in the audience. To some extent, the outcomes are dependent on the sociological characteristics and psychological predispositions of the receivers. The impact also depends on the quantity of the content and the qualities of the source, message, and channels. Transitory effects are pervasive, and extensive cognitive learning also occurs. The degree of direct influence on attitudes and behaviors is modest, but many of these consequences are socially, economically, and politically significant.

Answers to true-false questions:

1. F	7. F
2. F	8. T
3. T	9. F
4. F	10. T
5. T	11. T
6. T	

TERMS AND CONCEPTS FOR REVIEW

agenda setting	mass-communication receiver
attitudinal consistency	mass-communication source
audience effect	obstinate audience
change	orientation
cognitive, affective, behavioral effects	persisting change
competing messages	persuasive content
credibility	psychological defenses
entertainment content	reinforcement
entertainment value	relaxation/excitement

escapism/companionship
familiarity
informational content
interest value
learning
mass-communication channel
mass-communication message
mass-communication process

relevance
selective exposure
selective perception
selective retention
stability of orientation
status conferral
transitory change
two-step flow

REVIEW QUESTIONS

1. How do the media affect a person's thinking and behavior at the conscious level?
2. What subtle and unintended effects may be produced by the media on individuals?
3. How do audiences respond to mass-media informational content, persuasive content, and entertainment content?
4. What are the key research conclusions regarding the media-related social issues of the impact of TV violence and political advertising on media users?

REFERENCES

Atkin, Charles, John Galloway, and Oguz Nayman. "News Media Exposure, Political Knowledge, and Campaign Interest." *Journalism Quarterly*, 1976, 53, 231–237.

———, and Gary Heald. "Effects of Political Advertising." *Public Opinion Quarterly*, 1976, 40, 216–228.

———, and Bradley Greenberg. "Parental Mediation of Children's Social Behavior Learning from Television." Paper presented at annual convention of Association for Education in Journalism, Madison, Wisc., 1977.

Bandura, Albert. *Social Learning Theory.* Englewood Cliffs, N. J.: Prentice-Hall, 1977.

Bauer, Raymond. "The Obstinate Audience: The Influence Process From the Point of View of Social Communication." In W. Schramm and D. Roberts (eds.), *The Process and Effects of Mass Communication.* Urbana, Ill.: University of Illinois Press, 1971.

Booth, Alan. "The Recall of News Items." *Public Opinion Quarterly*, 1970–71, 34, 604–610.

Chu, Godwin, L. Erwin Atwood, and Sylvia Whitlow. "Television Coverage of Nixon's China Trip." Paper presented at annual convention of Association for Education in Journalism, Carbondale, Ill., 1972.

Comstock, George, and Marilyn Fisher. *Television and Human Behavior.* Santa Monica, Cal.: Rand, 1975.

Deutschmann, Paul, and Wayne Danielson. "Diffusion of Knowledge of the Major News Story." *Journalism Quarterly,* 1960, 37, 345–355.

Epstein, Edward. *News from Nowhere.* New York: Random House, 1973.

Greenberg, Bradley. "Gratifications of Television Viewing and Their Correlates for British Children." In J. Blumler and E. Katz (eds.), *The Uses of Mass Communications.* Beverly Hills: Sage, 1974.

———. "Person to Person Communication in the Diffusion of News Events." *Journalism Quarterly,* 1964, 41, 489–494.

———, Katrina Simons, Linda Hogan, and Charles Atkin. "Three Seasons of TV Characters: A Demographic Analysis." *Journal of Broadcasting,* 1979, 23, 345–354.

Hyman, Herbert, and Paul Sheatsley. "Some Reasons Why Information Campaigns Fail." In W. Schramm and D. Roberts (eds.), *The Process and Effects of Mass Communication.* Urbana, Ill.: University of Illinois Press, 1971.

Klapper, Joseph. *The Effects of Mass Communication.* Glencoe, Ill.: Free Press, 1960.

Lazarsfeld, Paul, and Robert Merton. "Mass Communication, Popular Taste, and Organized Social Action." In W. Schramm and D. Roberts (eds.), *The Process and Effects of Mass Communication.* Urbana, Ill.: University of Illinois Press, 1971.

Leibert, Robert, John Neale, and Emily Davidson. *The Early Window: Effects of Television on Children.* New York: Pergamon Press, 1973.

Lippmann, Walter. "The World Outside and the Pictures in Our Heads." In W. Schramm and D. Roberts (eds.), *The Process and Effects of Mass Communication,* Urbana, Ill.: University of Illinois Press, 1971.

Miller, M. Mark, and Byron Reeves. "Dramatic TV Content and Children's Sex-Role Stereotypes." *Journal of Broadcasting,* 20, 1976, 35–50.

Robinson, John. "Mass Communication and Information Diffusion." In F. Kline and P. Tichenor (eds.), *Current Perspectives in Mass Communication Research.* Beverly Hills: Sage, 1972.

Roper Organization. *Changing Public Attitudes toward Television and Other Media.* New York: Television Information Office, 1977.

Shaw, Donald, and Maxwell McCombs. *The Emergence of American Political Issues.* St. Paul, Minn.: Westing Publishing, 1977.

Weiss, Walter. "Effects of the Mass Media of Communication." In G. Lindzey and E. Aronson (eds.), *Handbook of Social Psychology.* Reading, Mass.: Addison-Wesley, 1969.

Part Three
COMMUNICATION
SKILLS

The last two chapters of the book discuss two communication skills: interviewing and public speaking. These two are identified as skills because there are steps involved which communicators can learn, practice, and evaluate to increase their competence. The fact that many people openly express a fear of interviewing or of speaking in public lends support for the learning progression model in the preface. For example, people who say they are not good public speakers are at the conscious incompetent stage in their development. They recognize that they are not as able as they would like to be in this communicative skill, yet know that some things could be done to enhance their competence. Chapters 8 and 9 point the way to improvement in both skills by describing what steps need to be taken and practiced in interviewing and public speaking.

Interviewing usually occurs in a dyadic setting but may be conducted in a group context and may be mediated (e.g., via telephone). Unlike most interpersonal exchanges, the source (or interviewer) has a distinct and serious purpose in engaging the other person in question-and-answer exchanges and in adapting to that receiver. Similar to interpersonal communication, interviewing is a transactional, symbolic process in which immediate feedback helps determine the next question of the source. As in other forms of communication, selective perception and retention can affect the messages received, but the interviewing techniques supplied in chapter 8 should help the interviewer to overcome potential or real communication barriers.

Public speaking is also a transactional, symbolic process. The speaker's first step is to conduct a careful audience analysis by gathering as much cultural, sociological, and psychological data about the receivers as possible. From this analysis, the receivers' attitudes, beliefs, and values are inferred. Then, using the principles of message construction (as discussed in chapter 3), the source builds an argument, the claim, data, and warrant of which will be most acceptable to the audience. Motivational appeals and organization are also adapted to the audience. Upon delivery, the speaker interprets the feedback provided by the audience and adds, subtracts, or alters material accordingly to obtain the desired response. A final evaluation by the audience and the speaker of the message should enable the source to assess the effectiveness of the speech and modify content, delivery, adaptation, etc. on future occasions.

Thus interviewing and public speaking are communication skills which incorporate principles of communication and can be assessed and improved. The theoretical understanding of the fundamental information in the principles and contexts sections of this book should aid you in adapting to your receivers in either the interview or public-speaking situation.

The Interview Defined

Interviewing Purposes
INFORMATION-GATHERING INTERVIEWS
INFORMATION-GIVING INTERVIEWS

Distortion of Information
INTERNAL DISTORTION
EXTERNAL DISTORTION FROM
INTERACTION OF PARTICIPANTS
EXTERNAL DISTORTION FROM
ENVIRONMENTAL INTERFERENCE
WAYS TO COUNTERACT DISTORTION

Managing the Interview
IDENTIFYING REWARDS AND COSTS FOR
PARTICIPANTS
SOCIAL EXCHANGE MODEL

Steps in Interviewing
DETERMINE THE GENERAL OBJECTIVE
DETERMINE SPECIFIC INFORMATION
NEEDED
SELECT THE INTERVIEWEE
PREPARE QUESTIONS
SELECT APPROPRIATE INTERVIEWER
ARRANGE THE INTERVIEW
OPEN THE INTERVIEW

ADAPT TO THE STYLE OF THE
INTERVIEWEE
CLOSE THE INTERVIEW
EVALUATE THE INTERVIEW
TABULATE THE INFORMATION

8
Interviewing

After reading this chapter, you should be able to:

1. Plan, organize, conduct, and evaluate any one of the three types of information-gathering interviews.
2. Explain how information distortion arises and how to counteract it.
3. Explain the level of control which each participant retains in the interview.
4. Forecast the dynamics of the interview by analyzing the situation through the social exchange model.
5. Develop rationales for selecting interviewers and interviewees.
6. Plan question strategies.
7. Arrange interviews and accommodate interviewees.
8. Explain processes of tabulating and interpreting the information obtained in an interview.

In this age of information overload we are constantly bombarded with messages—advertisements tell us what to buy and where to go, newspapers pile on our doorsteps, and bookstands fill our shopping malls. The irony is that while words and ideas fill our environment, it is often a real problem for us to obtain information we need. For example, students, journalists, researchers, and personnel executives often need or want to ask questions like the following:

"Who is responsible for embezzling public tax revenue?"

"What is the public opinion on building codes?"

"How do husbands and wives communicate with each other?"

"Who is the most qualified applicant for the public-relations position?"

Finding answers to these and other questions is a difficult process. Knowledge that is complete, relevant, and undistorted is not always available in books, journals, or through the mass media. At times it must be obtained from other persons who have the information we need. Hence, a useful but often abused method for acquiring information is the *interview.*

An interview only provides a structure or a method for gathering information. The tool we use to gain that information is *communication.* In general, the more sensitive the information we need, the more delicate we need to make the communication process. Just as a surgeon chooses his tools carefully to perform an operation, so good interviewers plan their communication strategy with care. They do this by (1) assessing the type of information they need; (2) analyzing the situational constraints surrounding the interview; and (3) selecting the best questions to elicit desired information from the interviewee.

This chapter will look at the various *forms* of interviewing, the ways in which information is subject to *distortion,* the types of *question formats* which may be effective, and the *steps* in planning a successful interview. By learning these basic principles, students can improve their skills at gaining control of interviewing situations.

The Interview Defined

Richetto and Zima paraphrase Goyer, Redding, and Rickey in their definition of an **interview** as "the interaction of two people, one of whom has a distinct purpose, and both of whom speak and listen from time to time and make moment to moment adaptations" (1976, p. 3).

This definition fits the transactional perspective of communication provided in chapter 1. The **interviewer,** or initiator of an interview, takes control of the exchange with an interviewee for a defined purpose and adapts to the messages of the interviewee as the interaction develops. Further, the interviewer introduces the interview, establishes rapport with the interviewee, specifies the purpose of the interview, keeps the conversation moving, and closes the interview. The **interviewee** is responsible for giving accurate information to the interviewer. However, he or she has the right to refuse comment or to terminate the interaction and hence retains some control of the situation.

An interview is most generally structured to be a dyadic exchange between one interviewer and one interviewee. There may, however, be times when an interview is arranged between two or more interviewers with one interviewee or between one or more interviewers and several interviewees.

Interviewing Purposes

Interviews fill several purposes. First, most people interview other people to gather information of some kind. For example, newspaper reporters conduct investigative interviews and professional interviewers such as Mike Wallace and Barbara Walters question national and international figures, as well as the man or woman on the street, for news and feature stories. Students sometimes do investigative interviewing of certain authorities to obtain data for theses and reports.

Second, many people conduct information-gathering interviews for the purpose of social-science research and public-opinion polling. Investigators who want to know regularities in human behavior or the opinions of large numbers of people create sets of questions to ask each person interviewed. Responses are tabulated and a composite response for each question is reported. Although only a select number of people are sampled, they represent a larger population. The sampled opinions, such as those of the Gallup polls, can quite accurately reflect the views of the whole.

A final purpose for interviewing is to hire new employees. Employment interviews are also used to gather information, because the employer needs to determine if the applicant has the requisite skills or capabilities to perform the job. In addition, the applicant usually wants to find out about the job and its benefits during the interview. While both participants in an employment interview seek information, they may also try to impress each other with their personal characteristics or advantages of the job.

Although the focus of this chapter is on **information-gathering** inter-

views, there are four types of interviews which have the primary purpose of **information giving.** First, *orientation* interviews are conducted to introduce people to a new environment or set of responsibilities. Second, *counseling* interviews are used by people to advise others or to help in personal problem solving (e.g., a guidance counselor may help a student select a college). Third, *persuasive* interviews occur when one person's primary goal is to change the behavior, opinions, or feelings of another by questioning and convincing. Door-to-door salespeople, telephone campaigners, and people getting signatures on petitions are examples of people who use persuasive interviews. Finally, the *appraisal* interview occurs when one person, usually a supervisor, evaluates the performance of another in a dyadic situation. Although the interviewee may be given the opportunity to explain his or her behavior and attitudes, the primary function of this type of interview is for the interviewer to communicate an assessment of the interviewee.

Distortion of Information: Causes and Preventions

As with most resources, information is most valuable in its purest form; that is, when it has not been distorted. Information is almost always subject to distortion. Think for a moment about rumors you have been told that were inaccurate or incomplete. Or remember when you asked someone for directions to somewhere and, upon following them, ended up even farther from your destination. In each of those cases you received information that was distorted, probably unintentionally.

Information may be distorted in different ways. **Internal distortion** occurs as the result of biases within the interviewer. The axiom "Meanings are in people" should provide the first caution for an interviewer. We see things and interpret events from our own perspective. Because our personal traits, experience, expectations, selectivity of exposure, perception, and retention all affect the way in which we interpret new information, it is always possible for us to change or distort new data. For example, if we interview a man whose political beliefs oppose our own, it is likely that we will only partially hear what he is saying because we are internally refuting his viewpoint and defending our own. Or, if we interview a woman we expect to be rigidly conservative, we may fail to recognize some liberal views she may hold.

A second form of distortion is **external distortion,** which occurs as the interviewer and interviewee *interact.* External distortion can arise from several factors. One of these is the violation of cultural norms, such as those affecting spatial distance or punctuality. If the interviewer is upset due to the violation of his cultural norms, he may react angrily towards the interviewee. Subsequently, he may not listen carefully or record the information properly. On the other hand, if the interviewee's norms have been violated, he may clam up and choose not to provide the interviewer with accurate or complete information.

Verbal and nonverbal behaviors of the interviewer or interviewee can also cause external distortions in information. These behaviors may include distracting physical mannerisms (such as nervous hand gestures or foot tapping), harsh voice characteristics or vocalized pauses (ah's and um's), or vocabulary choices (that the receiver finds unfamiliar, insulting, or offensive). In addition, verbal or nonverbal behaviors which provide added information about background or social status may also cause an interviewer or interviewee to distort messages. If the interviewee gets the idea that the interviewer lacks objectivity, the interviewee may cut short his answers or distort them to fit what he thinks the interviewer wants to hear. Or, if the interviewer is in awe of the status of the interviewee, he may not feel comfortable enough to probe for detailed or sensitive information. If the interviewee is in awe of the interviewer (such as a newspaper or television reporter), he may become speechless or forget details. Conversely, if the interviewee perceives the interviewer to be of lesser status, he may not feel obliged to take time to give details. Or, he may take the opportunity to inflate his importance, which would provide an inaccurate message.

Finally, distortion can occur when interference arises from conflicting messages sent by multiple channels. For example an interviewee may say he likes something but his vocal hesitation and strained facial expression indicate dislike. During such times an interviewer may become confused and fail to clarify and document the actual view of the interviewee.

The third form of distortion is external distortion that is caused by **environmental interference,** such as other people talking, general sounds, or physical discomforts due to the surroundings. For example, a person being interviewed in a noisy office may not hear the interviewer's question, or the interviewer may inaccurately interpret a response.

While absolute neutrality or objectivity in recording information is impossible, a successful interviewer recognizes the problems and works to hold them to a minimum. The following are ways to reduce the probability that distortion will occur.

To reduce the errors due to internal distortion, a good interviewer will:

Restate facts as he heard them and ask the interviewee for verification.

Take notes during the interview or ask the interviewee for permission to tape-record the interview (most interviewees are amenable to taping sessions because they know the information will be more accurately recorded).

Corroborate the accuracy of the information that the interviewee provided by checking reliable sources—experts, statistics, etc.

To reduce the distortions due to external causes, the interviewer should:

Analyze his own behaviors and work to change distracting gestures or vocal characteristics.

Be aware of potential differences in cultural norms or role differences between himself and the interviewee, and adapt his behavior to the interviewee accordingly.

Be prepared to alter the environmental conditions under which the interview takes place to avoid noise and distractions from sound, lighting, seating arrangements, room temperature, etc. (In extreme cases it may be wise for the interviewer to request the interview be held in a different location or at a different time.)

Managing the Interview

In the interviewing process, as in any communication transaction, there is a give-and-take between participants. However, since the interviewer approaches the interviewee and requests a valuable resource (information), interviewers should consider the dynamics of an interview in terms of its **rewards** and **costs** to each party involved. Rewards and costs may be **tangible** (e.g., monetary payment, loss of job) or **intangible** (e.g., high self-esteem, loss of face).

The concept of reward and cost in interviewing is best captured in the "social exchange" model. This framework is useful for crystallizing not only the communication exchange, but the payoff (or profit) for each participant. The potential payoff is generally greater for the interviewer than for the interviewee, since the interviewer gets the scarce commodity, the information, from the interviewee. The following model represents the social exchange framework:

Person 1   Person 2

$$\text{Rewards} - \text{cost} = \text{profit} \qquad \text{Rewards} - \text{cost} = \text{profit}$$

As this model indicates, ideally persons 1 and 2 should perceive that the profits accruing to each are equal. If one perceives an imbalance favoring the other, that person is likely to terminate the relationship. Similarly, in an interview, the interviewee may feel there is more cost (and less profit) in divulging sensitive information to an interviewer (e.g., the interviewee may lose face publicly or be criticized by his or her superiors for giving out information). As a result, it is likely the interviewee will refuse to answer some of the interviewer's questions or curtail the interview altogether.

In order to clarify this framework, let's consider some costs and rewards of an interview, first for the interviewer and then for the interviewee:

Rewards for the interviewer are numerous. Clearly, if the interview goes well, the interviewer obtains the needed information and completes the assignment. News interviewers like Barbara Walters who secure interviews with people who rarely grant interviews are considered stars, and their talents gain them million-dollar contracts. Interviewers engaged in research gain important data for completing their studies. Finally, while students who conduct interviews for class projects may not have such good fortune as Barbara Walters or Lou Harris, they may find that their interviewees are valuable contacts to have.

But nothing comes free, and interviewing also costs the interviewer. The time needed to plan, research, conduct, and report on the interview, if well done, is considerable. If the interview is handled in a nonprofessional manner, it can cause stress for the interviewer. Most importantly, poor planning can result in the interviewer getting wrong or incomplete information and having to resort to other ways of getting information. He may even have to return to the interviewee for more data. Whether the interviewer is a reporter, a researcher, or a student, errors he commits in recording or reporting information provided by the interviewee can cause the interviewee to sue for libel or refuse to provide information in the future. Thus although the interviewer has a great deal to gain by interviewing, mistakes can make the costs greater than the rewards.

In contrast, it is likely that the costs of granting an interview will almost always outweigh the rewards for the interviewee. Most interviewees are selected because they are authorities on a subject. Once recognized as experts, they are asked for an increasing number of interviews. However, as active people, it is costly for them to devote much time to being interviewed. If they perceive that the costs are too great, especially in comparison to the minimal rewards they are likely to gain, they may refuse to be interviewed, cut the interview short, or give inadequate responses. If the interview is conducted in a nonprofessional manner or the interviewer argues with the interviewee, it becomes an irritating experience for the interviewee. This is particularly true when interviewees feel they are doing the interviewer a favor.

A final source of cost is the "uncertainty" an interviewee experiences. Until the interviewer has clearly identified the purpose of the interview and has asked questions directed toward that goal, interviewees may feel uncomfortable. They may wonder why they have been selected to be interviewed and worry about how their responses will be used. As a result, they may be reluctant to answer questions honestly. This, of course, causes stress for both interviewee and interviewer. In essence, time-consuming and annoying interviews that do not seem to benefit the interviewee are not likely to be productive for either party.

How can an interviewer make an interview rewarding and pleasant for an interviewee? Several ways are immediately evident. First, the interviewer should be punctual, polite, and appropriately dressed. Second, the interviewer should clearly identify the purpose of the interview and how the information will be used. The interviewer should build the interviewee's esteem by stressing that his or her ideas are important. The interviewer should show interest in the interviewee's statements as well as appreciation of the interviewee's willingness to share them. An interviewee may be especially willing to cooperate with an interviewer who will publicly report the interviewee's ideas and opinions. As indicated in chapter 1, two goals fulfilled by communication are the establishment of human contact and the reinforcement of attitudes and behaviors of others. Both of these goals can be satisfactory rewards for interviewees who are made to feel that their ideas are valued and are useful to others. Finally, in some interviews, interviewees may be rewarded by learning something through the transaction—by the exchange of ideas with the interviewer, by having to think about old ideas in new ways, or by having new ideas emerge as they hear themselves explain their own plans.

In summary, the task of the interviewer may be thought of as an attempt to balance the social exchange paradigm of interviewer and interviewee by having each satisfy personal goals. To the extent the rewards can be made to outweigh the costs to the interviewee, the interviewer is most likely to gain the necessary information and receive undistorted facts and opinions. The good interviewer will convince an interviewee that the interview is worth the time and effort and that the interviewer does not have an unfair advantage or benefit in the exchange.

Steps in Interviewing

1. Determining the General Objective

As indicated earlier, interviews may be conducted for different purposes. When interviewers wish to gather information, they need to determine the type of information needed and then structure the interviews accordingly.

Investigative interviews are those conducted by reporters with individuals who (because of their expertise or relationship to the event or person about which data is being gathered) are considered knowledgeable on a specific topic. Woodward and Bernstein conducted numerous investigative interviews in their reporting of the Watergate break-in and the related events that preceded the resignation of Richard M. Nixon as president of the United States.

Polling, or *surveying,* large numbers of people representative of a larger population is a second type of information-gathering interview. Social-science researchers often depend upon sampling people's opinions via face-to-face interviews, telephone surveys, or written questionnaires to collect data that will provide them with a composite statement of the views or behaviors of people sharing certain demographic characteristics. The information is usually summarized or averaged so it remains relatively anonymous. People interviewed in polls are not chosen because of their expertise, but because they represent a mass of people. For example, a group of researchers may want to sample various opinions of middle-class midwesterners. They would first choose a small town in the Midwest where the average income is in a certain range, and then randomly select several hundred names of persons from the telephone book to interview.

Employment interviews enable personnel men and women or company representatives to determine if an applicant has the qualifications necessary to handle a job. In the interactive exchange of interviewer and interviewee, the applicant also has the opportunity to ask questions about the job, working conditions, benefits, and other personnel. Thus

the employment interview usually allows both participants to gather needed information.

2. Determining the Specific Information Needed

The problem suggested by the axiom "If you don't know where you're going, you're likely to end up somewhere else" is often faced by interviewers who have not determined the information they need or want to know. Thus interviewers should decide what information will be critical to have at the end of the interview, particularly what information *must* be gathered from the interviewee because it is not available from other sources.

Stating the general topic on which the interviewer intends to interview a person is not sufficient for conducting and managing the exchange. It is one thing to interview someone on the process of converting uranium to nuclear power. But it is another to interview on the economic hazards and resource limitations of continued use of nuclear power. Knowing the precise information needed enables the interviewer to (1) determine the most appropriate person(s) to interview; (2) research the topic and the background of the interviewee; (3) plan the questions and overall strategy to be employed; and (4) assess when an adequate amount of information has been obtained. An interviewee is more likely to respect and respond positively to an interviewer who has a well-defined, justifiable objective for conducting the interview.

In an employment interview, the interviewer should tell the applicant about the position(s) available. It can be frustrating for an applicant if the interviewer only asks questions about the applicant's skills and background and fails to say that the company has several positions open (and that the interviewer is trying to determine which position the applicant is most suited for). From an interviewee's perspective, knowing the specific goal of the job interview can help make the interview a positive and encouraging experience. Similarly, an interviewer who knows the kind of person who is needed can have more confidence and composure and can construct the most appropriate questions. The interviewer who has a specific objective is better able to plan in advance how to best use the information gathered during the interview (e.g., compare the interviewee with other candidates, recommend the interviewee for one or more specific jobs).

3. Selecting the Interviewee

We've already suggested that it is important to identify interviewees who have the desired information because it avoids cost to both interviewee and interviewer. To find the right interviewee, the interviewer must research prospective interviewees to insure they have the information. Interviewees selected for investigative interviews are usually chosen because they are authorities in certain areas. For example, a reporter wanting to get at the heart of some controversial legislation would want to interview the author of the bill. This person could best clear up any ambiguities.

In social-science research, interviewees are usually chosen at random. This and other methods are used to insure that they are representative of the group or population to which their comments will be generalized. For example, George Gallup has said his organization randomly identifies respondents based on their demographic characteristics. His researchers decide what sets of demographics they want in their study (e.g., income, sex, race, education levels) and then select communities where the majority of people fit those characteristics.

In the employment situation, candidates usually have applied for the position earlier. This indicates they are willing to work and have some interest in the specific job. While this self-selection process is common, it is possible for employers first to seek out specific individuals who they feel are qualified. They may also screen candidates on the basis of some criteria prior to interviewing them. Many job-hunting college graduates lament, "If only I could get my foot in the door . . ." Indeed, just getting an interview with certain personnel directors, principals, or other officials seems at times the impossible task.

4. Preparing Questions

After identifying the general purpose, determining the precise data needed, and selecting the interviewee, the interviewer is ready to prepare questions which are most likely to elicit the desired information. As in any communication event, the interviewer should carefully analyze the interviewee and adapt the questions to the experience, knowledge, attitudes, and communication skills of that person. It may be necessary for the interviewer to provide a frame of reference so the interviewee knows the context of the question. It may also be necessary for the interviewer to adapt to the language and style of communicating of the interviewee. And, it is critical for the interviewer to avoid alienating the interviewee by asking offensive, or misleading questions.

The questions should be worded to avoid distortion or bias. **Leading questions** should be avoided because they may make the respondent take a particular view or say what the interviewer expects to hear. For example, the question "Of course you agree that medicare should be provided to all people over sixty-five, don't you?" is a leading question because it implies that the respondent should answer yes rather than express an opinion independently.

Loaded questions which put the interviewee in a double-bind situation should also be avoided. For example, "Have you stopped wasting money playing pinball?" is loaded because it assumes the person played pinball machines in the past. It adds an overtone of criticism by implying that the money one spends playing pinball is "wasted." Similarly, loading a question with options, such as asking which of two candidates is preferred, limits the response of the interviewee, especially if the person does not like either candidate. It pushes the respondent into either saying what the interviewer wants to hear or refraining from answering.

The main point is that the interviewer should first decide what information is wanted and make sure the questions are constructed so as to obtain it. The questions should be phrased to allow interviewees to fully express their knowledge or opinions.

The interviewer may prepare both open-ended and closed-ended questions. **Open-ended questions** call for a broad response and allow answers in any direction. For example, "What do you think about abolishing general-education requirements?" or "What do you think should be done to the curriculum?" are open-ended questions. They give the interviewee maximum flexibility in responding.

In contrast, **closed-ended questions** require more direct, precise responses from the interviewee. The response to a closed-ended question may be one word, a few sentences, or a yes or no. For example, "Do you think general-education requirements should be abolished for graduation from college?" is a closed-ended question requiring only a yes or no response (although an interviewee may choose to elaborate). "Which of your previous research projects most directly contributed to your current research?" is a closed-ended question requiring a specific answer. Preparation of a range of open- and closed-ended questions provides the interviewer with more flexibility to adapt to the communication style and knowledge of the interviewee. This helps the interviewer to zero in on the desired information.

In addition, it is a good idea to have more questions prepared than can be covered in the interview. A surplus of questions allows the interviewer to adapt more readily to unexpected information provided by the interviewee. Mike Wallace may use only ten questions in the course of an interview, although he may have developed as many as fifty beforehand.

Once the questions have been prepared, the interviewer should create a strategy to reach the desired goal by *sequencing* the questions so they are logically connected and build on one another. The **funnel approach** begins with open-ended questions and moves to closed-ended questions. This approach may help relax interviewees if they know the topics well. It also helps them feel their ideas are of interest to the interviewer. The funnel strategy permits the interviewer to learn about the respondent's views in general, which can then serve as a basis for more specific questions. The following is a sample set of funnel questions:

Tell me what you know about the Equal Rights Amendment.

—What do you mean by that?
—Why did you say that?
—How long have you felt this way?
—What influenced your decision?

The **inverted funnel** begins with closed-ended questions and gradually asks more open-ended questions. This sequence may help the interviewee feel comfortable enough with the topic and interviewer to open up. When an interviewer asks specific questions first, it can give an interviewee a good idea of what the interviewer is interested in hearing. The following is an example of this line of questioning:

Do you agree with the philosophy of the Equal Rights Amendment?

—How long have you held that opinion?
—Why do you hold that opinion?
—What else do you know about equal rights legislation?

George Gallup reported the use of the **quintamensional plan** of questioning (1974, p. 385). This is a method for probing the knowledge and intensity of attitudes of people. While this approach could be used in any of our information-gathering settings, we'll take an example from the employment situation. The five types of questions to ask in sequence are:

1. *Awareness:* "Tell me what you know about working with the aged."
2. *Uninfluenced attitudes:* "What, if any, contributions are made to the Center for the Aged by private citizens?"
3. *Specific attitude:* "Do you approve or disapprove of giving meals away?"
4. *Reason why:* "Why do you approve . . . or disapprove?"
5. *Intensity of attitude:* "How strongly do you feel about improving physical and social conditions for the elderly?"

The funnel, inverted funnel, and quintamensional plan are the three most common means of gathering in-depth responses to questions. However, other sequences, such as asking all closed-ended questions on a questionnaire may be used, depending on the purpose of the interview. Such questions could have the following formats:

1. How many years of school have you completed?

    _____ 1–6

    _____ 7–9

    _____ 10–12

    _____ 13–16

    _____ 17+

2. In general, who do you feel gives more to your relationship?

    _____ My spouse gives much more than I do

    _____ My spouse gives slightly more than I do

_____ We both give about the same

_____ I give slightly more than my spouse

_____ I give much more than my spouse

5. Selecting the Appropriate Interviewer

As manager of the communication event, the person responsible for gathering information may be able to select an interviewer who is most likely to be well received by the interviewee. There are several factors that the manager should keep in mind. First, interviewers should not have personal characteristics which would threaten or antagonize interviewees or bias their responses. Nor should the role of the person conducting the interview affect the interviewee's responses. For example, if a first-year teacher is interviewed by the superintendent of schools, the teacher may be less confident and more uncomfortable than if the interview were conducted by the principal of the school.

Sometimes it is necessary to select an interviewer who has the ability to be direct and persistent enough to get to the heart of the issue. Mike Wallace on the television program "60 Minutes" often interviews people he believes are withholding significant information. In the employment interview, personnel people may need to take a hard line in their questioning to identify the person who can withstand pressure.

In short, it is necessary to assess the communication styles and personalities of the interviewees, the situation, the purpose of the interview, and to identify an interviewer who can best handle the needs of the situation.

When two or more people interview one or more interviewees, the interviewers should plan beforehand who will take the lead and what sequence of questions they will use. Although they will still have to adapt to certain occurrences, they should discuss how they expect to adapt. Vying for leadership or contradicting each other can hamper the interview or disturb the interviewee(s). Team interviewing should be carefully planned so as not to intimidate or overwhelm those interviewed.

6. Arranging the Interview

Once the interviewer has selected the interviewee, he should contact the person and arrange for the interview to be held. The interviewer should identify himself and indicate the reason for calling that particular individual. He usually should state the purpose of the interview and how the information will be used. The interviewer should indicate the amount of time he anticipates will be necessary to conduct the interview and then schedule a time and place that is convenient for the interviewee. (Remember, the interviewee is doing the interviewer a favor in granting the interview.) Thus one way to make a good first impression is to accommodate the interviewee. In some employment interviewing, such responsibilities for arrangement may be shifted to the interviewee but the guidelines remain the same.

7. Opening the Interview

It is crucial to set a smooth tone at the beginning of the interview. The interviewer should work to build *rapport* with the interviewee by introducing or (reintroducing) himself and possibly (if time permits and the situation is appropriate) making enough small talk with the interviewee to reduce anxiety and to establish a foundation for communicating. The interviewer should restate the purpose of the interview and his intended use of the information. He should establish personal and professional credibility so the respondent trusts him. The interviewee should understand why the interviewer is interested in the topic. If the interviewer is relaxed, yet in tactful, businesslike control of the situation, the respondent is usually more at ease and interacts more freely.

In the beginning the interviewer should arrange the seating so both participants are comfortable. They should be within hearing distance and be able to maintain eye contact with each other. All external distractions should be eliminated. If there is noise in an adjoining room, the interviewer may ask the interviewee if the door can be closed. In another person's office or home, the interviewer may need to request that the interview be conducted in private. In short, it is desirable to free the environment of any distractions that could interfere with the interviewer's accurate reception of the message or that could distort or bias the information provided by the interviewee.

8. Adapting to the Style of the Interviewee

People have various communication styles, and sometimes the interview situation triggers communication behaviors that even the person interviewed did not anticipate. Upon the mention of a favorite topic, one person may take off and ramble for hours. Another person may fear disclosing too much information or discrediting himself and refuse to talk. The good interviewer will spontaneously adapt to these and other reactive communication behaviors of the interviewee.

To gain in-depth information and encourage the interviewee to discuss his opinions and knowledge openly, the interviewer should be careful not to cut off the interviewee's comments or to interrupt him. The interviewer may also develop **probing questions** which ask the interviewee to extend, clarify, or provide an example of his points. "Why do you say that?" and "Can you give me an example?" are probing questions. Many investigative, research, and employment interviewers use this technique of probing frequently. As Barbara Walters says, the key to good interviewing is not the written question but the follow-up question of "Why?" or "What do you mean?" She says that it is this *second* question that opens up her respondents.

A technique related to probing is the use of **mirror (restatement) questions.** Questions which begin with such statements as "Let me make sure I understand you correctly. Did you say . . . ?" allow the interviewer to check the accuracy of his understanding and provide feedback to the interviewee. Such mirror questions also encourage the interviewee to extend or clarify his comments on an issue.

If the interviewee is withdrawn, the interviewer may ask open-ended questions which prompt the interviewee to respond. However, if the problem persists, the interviewer may need to reassess whether the interviewee actually possesses the necessary information or is just reluctant to talk. If lack of information is the problem, the interviewer may change the focus of the interview or curtail it. If the interviewee does seem to possess the knowledge, more specific questions may help. If the situation continues, the interviewer should quickly evaluate his interviewing techniques. He may find that he has asked too many questions, has not given the interviewee adequate time to think about the answers and then respond, or has used terminology which is unfamiliar to the interviewee.

Not all interviewees need to be given encouragement to talk. Sometimes it is necessary to subtly and politely redirect the discussion back to the intended purpose of the interview. If the interviewee rambles, the interviewer should refocus the discussion by asking closed-ended questions: open-ended questions encourage discursive responses. However, the interviewer should show his appreciation for the interviewee's willingness to provide information.

As has been stressed earlier, it is important for the interviewer to remain as objective as possible throughout the interview. An interviewee agrees to provide information, not to argue. Thus the interviewer should avoid interjecting his opinions during the interview. In addition, the interviewer should consciously avoid allowing himself to be biased by his reaction to the interviewee's personality, dialect, race, etc. Instead, the interviewer should try to listen and record the information objectively. If the interviewee reacts emotionally to an issue or question, the interviewer may wish to seek an explanation for that response. Attention to the information and to the interviewee should consume the interviewer, but not to the extent that he loses sight of the interview's purpose.

People remember what they want to remember, and interviewers are no exception. Thus we caution an interviewer against depending on his memory for recording the information after the interview. Tape-recording, with the interviewee's permission, is perhaps the most accurate record of the interview, but it can cause some interviewees to respond less spontaneously. An interviewer should be skillful in using the tape recorder and should know it works before taking it to the interview. Taking notes during an interview can be an efficient way of recording the interview if the interviewer has planned for the interview, has a set of questions prepared, and attempts to record only key phrases of the answers.

Throughout the interview (however recorded) there may be times in which the interviewee provides sensitive information that he does not wish to have publicly reported. The interviewer should honor the interviewee's request for certain opinions or facts to be "off the record." Such background information may be valuable in helping the interviewer understand the context of the issues. It should *not* be used against the will of the interviewee. It is useful to consider the social exchange paradigm in such situations. The interviewer could greatly increase the costs of the interview to the interviewee by publicly disclosing such confidential material.

9. Closing the Interview

As in public speaking or writing a paper, it is necessary to bring an interview to a close. The interviewer may accomplish this by summarizing the information if it is not too lengthy or highlighting the key points. The interviewer should thank the interviewee for his time and willingness to provide the needed information. It is also important for the interviewer to leave the interviewee with a sense of gratification, compensation, or both. For example, while reinforcing that the interview helped the interviewer, he may also point out that the information given by the interviewee may be valuable to others. Or, in some polling or research situations, interviewees are paid a monetary stipend for participating in the study.

10. Evaluating the Interview

Since the interviewer is ultimately responsible for the success or failure of the interview, it is in his best interest to evaluate the outcome of the interview. The first question should be, "Did I obtain the desired information?" If the answer is yes, the interviewer might ask if he could have improved the information-gathering procedures. If the answer to the former question is no, the interviewer might ask several questions: (1) "Was the interviewee able to provide the information?" (2) "Were the questions or the sequence of questions in any way inappropriate?" (3) "Did I adapt to the interviewee and to the situation?" or (4) "Did I do too much of the talking?" In analyzing the interview, the interviewer might consider the following guidelines for avoiding distortion of information:

1. Avoid asking leading and loaded questions.
2. Do not induce defensiveness.
3. Take notes—do not depend on memory.

4. Do not talk so much that you do not elicit information from the interviewee.
5. Begin objectively without preconceived perceptions of the interviewee.
6. Explore important comments to elicit information (probe) rather than make inferences.
7. Adapt the rate of the interview to the interviewee's pace.
8. Use mirror questions to insure accuracy.
9. Analyze your own personal characteristics which could bias the responses of the interviewee or in other ways affect the interview.

The interviewer may obtain the desired information but still feel that the interviewing process was not as successful as he would have liked. Problems have often occurred in interviews where the interviewer:

Was not prepared.

Became so tied to prepared questions that he did not adjust.

Failed to treat the interviewee with respect.

Gave the impression of not caring about the topic.

Did not keep the respondent on the topic.

Left issues unresolved or unexplored.

On the other hand, generally successful interviews have been those in which the interviewer:

Was adequately prepared.

Adapted to the response rate of the interviewee and did not rush.

Showed interest in the respondent and in the topic.

Planned more questions than needed.

Listened well.

11. Tabulating the Information

Upon completion of the interview, the interviewer must use the data to write a report, tabulate a survey, or select a candidate for a job. In the investigative interview the interviewer may want to confirm the information with another source before writing or presenting the final report. In social science research the researcher will compile the findings to quantify people's responses into percentages. He may then generalize from the sample to a larger population. In employment situations the employer will compare the qualifications and resonses of interviewees with each other or against a set of criteria to select the best candidate for the job.

While methods for tabulating information are usually objective, difficulties may arise in the interpretation or analysis of what the information means. In analyzing the data, the interviewer puts it in perspective with other pieces of information and draws conclusions. Throughout the process of tabulation and analysis it is the responsibility of the interviewer not to violate the confidence of the interviewee nor to distort the information. Thus the information reported is only as accurate or complete as that which the interviewer is able to provide from the stages of questioning, tabulating, and analysis. One should be aware that distortion is liable to occur at every juncture.

Conclusion

The interviewing process is a transactional exchange between an interviewer and an interviewee. The purpose of an interview is to obtain or provide information. As in any communication event, however, the messages transacted contain information which is constantly subject to distortion. While total objectivity is impossible, there are precautions one can take to safeguard against more serious errors of distortion.

We have emphasized the transactional nature of interviewing for a reason. Interviewing is a communication *event* in which both parties give and receive information. Too often, however, interviewers fail to listen to their respondents. When this occurs, the dyadic exchange nature of the interview falls apart. If the interviewer fails to engage the interviewee in discussion or fails to actively listen to him, the interview becomes little more than a monologue by the person conducting the interview. As veteran interviewer Sander Vanocur commented, the secret of good interviewing is that the interviewer is able to withdraw rather than advance on the person being interviewed. The interviewer is there not to listen to himself, but to listen to the interviewee.

TERMS AND CONCEPTS FOR REVIEW

closed-ended questions
employment interviews
environmental interference
external distortion
funnel approach
information gathering
information giving

internal distortion
interview
interviewee
interviewer
inverted funnel
investigative interviews
leading questions

loaded questions
mirror questions
open-ended questions
polling (surveying)

probing questions
quintamensional plan
rewards/costs
tangible/intangible

REVIEW QUESTIONS

1. How would you plan, organize, and conduct the three types of information-gathering interviews?
2. How does information distortion arise and how can it be counteracted?
3. What is the level of control that each participant retains in an interview?
4. How can the interview be forecasted?
4. How can the dynamics of the interview be forecasted by analyzing the situation through the social exchange model?
5. What rationales would you follow in selecting interviewers and interviewees?
6. What question strategies would you follow?
7. What are the processes of tabulating and interpreting the information obtained in an interview?

REFERENCES

Gallup, George. "The Quintamensional Plan of Question Design," *Public Opinion Quarterly,* 11, Fall, 1974.

Goyer, Robert S., W. Charles Redding, and John T. Rickey. *Interviewing Principles and Techniques: A Project Text.* Dubuque, Iowa: Wm. C. Brown, 1964.

Kahn, Robert L., and Charles F. Cannel. *The Dynamics of Interviewing.* New York; John Wiley & Sons, 1967.

McMillan, Penelope. "Some of TV's Best Interviewers Reveal the Tricks of Their Trade." *TV Guide,* August 13, 1977, pp. 6–10.

Richetto, Gary M., and Joseph P. Zima. *Fundamentals of Interviewing.* Chicago: Science Research Associates, 1976.

Stewart, Charles J., and William B. Cash. *Interviewing Principles and Practices.* Dubuque, Iowa: Wm. C. Brown, 1974.

Analyzing and Adapting to Your Receivers

RECEIVERS' ATTITUDES, KNOWLEDGE, AND BEHAVIORS TOWARD TOPIC

THE SETTING OF THE SPEECH

RECEIVERS' KNOWLEDGE AND ATTITUDES TOWARD SPEAKER

CHECKLIST FOR ANALYZING AND ADAPTING TO RECEIVERS

Choosing and Adapting Your Subject and Purpose

CHOOSING A TOPIC

IDENTIFYING THE PURPOSE

SPEAKING OUT OF AN EXIGENCY

LIMITING YOUR SUBJECT

THE PURPOSE SENTENCE

Developing the Content

MATERIALS OF PERSONAL PROOF

MATERIALS OF DEVELOPMENT
  Factual evidence and opinion evidence
  Repetition, restatement, comparison, and contrast
  Reasoning by analogy, example, cause, and sign

MATERIALS OF EXPERIENCE
  Motivational appeals

Arresting and holding the receivers' attention
Techniques of composition
Techniques of delivery

Structuring Your Speech

PURPOSE SENTENCE

BODY

CONCLUSION

INTRODUCTION

Delivering Your Speech

IMPROMPTU DELIVERY

MANUSCRIPT DELIVERY

MEMORIZED DELIVERY

EXTEMPORANEOUS DELIVERY

IMPROVING YOUR DELIVERY
  Vocal delivery
  Nonverbal delivery

Evaluating Your Speech

Speech Evaluation Form

Sample Deductive Speech Plan

9

Public Speaking

After reading this chapter, you should be able to:

1. Identify and explain the six steps in preparing a formal speech.
2. Discuss analyzing and adapting to the receivers.
3. Explain and give examples of materials of personal proof, materials of development, and materials of experience.
4. Give examples of the four modes of delivery and explain when each mode should be used.

Some of the material for this chapter is adapted from Kenneth G. Hance, David C. Ralph, and Milton J. Wiksell, *Principles of Speaking,* 3rd ed. Belmont, Cal.: Wadsworth, 1975. The author is indebted to his co-authors and his publisher for their kindness in permitting him to condense and adapt this material.

If the message you will deliver is an oral one; if it is primarily original with you; if you are the sole source or the main source or the source for a considerable part of the message; if you have to organize your ideas and adapt them to a person or persons who will receive them and who have a potential for responding; if you have a purpose for speaking and seek to disseminate knowledge or advocate a more or less specific behavioral change, you are probably delivering a **public speech.**

How do you do it? That is the subject of this chapter. For the formal and detailed study of speechmaking, which you will need if you want to become a lawyer, teacher, public-relations person, salesperson, manager, personnel officer or foreman or, indeed, any person who participates to a considerable degree in society, you will want to study a textbook on public speaking or enroll in a course devoted to public-speaking skills. However, a careful study of this chapter, combined with reference to chapter 3 on "Message Construction," will get you started toward successful public speaking. Take advantage of every opportunity to put these principles into practice, using chapters 3 and 9 as your guide. Principles plus practice are the keys to effective public speaking.

There are certain steps in preparing a formal speech which all speakers go through: (1) choosing and adapting the subject and purpose, (2) developing the speech content, (3) structuring the message, (4) delivering the speech and (5) evaluating the speech. However, one required step does not fit neatly into a time sequence and we turn first to a discussion of that step.

Step "X": Analyzing and Adapting to Your Receivers

The receiver must be considered at every step of the speech preparation process, from the moment you realize that you will be speaking until the end of the evaluation process following your speech. The selection or adaptation of your topic, organization, word choice, and delivery depends upon what you know or can predict about your receivers' probable reactions based on the cultural, sociological, or psychological data you can gather about them.

Speaking in public is a matter of continual compromise between you and your listeners, wherein you try to state your beliefs as accurately and honestly as you can, while at the same time striving to hold your listeners' attention and keep their minds open and receptive to you. Given that your goal as a speaker is to persuade your listeners and make your message clear, you should try to understand your listeners before, during, and after your speech in three areas: (1) their attitudes, knowledge, and potential or actual behaviors toward your purpose, that is, what you want them to do or believe, (2) the circumstances under which your speech will be delivered which might influence their attitudes and behaviors, and (3) their knowledge and attitude toward you.

Many speakers find it useful to classify their receivers as "friendly," "apathetic," "neutral," or "hostile" toward the goal the speaker seeks. Categorizing individual listeners is a chancy matter, however: individuals may change their minds, may deliberately or unintentionally mislead you, may not be sure of how they feel. Other speakers prefer a more specific category system, perhaps involving percentages of favorable audience members. Still others seek a definite response, preferring to know in advance exactly who believes in what. Obviously, the more specific your analysis of audience attitudes is, the more adaptations you can make in your message.

The degree of knowledge which individuals in a listening group may possess about your topic is important. A youngster may have a highly favorable attitude toward his football coach—he is a "friendly" audience. He may have a strong desire to believe and emulate his coach and learn from him how to catch a pass. But if he doesn't understand what a "simple down" and "in pattern" means, his coach's instructions (a form of public speaking) may not result in a successful catch. Again, as with the analysis of attitude and behavior, some system of categorizing your listeners' knowledge should be helpful—"specific knowledge," "general knowledge," and "little knowledge" is a simple system that has been found useful in determining how much detailed explanation of an idea or subject is necessary before persuasion or learning can take place.

In general, as a speaker you should collect as much data about your receivers as possible and then try to reason out what their views toward the topic are likely to be. Demographic data such as age, sex, race, place of residence, and occupation allow preliminary predictions on the cultural and sociological levels. Knowledge of group memberships of the receivers allows you to predict how the receivers might view the specific topic or related topics based on the goals of the groups to which they belong or the behaviors exhibited and opinions expressed by the group as a whole. Finally, personal knowledge of individual audience members may provide valuable insights into the rest of the audience and allow you to more specifically adapt to your receivers. Basically, then, adapting to an audience is a matter of gaining as much information about the audience members as possible. Once their attitudes and values have been predicted, you choose words, examples, and reasoning that the audience is most likely to accept. In other words, you work from their perspectives to get them to see and agree with yours. You should remember that to adapt you must determine with each audience those things that cannot be said, those that must be said, and those that can be said.

The setting—the occasion—of the speech is important. People expect to hear certain messages in certain locations. For example, people expect to hear patriotic speeches on the Fourth of July or a campaign

speech at a political rally before an election. In the example of the boy
and the coach, the explanation of how to catch a pass and the exhorta-
tion to "watch for the ball" may be delivered on a crowded playground,
with background noise from the street and competing instructions from
other coaches interfering with the normal source-receiver relationship.
Thus the speaker must adapt the message to the expectations of the audience and the demands of the setting.

What the receivers think about the source is also important, for a
speaker with low credibility will be unlikely to move the audience to action. On the other hand, a highly credible source may be able to readily
win over his audience. You can insert comments in the speech to enhance your credibility with the audience if you can indicate your knowledge of the topic, link yourself with the audience, prove your trustworthiness, and be dynamic in your delivery.

The following checklist may be useful in analyzing and adapting to
your audience:

1. Make a preliminary guess concerning your receivers' reactions to
   and knowledge of your subject and goal. Use the rest of the checklist to attempt to confirm or deny that guess.
2. Try to determine what your credibility with your receivers is. Do
   you have any? Have you earned their respect in your previous contacts with them? Do they think of you as a leader? Do they know

how much you know about your subject? Have you blown it badly with them in some way—for example, by failing to do your share in preparing a group project within your class?

3. Consider the physical setting of the place where you will speak. Are you familiar with it? Is it noisy? Can you rearrange the chairs if you want to? Can everyone hear you easily, or will you have to speak up or use a mike? Can you have physical contact with your receivers if you want it? Is a chalkboard available? How about electrical outlets and extension cords for your overhead projector?

4. Be sure you know the true purpose of your speech. Sometimes you may have a goal in speaking which differs from the topic you've agreed to speak on—sometimes you may not even realize this yourself. But it can make quite a difference in the way you work with your audience.

5. What is the group gathered for? To hear you only, or are you one of several speakers? To hear the subject you intend to talk about, or something else? In other words, item four asks what you're there for—this item asks what they are there for, and there might be a significant difference.

6. What are your listeners' occupations? If they are all students, you might be better off if you know what their parents do for a living. Better still, what majors are you talking with? Students who are majors in the college of agriculture and natural resources might hold somewhat different beliefs in environmental matters from students who are majoring in the college of arts and letters.

7. Find out what you can (by survey or interviews) about the social conditioning of your listeners. Education, economic status, religion, social class, and living style all may make a difference in their reaction, for example, to a speech about success and money. And this leads to learning as much as you can about the strongly held attitudes and beliefs of your receivers. How do you suppose the student who was born and reared in the Panama Canal Zone will feel about your support for turning the canal over to Panama?

8. What do you know about your receivers' behavioral patterns? How will they react when you express delight that additional support for the relationship between cancer and cigarette smoking has been found? Will they share your pleasure as they sneak a smoke in the hall before your speech or dream about the one they'll have while running to the next class? Of course, the more homogeneous your group is, the more useful your knowledge of their probable behavior will be.

9. Determine your receivers' predominant physical characteristics— are they young, old, mixed, male, female, athletes, or spectators? It is far easier to construct a message about disco dancing for an au-

dience of young people than it is for a group of older people in a convalescent home.

10. While you are speaking, study your receivers' nonverbal cues—are they attentive, do they look bored, puzzled, angry, pleased? American audiences do not normally hiss and boo and throw shoes, but they will tell you whether you're getting across or not.

We have talked about some of the things you need to know about your audience and how you can go about finding these. Adapting to your audience will be a prominent part of each of the steps in speech preparation and presentation.

Step One: Choosing and Adapting Your Subject and Purpose

Speakers end up with a subject in one or a combination of three ways. Traditional courses in speaking encourage students to "choose a topic"; that is, it is assumed that speakers have a free choice in what they talk about. A speaker looks over all the goodies of the world and after thinking for awhile, says, "I have decided to speak about supporting your public television station." The problem here is that in the real world, speakers don't choose topics—topics choose speakers.

The second approach to obtaining a subject for your speech is to put purpose foremost in your mind. What do you want to accomplish in your speech? What behavioral changes would you like to encourage your listeners to make? What attitudes in your listeners would you like to develop, create, change? What personal goals have you set for yourself? What are you interested in that you would like others to know about? A public speech, after all, is a way of expressing your thoughts, your ambitions, your hopes; it is a way of offering support for a conviction you have; it is a way of explaining an idea or a process in just the way you want to. Your purpose in speaking is a solid basis for deciding upon your subject, and, of course, every speech should have a purpose and should be delivered for a purpose.

In real life most public speakers speak out of necessity. Their subject is not chosen by them but *for* them. The boss may order you to report to the board on the slumping sales in your department. Your job may call for you to instruct rookie firemen in a new technique of fighting oil fires. The PTA may request that you, as a real estate agent, explain the effect of the millage proposal on homeowners. Or, an event in the Middle East may compel you to express your strongly held views on the Arab-Israeli conflict.

We call this approach to the subject speaking out of an **exigency.** In its simplest form, this means that you speak because something has happened which requires you to speak. "Require" may mean outside pressure or pressure from within you. In either case, you speak on this subject because you feel compelled to speak.

Whether you choose your topic, determine the purpose, or respond out of exigency, the main test of any topic must be applied: how will it go over with your listeners? There are several possible answers to this question, ranging from total rejection of the subject because it doesn't fit the receivers' needs or will never be acceptable to the receivers or is over their heads, to total acceptance because it fits all three criteria. Or, you may decide that the subject is so vital to you that you will talk on it even if you know in advance that you will lose. Finally, you may have no choice. The exigency is so strong that your personal decision and the receivers' interests are irrelevant—you will talk on this topic because the boss ordered you to or because something inside you says you must. Most of the time, fortunately, you can modify your subject to help increase the probability that you and your audience can get together on it.

Limiting Your Subject

You must *limit* your subject, no matter how you arrived at it. You can't begin to make a stab at all the issues involved in "The Middle East." "Apathy and indifference versus open revolt among college students" is a great subject for a book, but you'll have to deal with some aspect of that subject in a speech of any reasonable length. "Technological advances without moral commitments" is a whale of a subject for a group of people to consider in a series of meetings, but you'll have to content yourself with a small part of it. Limiting the subject, as we have suggested a bit earlier, is necessary also because for each audience there are aspects of the subject that are inappropriate—too complicated, unnecessarily controversial, a taboo of that group, not germane, not persuasive.

Composing the Purpose Sentence

The way you limit your subject is to come up with a single sentence which sums up what you want to explain or the attitude you want to foster in your listeners or the behavioral change you are after. Public speakers call this statement the **purpose sentence.** ("Proposition" is the term used in chapter 3 to designate a persuasive purpose sentence.) It is useful because it helps you to straighten out your thinking about your subject, forces you to consider the main points of your speech, and guides you as you organize it. Constructing the purpose sentence can help you to visualize the subject and the receivers together—and to check the compatibility of the two. Finally, and sometimes most important, the purpose sentence forces you to concentrate upon the *purpose* of your speech or the behavioral change you want to effect in your audience.

The rules for composing the purpose sentence are simple but important:

1. Make it a complete sentence, with subject and predicate. A phrase or clause allows sloppy thinking; a complete sentence makes you think carefully about what you are writing (and ultimately saying).
2. Make it an affirmative sentence, not a negative one. Even if you are against something rather than for it, state your purpose affirmatively; "Higher education today fails to prepare young people for coping with the complexities of modern life," not "Higher education does not prepare young people to cope with the complexities of modern life."
3. Make the sentence complete and specific in the sense of describing exactly what you are going to talk about, exactly what behavioral change you expect in your listener: "Ecological considerations must give way to energy considerations when our existence is in danger and when our economic development is in danger." This purpose sentence dictates that your argument will have two basic parts; thus, in a short speech, you would expect to have two main divisions to your speech plan (I, II).
4. Make the sentence as succinct and clear as possible, preferably a straightforward declarative sentence, not a long-winded compound or complex sentence: "Americans must learn to live with their relative affluence," not "Americans, who are relatively affluent, must learn to live with it."

An example of how a broad subject is limited may help you to see the importance both of limiting your subject and composing your purpose sentence:

Suppose that while crossing at a busy intersection on a crowded campus, you narrowly escaped being run over by a car. You picked yourself up, perhaps uttered a prayer (or a curse), and went on to class. But during the professor's lecture your thoughts kept returning to your near accident. "Somebody ought to do something," you muttered. "Cars should be eliminated altogether—they burn up gas, anyway. At least they should be banned from campus. But some of the profs are too old to walk, and, besides, it's a long way for a student to run, from Bogue Street to Beal Street. Somebody ought to do something—get everybody to buy bikes, or something. Think I'll bring that up at the student government meeting—maybe the *State News* would run an editorial. A ten-speed for everybody would be a good idea, anyway—good exercise; you can ride a long way without getting too tired. But they're expensive as the dickens, the good ones, anyway, hard to repair unless you're an expert. What about the Zenith? It's on sale; it's a pretty good bike, and they do their own repair work right where you buy it—guaranteed, too, for a year or something like that. Hey, ten thousand Zenith ten-speeds, all on one campus. Wouldn't solve the whole problem, of course. Pedestrians could get killed by a ten-speed; but it would help some. If I just complain about cars, I won't get anywhere, but if I told them about the Zenith—let's see: Crowded conditions on campus make it difficult to get to class without getting killed. I could talk about that for an hour, but it would make a good reason for buying a ten-speed; and the Zenith is the one to get, because it's cheap and good and you can get it fixed quickly and for not too much money. I've got the reasons but reasons for exactly what? I know—*Buy the Zenith ten-speed bicycle.*

This is just one way of limiting a subject, just one way of arriving at a purpose sentence. But in this case it did provide the speaker with a subject: it arose out of an exigency, so it interested the speaker; the speaker knew something about ten-speeds and could find out more; the subject had potential interest for an audience of college students; limiting the subject helped the speaker to straighten out his thinking, led him to possible main points in his argument, started him on the road to organizing the message, gave him a specific purpose to which he could refer as he developed the speech, and helped him to relate the subject and purpose to his and the audience's possible involvement with the subject. The purpose sentence which emerged from his thinking was a complete, succinct, affirmative sentence. Since the speech was to be persuasive, a proposition, or persuasive purpose sentence, was needed, and that's what evolved.

Step Two: Developing the Content of Your Speech

Begin the development of your speech content with the purpose sentence, which you will literally write out at the top of a blank sheet of paper. Your problem now is to decide what kinds of materials you need to achieve the goal in your purpose sentence. We shall assume a persuasive purpose, although the development of so-called expository speeches is not very different. Let's use the purpose sentence we developed in step one: "Ecological considerations must give way to energy considerations when our existence is in danger and when our economic development is in danger." You must ask yourself three subquestions concerning the materials you need.

1. "What do I need in my speech which will influence my receivers to respect me, to believe me, to think I know what I'm talking about, to believe that I'm working in their best interests as well as expressing my own personal beliefs?" We call this kind of message material **materials of personal proof,** and their purpose is to increase or maintain your credibility as the source of the message.

2. "What do I need in my speech which will help prove my case rationally, logically?" Chapter 3, "Message Construction," considers
   this basic question in detail. We call this kind of message material
   materials of development, because they are intended to help you
   develop the rationality of your message.
3. "What do I need in my speech that will hold my receivers' attention, motivate them to want to believe me and follow me, make it
   easier for them to experience what I'm talking about?" We call this
   kind of message material **materials of experience.**

As you consider each of these questions in detail, you will want to
check back constantly with your purpose sentence to be sure that you're
not wandering from your goal, that you're not throwing in extraneous
material just to pad the speech or just because you happen to like it.
While we shall look at each of these kinds of materials separately, you
must remember that they won't necessarily appear in the speech separately, i.e., they will be mixed in a judicious manner, calculated to advance your argument and appeal to your receivers at the same time.
Your problem in Step Two is to lay out the materials, not worrying especially about the ordering or structuring of them—that difficult problem
we'll reserve for Step Three.

Materials of Personal Proof

You have encountered situations where you knew that what someone
said was accurate, but you didn't want to believe him because you didn't
respect him or because he had been wrong before. If your own reputation with the group you're speaking to is positive, your battle is half
won; if you have failed with them before, you have a difficult job before
you.

Research into personal proof has strongly suggested that high credibility is usually a real asset to a speaker. You can be reasonably safe in
assuming that you want to include material in your message which shows
the receivers that you know your subject well (you have factual information which you can substantiate). For example, you can respond to questions, going further than your formal message intended.

You also want to show your receivers that you are honest, that you
recognize that you are taking a position and that other positions are possible. Such statements as "Everybody knows . . ." and the cliché "I
have proved beyond the shadow of a doubt . . ." suggest a lack of openness, a lack of respect for the opinions of others, a certain contempt for
your listeners. On the other hand, statements such as "Most of the research I've been able to find suggests . . ." or "My own experience is
supported by a number of eminent students in ecology as well as by the
majority of business and financial leaders who have considered the
problem . . ." should tend to sustain or raise your credibility.

Finally, be sure that your message is organized, phrased, and delivered with enthusiasm, with confidence in yourself and in your receivers, with a courteous but firm determination that your position will be stated as well as you can state it. Personal proof is achieved in two ways: by the inclusion of certain materials deliberately designed to increase it and by the *way* in which you handle the entire public speaking event. In other words, much of personal proof is related to the way in which you organize your speech, deliver it, and behave under questioning. We shall return to this important matter when we consider Step Four. Note, too, that we don't have to talk about adapting materials of personal proof to the receivers; the attempt to create materials of personal proof *is* adapting to your audience.

Materials of Development

Materials of development are often referred to as the "guts" of a message and have already been discussed in chapter 3 under the heading "Rational Appeals." Therefore, our thrust here will be to help you adapt these materials to the receivers who will hear your arguments only once.

It is convenient to think of materials of development as stemming from two sources: those discovered by the speaker and those created by the speaker. Materials of development discovered by the speaker are commonly called evidence, or data, and evidence is used to support your arguments. While evidence may be considered in several ways (see chapter 3), we shall discuss only two: factual and opinion evidence.

Factual evidence usually refers to matters of fact, such as statistics, or matters which can be demonstrated: "The soil erosion resulting from overproduction can clearly be seen in this photograph, taken in 1937 in a county in western Oklahoma." **Opinion evidence** refers to the testimony of others concerning a claim or argument: " 'Soil erosion was minimal on my farm until 1936, when I removed a line of trees in order to provide more land for wheat,' said Ed Jones, prominent western Oklahoma farmer, as reported in *The Southwest Farmer* for June 1937." Opinion evidence refers to the opinions of other people or other sources, not your own. Your own opinion is important, of course, but it is not evidence.

Evidence is found in books, magazines, and special documents prepared on specific topics and is gathered through surveys and interviews (your own and others'). The library is an excellent source for evidence, as are your state or national representatives and senators and any person or institution interested in your subject.

Evidence is primarily used to back up your claims and arguments. Evidence may be arranged so that it follows a statement: "We definitely have a sales problem with our vacuum cleaner; Ed Ross, our sales manager, reports that vacuum sales are down 11 percent over the past three months." Evidence can also introduce the claim or argument: "Sales of the Peerless vacuum cleaner declined in Ohio this past year; Michigan reported a drop of 15 percent in sales; even Texas, our best market, noted only a minimal increase. We definitely have a sales problem with our Peerless vacuum."

To test the adequacy of the evidence, use the *tests of evidence* discussed in chapter 3.

Materials of development created by the speaker come in many forms: *repetition,* where you repeat a statement in the same words; *restatement,* where you say the same thing but in different words; *comparison,* wherein you point out similarities between two or more things; and *contrast,* where you emphasize differences.

In persuasion, however, the most common and most significant form in which materials of development created by the speaker appear is **reasoning,** or making an argument. Reasoning constitutes the backbone of most persuasive messages. The argumentative process is covered in detail in chapter 3; here we shall concentrate on four types of reasoning often used in public speaking and suggest ways of adapting reasoning to receivers. A succinct explanation of reasoning is given by Kenneth G. Hance:

> Reasoning may be defined as the *process of inferring conclusions from evidence or from other conclusions.* In the first instance (inferring from evidence), reasoning consists of using facts and opinions to reach a conclusion beyond that embodied in the evidence itself. . . . In the second instance (inferring from other conclusions), reasoning consists of joining two or more ideas or propositions to form a new idea (1975, pp. 93–94).

Reasoning by Analogy

Perhaps the oldest form of reasoning in our culture is reasoning by analogy, wherein the speaker makes a comparison between two cases that are similar in important respects and then infers that they are similar in other respects. Using the purpose sentence "Ecological considerations must give way to energy considerations when our existence is in danger and when our economic development is in danger," we might argue that since atomic plant Y has been in operation for ten years without a mishap, and since proposed atomic plant Z is similar in design to Y, we have no fear that proposed plant Z will suffer an atomic accident. This form of reasoning is fraught with possible danger and should ordinarily not be used alone. In any event, it should be tested by the speaker before using it. He will ask himself questions such as:

1. Are there actually points of similarity in the two cases?
2. Do the points of similarity outweigh (in quality, not necessarily in quantity) the points of dissimilarity?
3. Are the points of dissimilarity adequately explained?

Reasoning from Example or Multiple Data

A second form of reasoning used by the public speaker is called **reasoning from example or multiple data.** In this form the speaker infers conclusions from specific examples, cases, and illustrations. You have heard this form of reasoning used and have probably used it often yourself. We once heard a speech in which the speaker argued that during World War II the British gave up the beautiful and ornate Victorian iron fences surrounding their London homes and melted the metal down for use by the military; in the United States thousands of women turned in their gold and silver jewelry for use in the war effort; Russian women gave their scarce cloth for use as bandages. The speaker argued that, therefore, we must believe that the civilian populations of the democratic nations in World War II made the necessary sacrifices for the war effort. Probably a stronger form of reasoning than analogy, reasoning from example demands, nevertheless, that certain tests be met before we can consider it accurate reasoning:

1. Are enough examples cited? (Only the receivers can really answer this question.)
2. Are the examples typical? (Or is the speaker s-t-r-e-t-c-h-i-n-g to make them work?)
3. Are there negative examples, and, if so, are these rationally accounted for?

Reasoning from Cause

In **reasoning from cause,** probably the most commonly used form, we argue either that a certain phenomenon (a cause) has produced another phenomenon (an effect) or that a certain phenomenon (an effect) is the result of another phenomenon (a cause). If we argue that increased dependence upon Arab oil has badly hurt our economy, we are using the first of these forms (cause-to-effect reasoning). If we argue that the recent spiral of inflation was the result of sharply increased prices of Arab oil, we are using the second form (effect-to-cause reasoning). Again, there are three tests which the speaker should apply to the reasoning before incorporating it into the message:

1. Is the cause relevant to the effect?
2. Can this cause produce this effect?
3. Is there a *probability* that no other effect can result from this cause, or a *probability* that no other cause operated to produce this particular effect?

Reasoning from Sign

In **reasoning from sign** we infer associations between phenomena that are not causally related. We say that the presence of one phenomenon indicates the presence of another. For example, we note that since the pipeline went through, the bird population seems to have increased. Note that we do *not* link the two phenomena causally. Much reasoning must be sign reasoning, because there are no causal links or we cannot find any. Some of the economic indicators with which we predict the coming state of the economy are of this type. Although this type of reasoning is not strong, it is inevitable, and we must often depend upon it. It is inaccurate and unethical, however, to insert the word "because" into sign reasoning. At its best, this is misleading; at its worst, it may be a deliberate lie.

Between the more theoretical discussion of reasoning in chapter 3 and the more pragmatic discussion in this chapter, you can see how materials of development can be adapted to your receivers. For example, you may decide not to use a particular argument on the grounds that it is too complex to develop in a short speech, that it is not of primary importance as a means of proof, or that the receivers do not possess enough knowledge to understand the argument in the short time you have available to speak. You almost always use qualifiers like probably or mostly or often (see the third test of reasoning from cause), for in real life things are not often "always"; they are at best "mostly." You may simplify arguments, if you are careful not to distort them. You may elect to give the source of only part of your evidence, as long as you are prepared to give the source of any evidence which your receivers may challenge. You may use restatement to clarify obscure arguments. Unless you are speaking on a subject about which both you and your receivers are expert, you will rarely use straight argument exclusively. Instead, you will modify your materials of development, employ personal proof, and you will want to make use of a considerable amount of materials of experience.

Materials of Experience

Purposes of materials of experience are to attract and sustain the listeners' attention, to appeal to their basic beliefs, to increase their willingness to hear the rational message, to help them recall experiences similar to those the speaker is narrating, or to call up vicarious feelings which may render listeners more persuasible. Materials of experience add to the growing weight of evidence that meanings are not sent from a source to a receiver, but are aroused or called up in the being of the receiver.

Among the more general means by which you can help your audience receive your message and call up meanings similar to yours are the use of (1) **narration,** that is, telling a story to convey an idea or arouse attention; (2) **description,** by which you can paint a picture, set a scene, or re-create a mood; (3) **figures of speech,** including short, pithy, sometimes witty expressions that often impart more meaning than longer and more rational expositions; and (4) **the massing of detail,** by which the speaker piles incident upon incident, fact upon fact, to convey a general impression rather than present data that is meant to be remembered.

Motivational Appeals

Motivational appeals work upon the needs and drives that are a part of our being; they appeal to the socially conditioned part of us; they can be used to suggest indirectly ideas and behaviors that, as speakers, we choose not to present in a more direct manner. Although both biological drives and learned motives have been considered in chapter 3, we have selected for discussion here a half-dozen of these which appear to be among the most powerful influences in the persuasive-speaking situation.

Appeals to preservation. Perhaps the most powerful appeal is to self-preservation or to preservation of what we hold most dear. If you can relate your purpose sentence to your receivers' desire to save their own lives, you are probably strengthening your case. Thus, in addition to the rational statements about the necessity of tempering our desire to protect the environment with the recognition of the equal necessity of finding fuel, you can project for your listeners a picture of a world without enough fuel to heat their homes in the winter—a picture calculated to strike fear into the heart of any citizen of Michigan or Maine; you can picture a ban on all air conditioning—surely enough to frighten office workers from New York City to New Orleans.

Appeals to pride. One of our neighbors, who has several teen-agers in his family, consistently refused to mow his yard, clean up his weeds, or even paint his house. Since he has as much income as the rest of us, plus some cheap labor at hand, we launched a campaign in praise of our neighborhood for its cleanliness, its beauty, and its suburban charm. We advertised in our local weekly, took pictures, and displayed them in the near-by shopping center. Yes, you've guessed it; the neighbor did get his yard mowed, his weeds cleaned out, and his house painted. Of course, he hired people to get it done, while his teen-agers continued to loaf; however, the principles of successful public speaking are not always guaranteed to work exactly as planned by the speaker.

Appeals to altruism. Unlikely as it sometimes seems, we are motivated to do good for the *sake* of good and concern for others. The directors of CARE and United Fund know that. Several recent appeals both for the environment and for the discovery of new energy sources have urged us to do the *right* thing, even though it may cost us as individuals.

Appeals to sex. Advertisers know the value of appeals to sex, that is, of indicating you will be more likely to attract the opposite sex if you do—or buy—certain things. It is easy to see (even in our present liberated society) that Miss America can sell bathing suits better than our grandmothers can. Certainly many cigarette ads use physically attractive men and women to try to sell the products. A word of caution is in order, though. For reasons not entirely clear, it appears much more dangerous for a public speaker to make an overt appeal to sex than it is for a television advertiser. Perhaps we are still somewhat conservative in our expectations of what the speaker can and cannot say.

Fear appeals. In recent years considerable use has been made of fear appeals in selling ideas and influencing behavior. We are bombarded with messages that threaten us with impending doom, cancer, heart attacks, auto accidents and a host of other ills if we don't do certain things. We are warned to stop smoking, to have regular medical checkups, and to buckle up. The results of such appeals are inconclusive—sometimes the appeals seem to miss the mark and focus listeners' attention more on the fears than on the proposed solutions. Research tends to suggest that high fear appeals tend to work better when the personal proof of the source is high and when the receiver is deeply concerned about the message. But, at best, fear appeals, particularly high fear appeals, are chancy and probably should be avoided or used in moderation by the beginning speaker.

Reward appeals. Research here is not conclusive either, but there is evidence that a rational argument coupled with a promised reward seems to be more effective than using the argument alone. For example, both environmentalist groups and energy groups promise good things for us if we support their position.

Of course, there are many other motivational appeals, and careful thought should be given both to the possible motivational appeals you can use to enhance your speeches and to the potential danger of the overuse of these appeals.

Arresting and Holding Receivers' Attention

William James once wrote that what holds attention determines action. This is somewhat overstated, of course. But the converse is certainly true—if you can't arrest and hold attention, you will never determine action. Arousing and maintaining the receivers' attention seems to be one of the most difficult tasks confronting the beginning speaker. When we consider the conditions under which the student speaker often has to speak—"All right, speaker number 44, front and center"; "Ho-hum.

Yawn"; "How many more today to meet the quota?"—it's no wonder he or she feels discouraged about capturing and maintaining the receivers' attention.

In any public-speaking situation you must arrest your receivers' attention at the very beginning, no matter what the odds against you, no matter how many speakers have preceded you, no matter how boring your subject turned out to be. Then you must *hold* that attention throughout your speech, using techniques such as those we'll mention below and others of your own invention. You must do all this while maintaining your focus upon the heart of your message.

Here are some techniques of arresting and holding attention which have worked well for many speakers.

Techniques of Message Composition

1. Organize your message in an interesting manner; be inventive; adapt the basic principles of speech organization to fit your needs and those of your receivers.
2. Use materials of development that are germane to your purpose and actually develop your ideas.
3. Start with a reference to a preceding speech or to the chairperson's introduction of you.
4. Make your opening statement significant and meaningful—a quotation, a story with a point, a descriptive scene.
5. Use the massing-of-detail approach we talked about earlier—a barrage of facts or questions. (If they are questions, be sure you answer them in your speech.)
6. Use narrative material throughout your speech, wherever practical. A good story will almost always hold attention if it's well told and pertinent to the subject.
7. Try a little humor. It won't kill you, and chances are it won't kill your receivers. Be sure your humor is related to your subject.

Techniques of Message Delivery

1. Approach the platform or the front of the room deliberately, confidently, vigorously. Don't hurry, but don't sneak up there, either.
2. Pause before you begin to speak; look at your listeners; show that you're interested in them; smile if it's appropriate. Then begin.
3. Use expressive language whenever you can. Dull words turn people off, and they'll turn you off, too.
4. Try beginning your speech either with a little too much volume or a little too little, especially if the group's attention isn't entirely on you.

5. Ask your listeners to do something in unison—stand up, look out the window, focus on the chalkboard or on a visual you have, answer a question, whatever may be appropriate to your subject and the setting of your speech.

Of course, you can't use all these techniques in every speech! And you'll come up with many more of your own. The important thing for you to remember is that if you want your receivers to understand you and believe you and do what you want them to do, you have to show a genuine interest in them. You must use materials of experience to supplement your materials of development; and you must use personal proof as well, for you sell your idea only as well as you sell yourself.

Step Three: Structuring Your Speech

The major principles of structuring, or organizing, the message have been developed at length in chapter 3. In this chapter we shall utilize those principles, as well as the discussion of patterns of organization, to create the **speech plan,** the basic document from which the extemporaneous speaker prepares his speaking notes. In the next step (four) we shall discuss the different forms of delivery, but since most of your formal public speaking will be extemporaneous, our speech plan will be for that mode. We'll also assume that your speech will be persuasive, and we'll use the deductive approach to structure it.

What we call a speech plan you may have called an outline in high school, but we prefer to think of the term "outline" as describing the method you use in setting down the ideas of your speech in organized form. The organized form we call your speech plan. As you will see, the steps of preparing the speech plan do not follow the order of delivery.

The speech plan consists of four basic parts: the purpose sentence, the body of the plan, the conclusion, and the introduction. They are prepared in that order. In addition, you may wish to include certain internal summaries and transitional statements to help you tie the parts together.

The Purpose Sentence

Since your purpose sentence is already prepared (subject to modification, of course), place it, for the moment, at the top of the page. Refer to your purpose sentence constantly as you develop the remainder of the plan. Be sure that the speech plan accurately develops your stated purpose.

The Body

The **body** of your speech is where you develop your main arguments. Ask yourself what your first and most important point in support of the purpose sentence is. State this argument in a single declarative sentence and label it I. Leave about half a page of blank space and record your next major argument, labeling it II. In our example of a purpose sentence cited earlier, we concluded that the purpose sentence demanded two main divisions. In a speech of around five minutes you should not exceed three main arguments, and two are more easily handled.

Now, go back to main argument I and, using the principles of message construction from chapter 3, develop the subpoints which support main point I. In a deductive plan, your development in the plan body will appear like this:

I. x x x x x x x x x
    A. x x x x x x x x
        1. x x x x x x
        2. x x x x x x
            a. x x x x
            b. x x x x
        3. x x x x x x
    B. x x x x x x x x
        1. x x x x x x
        2. x x x x x x, etc.

The number of subpoints in a persuasive speech depends upon the development of your arguments, that is, you may have A, B, and C or you may have only A. In an expository speech, where dividing ideas and concepts into their parts is the key, you must always have a B when you have an A. It *is* important, however, to use parallel construction; that is, the symbols of like power must be arrayed directly under each other to indicate that they are of equal strength. Therefore, while you may have a 1, 2, and 3 under A, and only a 1 under B, the capital letters must be placed directly under each other, as are the arabic numerals:

Correct: I.
                A.
                    1.
                        a.
            II.
                A.
                B.
                    1.
                        a.
                        b.

Incorrect: I.
    A.
      1.
        a.
   II.
    A.
      1.

Complete the body of your speech plan by arraying all the subpoints under II.

The rules for composing the body of the speech plan are simple but important:

1. The indentation for a deductive plan proceeds from left to right in descending order, with equal symbols falling on the same vertical plane.
2. The symbols must be consistent. In the body of the plan, main arguments or main points are indicated by roman numerals (I, II, III, etc.). Second-degree points are indicated by capital letters (A, B, C, etc.), third-degree points by arabic numerals (1, 2, 3, etc.), and fourth-degree points by lowercase letters (a, b, c, etc.). Since the introduction and conclusion do not ordinarily contain main points, it is customary to use capital letters to designate the first-degree points, as we shall see a little later.
3. While some authorities permit the use of incomplete sentences, phrases, and even key words in the speech plan, it has been our experience that only by forcing ourselves to undergo the discipline of writing out complete sentences whenever possible are we able to think through the logic of our arguments. We strongly recommend, therefore, that you use complete sentences, *one sentence to a symbol,* in your speech plan.

You will remember that the organizational pattern we have considered so far is the standard deductive speech plan. As you learned in chapter 3, the deductive approach is one of the two basic forms of messages. In the inductive plan, you reverse everything. You start with the smallest degree points and work toward the main arguments:

```
            a.   x x x x
            b.   x x x x
         1.   x x x x x x
      A.   x x x x x x x x
   I.  x x x x x x x x x x
```

Several variations of the basic deductive and inductive structural patterns, appropriate for persuasive and informative speeches, are considered in chapter 3. Now is a good time to restudy those patterns.

The Conclusion

We have now developed the body of the plan, together with the purpose sentence, which, in the case of the standard deductive form, is located between the introduction and the body of the plan. Your next task is to plan the conclusion of your speech. Now that you know what the body looks like, this should not be a difficult task, for there are only a few basic forms in which the conclusion will appear. The purposes of the **conclusion** are (1) to sum up the main points or arguments you have made; (2) to urge the receivers in the direction you want them to go; and (3) to signal the end, a psychologically satisfying moment for speaker and listener alike. Ideally, the conclusion should accomplish all these goals; however, you must keep your receivers in mind at all times, and you may find it necessary to concentrate on one or another of these goals of the conclusion. Therefore you may wish to use (1) a *summary conclusion,* in which you sum up the arguments you have made; (2) an *appeal conclusion,* in which you appeal to the receivers to believe as you wish them to or to act as you wish them to; or (3) an *illustration-quotation conclusion,* in which you end by telling a story, describing an event, or quoting a well-known person or repeating a well-known quotation.

Your conclusion is your last chance to put your point across. Keep it short; hit your point; and as a great speech teacher once said, "When you quit, quit all over!"

The Introduction

Finally you are ready to prepare the introduction. A surprising number of speakers begin their speech preparation by designing the introduction, but this is often a futile move. How can you create an introduction to something you haven't yet composed?

The **introduction** has three basic purposes: (1) to arouse the receivers' attention; (2) to maintain or improve the source's personal proof; and (3) to direct the receivers toward what is to come in the speech. As happens with conclusions, however, circumstances may force you to emphasize or deemphasize one or another of the purposes. If arousing attention is a problem, you may want to use an *illustration-quotation* introduction, in which you try to catch your hearers' attention with a story, a description of an event, or a striking quotation. If maintaining or increasing personal proof is your immediate goal, often the *acknowledgment introduction* will work for you. Using this form, you devote all or a major part of your introduction to greeting distinguished guests or members and complimenting your audience. The *direct introduction,* in which you announce your purpose sentence first, almost like a title, is used when you assume that your listeners are strongly interested in your subject and when their attitude is most likely to be favorable. Obviously, if you need to conceal your real purpose in speaking, or delay revealing it, you will avoid the direct introduction.

Now you have completed all the parts of your speech plan. You simply rearrange your sheets of paper so that the order is the order of presentation: introduction, purpose sentence, body, and conclusion. After this exhaustive exercise, you may want to stop and look at the example we have included of a student speech plan at the end of this chapter. It's an honest effort by a student, and we've not altered it in any way. It is not perfect, but it served its author well.

The beauty of all this preparation of the speech plan is that now you've finished it, you are well on your way to delivering your speech. Ordinarily, you will not need much rehearsal time, because you know your material forward and backward. With that good news in mind, let's proceed to Step Four.

Step Four: Delivering Your Speech

Someone has said that the only problem with preparing a speech is that you have to give it. It is certainly true that all the preparation you've gone through, steps X, one, two, and three, are for nothing unless the speech is heard.

There are four forms of delivery appropriate for public speaking. We shall look briefly at three of them and then concentrate the remainder of this section upon the fourth.

Impromptu Delivery

In impromptu public speaking no formal preparation of any kind is made. An exigency arises, and you respond. Probably most daily public speaking is of that order—the phone rings and you're asked to go down the hall to explain the new budget forms to the executive committee. Somebody at a staff meeting says, "This is a bad paper you've prepared," and you're on your feet protesting. A citizen asks if there is anyone present who can suggest a solution to the problem of how to get the paramedic unit into the back lot of the hospital, and you're at the chalkboard, sketching in the route.

You will make many speeches of an impromptu nature during your life, but it's really not a frightening thing to think about. For one thing, you usually don't speak unless you know something about the subject, so it isn't like drawing a topic out of a hat and talking on it. For another, the study of public speaking in this course will improve your ability to speak impromptu, even though that's not the purpose of the course. You just follow as many of the steps described in preparing an extemporaneous speech as you can, in abbreviated form, and your impromptu speaking will improve.

Manuscript Delivery

In this form, you go through all the steps we have outlined in this chapter, and then you write out a manuscript from your plan, complete to the paragraphing and punctuation. You study and practice the written speech, and then you read it to your receivers. You may have some opportunity to use this form of delivery, especially if you occupy a position of importance within your organization; if you have a significant piece of information to relay, which demands absolute accuracy in the transmission of figures or in repeating what someone else has said; or if you wish to be quoted accurately. More likely, however, you will occasionally read such material as a small part of your extemporaneous speech.

Memorized Delivery

Once a major form of delivery, memorizing speeches is now largely confined to students who think that by memorizing, they are fulfilling the requirements of a course in extemporaneous speaking! On the very formal occasions when memorizing might be appropriate, the Teleprompter, which allows you to read the manuscript while appearing to have eye contact with your receivers, has replaced the memory. Normally, however, memorizing a speech is a bad practice, for it tends to make you "sound memorized."

Effective speaking is a conversation between you and your receivers or, at least, it ought to have the "feel" of conversation, even if you are doing all or most of the talking. Memorized speeches tend to lose this quality. Furthermore, if you memorize your speech, you lose the flexibility of adapting to your audience as you are speaking; you ordinarily cannot meet the situations which arise in a speaker-audience relationship. You cannot alter your organization, add interesting information which might occur to you, delete items which your last-minute audience analysis tells you will be harmful to your cause.

Extemporaneous Delivery

This is the form most often used in formal speechmaking, with the exceptions previously indicated. Your college instructor probably lectures this way; your minister may use extemporaneous delivery, although he may have a manuscript in front of him, for later publication. Speeches at committee and board meetings and at sales meetings are usually extem-

poraneous. Even papers "read" at conventions are now often in semiextemporaneous form—the speaker has his manuscript and distributes copies of it, but he often speaks extemporaneously from it.

In the extemporaneous delivery mode you do not memorize your speech; you do not write out a manuscript of all the words you intend to deliver. On the other hand, your speech is not unprepared; on the contrary, it is prepared well. Your topic chooses you, or you choose it; you analyze and adapt to your listeners as you prepare your message and also as you deliver it; you construct your purpose sentence; you gather your materials into a speech plan, in outline form, using complete sentences whenever possible; you practice and refine your speech; you develop a set of reminder notes. Then you deliver your speech, choosing most of the words at the moment of delivery.

The suggestions concerning delivery we shall be making here will assume a semiformal situation in which you will speak extemporaneously from a set of notes. Your notes are your own private property, prepared in your own personal way, to serve you. They will vary in form and length, depending upon the eccentricities of the individual speaker. However, they will all share in common the fact that they, the notes, are developed from a speech plan, which is in turn developed from a study of the receivers and the subject and from the gathering of materials of personal proof, development, and experience.

Preparing your speaker's notes and practicing your speech stem directly and naturally from the composition of your speech plan. Indeed, as we have suggested earlier, if you prepare the speech plan properly and in detail, you are well over halfway toward being prepared to deliver the speech. We suggest that you run through the speech the first time, using your speech plan as your guide. Stop and make marginal notes on your plan wherever you are having trouble—a thought won't come, something seems out of order or missing or too detailed, a word is "jargonese." For your second run-through, have your speech plan handy, but try not to refer to it. Make notes on a separate sheet of paper as you practice, jotting down points that you forget or stumble over, special words that you tend to forget or know you must remember exactly, and any other relevant matters. Then sit down and make out your speaker's notes. Make them as brief as possible, and use a typewriter (all caps if your vision isn't the best) or print with a dark pen or pencil. The best rule to use in making these notes is to plan them so you can see at a glance what you want to pick up. Never use your speech plan as a substitute for your speaker's notes. The speech plan is exactly that, a full plan of your speech—it's the worst thing in the world to use when you need a quick reminder of what's coming up next in your speech.

How many times should you practice your speech? There is no magic number; it depends upon you. A general guide is that you should practice until you feel you know your organization perfectly but not so much that you're starting to recall the exact wording that you used in your previous practice.

Suggestions for Improving Your Delivery

Delivering a speech is, in large measure, an intensely personal experience; and the style of speaking which is right for one speaker may be all wrong for another. Therefore only a few basic suggestions are appropriate for all speakers. You will want to develop your own style as soon as you can, for, after all, it's the *you* in speaking that makes the difference between adequate speaking and good speaking.

There are three important differences between the standard essay you may write for your English class and the extemporaneous speech you will be giving. Speeches (1) require instant intelligibility, (2) are personal, and (3) are conversational.

With an essay the receiver has an opportunity to read your words over and over until he can call up meaning that approximates the meaning you intended; in a speech the receiver must get the message on the run—he has one chance only. So, you must strive always for *instant intelligibility* in speaking. Instant intelligibility may often be achieved by using short words, phrases, and sentences. Pauses, drawing out the pronunciation of key words, stories, and illustrations also help to achieve instant intelligibility.

While the essay often strives for objectivity, sometimes using the impersonal third person form of address, in speaking you most often work for the immediate, the highly personal, the "you." In an essay you might say, "The effective speaker strives for correct usage of language in his oral compositions." In a speech you would say, "You must learn how to use the right words when you speak."

In an essay, you might strive for correct sentence structure, abiding by all the formal rules of grammar. In speaking, you often use sentence fragments, contractions, and other techniques of conversation. In fact, conversational quality is one of the most important parts of oral style, and you use as much of it as the nature of the subject and the occasion of the speech will permit.

What are the characteristics of good oral style? In four words, they are clarity, forcefulness, vividness, and adaptability. **Clarity** demands that you use words, phrases, and sentences that are precise and accurate and that can be easily understood by your receivers. **Forcefulness** implies drive, excitement, and urgency. It sometimes but not always means loudness. **Vividness** calls for language that helps the listener see, hear, feel, and even smell and taste the images you produce in your attempt to make your ideas real to your audience. By **adaptability** we mean that you must be ready to use the language and the style that best fits the situation in which you are speaking, that will work for your subject, and that will be most comfortable and effective with your receivers. For example, "bitch" may be the only acceptable word at a dog show; it would probably offend your mother and her friends at the afternoon flower show.

Vocal Delivery

We can make five suggestions to help you improve your vocal delivery in public speaking.

1. Articulate so you can be understood. Pronounce your words correctly, in a manner acceptable to the majority of your receivers. Poor articulation is most often the result of carelessness, incorrect pronunciation the result of ignorance. Put your speech on tape and listen to it. Let someone else, not a relative or close friend, listen also. You may be shocked at what you hear. Take your problem words to your instructor for assistance.
2. Talk loudly enough to be heard in the back of the room; vary your loudness to emphasize important points. If you can't be heard, you won't be believed; and the same loudness for all words will turn off your receivers.
3. Seek a basic pitch level which is right for you; vary your pitch to avoid monotonous speaking and to achieve emphasis. You can use a tape recorder to practice pitch variety; but if your basic pitch does not seem right for you, consult the speech and hearing de-

partment at your college. Don't try to make drastic alterations in your basic pitch without professional help, or you can do serious and permanent damage to your vocal apparatus.

4. Work to improve your time (your overall rate of speaking). You should avoid a sameness in time, which is monotonous sounding; too fast a rate, which hinders intelligibility; and the slow plodding rate which bores an audience. Vary your rate of speaking to assist you in emphasizing important points and also to hold the audience's attention.

5. Work to improve the quality, or tone, of your voice. Terms like "resonant," "pleasing," and "warmth," describe pleasant quality. "Harsh," "nasal," and "hoarse" describe unpleasant quality. If you have poor quality, you will probably want to seek professional help from the speech and hearing department.

Nonverbal Delivery

Usually a public speaker is seen as well as heard, and what the receivers see may be as important in determining the outcome of the speech as what they hear. Again, nonverbal delivery is a personal matter—what looks good on one speaker may look bad on another. There are, however, some principles which are generally applicable to good nonverbal delivery.

1. *Personality.* Obviously an interesting personality is preferable to a dull one. But how does a speaker develop "good" personality? For one thing, if you have a positive attitude toward yourself, toward your subject, and toward your receivers, some of this will most likely show up in your behavior in the public-speaking situation. A neat appearance (or one suitable to the particular group of receivers), a reasonably relaxed posture, and a lively delivery style will help. For most formal occasions, posture somewhere between that of the modern major general and the street-lamp lounger will do; but there are many occasions when you will want to stand straight and tall, and many others when you will want to sit on the desk or table or even on the floor. The circumstances of the speech will dictate what you do, and with a little thought you should readily be able to adapt your behavior.

2. *Movement and gesture.* Stationary speakers don't persuade as well as speakers who move about. Too much movement is distracting and causes irritation among your receivers. Stepping forward to make an important point, walking to the chalkboard to illustrate a concept, using a gesture to emphasize an idea serve to improve your chances of success, if these can be done naturally and without embarrassment. Movement can also help relax you and assist you in

reducing the tension so often associated with public speaking. However, you should practice these moves in private and then "forget" them in public. They will come when they will come, and you can't force them.

3. *Facial expressions.* The same advice holds for facial expressions. Obviously a speaker whose features are animated will be more persuasive than one who has a deadpan. Just as obviously, faking or acting out facial expressions in public speaking can be disastrous (unless you're a good actor). Remind yourself of what you look like by practicing parts of your speech in front of a mirror and trying different facial expressions. However, when the time to speak arrives, forget about facial expressions and just get up and talk with your audience. You will improve in this way without the embarrassment of overacting or grimacing.

4. *Eye contact.* Surely the most important part of nonverbal delivery in public speaking is **eye contact.** Almost all of us have been subjected to the speaker who looks out the window or door, down at the floor, at his notes constantly, or, even worse, has been taught to fake eye contact by looking just over the heads of his receivers. We have all seen the poor use of teleprompters on television where the speaker is earnestly soliciting our attention while obviously not looking at us. It is somewhat insulting to be told that we are important, that the speaker's ideas are important, that we must listen, and then find that the speaker either can't or won't look us in the eye. In our culture, anyway, direct eye contact suggests honesty and the desire for communication; eye-contact avoidance suggests dishonesty, something to hide.

Perhaps even more important than the psychological effects of eye contact is that it enables you to "read" how you are doing. By looking at your receivers, you can often tell if they are bored or puzzled, interested or convinced, that they need more or less information, that you must exert more overt effort or that you're coming on too strong.

Finally, we believe that in the face-to-face speaking situation, at least, without eye contact there is no public speaking going on. Public speaking is a two-way process; it requires the efforts of a source and a receiver to make it work. And even though one person is primarily the source and the others primarily the receivers, there *is* interchange between them. Moreover, the real thrill of public speaking is in the give-and-take of the speaker-audience relationship. Without eye contact, this joy is absent.

We have assured you throughout this chapter that analyzing and adapting to your receivers would be constantly emphasized. It should be apparent that delivering the speech is almost entirely a matter of adapting to your audience—the speaker-audience relationship determines the style of the speech, the choice of words, and the vocal and nonverbal delivery.

Step Five: Evaluating Your Speech

As with most activities, speechmaking is not complete until the decision is in. Upon completing your speech you will want to know how successful you were in carrying out the task. In real life this is often difficult to achieve, for American audiences are usually polite; they applaud you; they even come up and tell you that you did a great job. Rarely do you know whether you were really successful, unless your speech results in some overt action such as a vote or contribution. It is a good idea to check up on yourself by talking privately with individuals whom you've asked in advance to evaluate you honestly. Under some conditions a follow-up survey is possible, wherein your receivers will react to questions you ask them.

In the classroom, which is a learning environment, it is often possible to obtain feedback of several kinds. More than likely, your instructor will evaluate you orally or in writing. In many classes, your peers are asked to make an evaluation and sometimes even grade you. The use of both methods benefits you two ways: the expert reaction will help you to improve when next you speak; the peer evaluation will let you know more about how well you would do with a "real" audience.

In addition, you should make your own evaluation. As soon as you can, preferably before you receive evaluation from anyone else, jot down your "gut" reaction to your own speech. Later, after you have received the criticism of your instructor and your peers, make a formal evaluation of your preparation and delivery.

The criteria for evaluating your speaking are all in this chapter, but to simplify your task, we offer a speech evaluation form. Be honest in completing it. When you study the forms completed by your peers, be a little cautious. Don't become angry or feel guilty because one colleague says that your organization is poor; don't rate yourself as an expert speaker because another praises your personal proof as the best he's ever heard. Even in the Olympics it is customary to throw out the high and low scores and take the mean of the others. Follow a somewhat similar procedure. If a substantial number of your peers find fault with your loudness, assume you'd better look into that. If most of them liked your narrative, consider that it was probably a good one. If not many marked the question concerning your materials of development, you will want to further question some of your listeners.

Conclusion

The ability to speak effectively in public is a valuable asset to every woman and man. One chapter on public speaking in a book on general communication will not make you a superior speaker. It should, however, assist you in improving your ability to prepare, deliver, and evaluate a speech. If you need or want further instruction and experience, we urge you to enroll in the public-speaking course at your college. You will probably find it not frightening at all but an enjoyable experience—and the better speaker you are, the better you can express your ideas, persuade others, and evaluate the speaking to which you will most certainly be exposed all your life.

Speech Evaluation Form

1. *Audience analysis and adaptation*

   a. Did the speaker do a good job in judging your attitude toward the speaker and the subject?   Yes /__/__/__/__/ No

   On what basis do you make this statement? _____

   _____

   b. Did the speaker do a good job in judging your knowledge about the subject?   Yes /__/__/__/__/ No

   c. At the beginning of the speech, what was your attitude toward the speaker and/or his/her speech?   /__/__/__/__/
   Friendly Neutral Apathetic Hostile

   Explain your answer _____

   d. At the conclusion of the speech, what was your attitude toward the speaker and/or his/her speech?   /__/__/__/__/
   Friendly Neutral Apathetic Hostile

2. *Subject*

   a. What was the subject? _____

   b. Did the subject interest you?   Yes /__/__/__/__/ No

   c. Did the speaker seem prepared?   Yes   No
                                                  / / / / /

   d. Can you state the purpose sentence? _____

_____

   e. Did the purpose of the speech come cross?   Yes   No
                                               / / / / /

3. *Message content*

   a. Did the speaker use materials of *develop-* Yes   No
     ment? Was there sufficient evidence and / / / / /
     reasoning to persuade you?

     Give example _____

_____

   b. Did the speaker use materials of *personal* Yes   No
     proof?   / / / / /

     How did he/she establish his/her credibil-
     ity? _____

_____

   c. Did the speaker use materials of *experience?* Yes   No
                                         / / / / /
     How did he/she hold your attention? ____

_____

   d. What motivational appeals did the speaker
     use? _____

4. *Organization*

   a. Was the speech well organized?   Yes   No
                                               / / / / /

   b. Was the approach inductive? deductive?
     other? _____

   c. Was the organization appropriate for the Yes   No
     subject?   / / / / /

d. Can you remember the introduction? Yes / / / / / No

e. Can you remember the conclusion? Yes / / / / / No

f. Were the transitions smooth? Yes / / / / / No

5. *Delivery*

   Vocal

   a. Was the speaker sufficiently loud? Yes / / / / / No

   b. Did the speaker have good articulation? Yes / / / / / No

   c. Was the speaker's rate of speaking appropriate to speaker, subject, and audience? Yes / / / / / No

   d. Did the speaker employ pitch variety? Yes / / / / / No

   e. Was the speaker's voice quality pleasing? Yes / / / / / No

   f. Overall, did the speaker's verbal delivery enhance or detract from the speech? _____

   g. The speech was to be delivered extemporaneously. Was it? Yes / / / / / No

   Nonverbal

   a. Did the speaker utilize appropriate facial expressions? Yes / / / / / No

   b. Did the speaker's use of gestures aid in delivery? Yes / / / / / No

   c. Did the speaker maintain good eye contact? Yes / / / / / No

d. Was the speaker's appearance appropriate?　Yes　／　／　／　／　／　No

e. Overall, did the speaker's actions and appearance enhance or detract from the speech? _____

How would you rate the speech as a whole?

Good/ / / / / / /Poor
　　　7　6　5　4　3　2　1

A Sample Deductive Speech Plan

It Takes Only Four Minutes
by Dianne Feeney

Introduction

　　A. According to the National Safety Council, foreign-body obstruction of the breathing passage is the sixth greatest cause of accidental deaths in the United States.

　　B. For the victim unable to breathe, death occurs in four minutes.

Purpose　　C. Everyone should learn to help a person who is
Sentence　　　　choking.

Body

　　I. Foreign-body obstruction usually occurs during meals.

　　　A. Most adults choke on meat.

　　　B. A high level of alcohol is often found in these victims.

　　II. There are several habits you can develop to help prevent choking.

　　　A. Chew meat slowly and thoroughly.

　　　B. Avoid laughing and talking while chewing.

　　　C. Avoid excessive alcohol before and during meal.

　　　D. Restrict children from running while eating.

III. There are two types of blockage.

    A. In partial blocking the person can still speak.

        1. He should not be interfered with.

        2. Never hit this type of victim on the back.

    B. In total blockage the victim cannot breathe and fast action is urgent.

        1. Stand behind the victim.

        2. Place your fist against the abdomen.

        3. Grasp your fist with your other hand and thrust upward three times.

        4. Do not practice on a human subject.

        5. The above technique is taught by Red Cross.

Conclusion

A. You may need to know and use first aid on a choking victim at any time or place.

B. The local Red Cross and heart associations offer classes.

C. The Health, Physical Education, and Recreation department here on campus offers a first aid class.

D. It is urgent to know how to act quickly, for it takes only four minutes to die.

TERMS AND CONCEPTS FOR REVIEW

adaptability
body
clarity
conclusion
description
exigency
extemporaneous delivery
eye contact
factual evidence
figures of speech
forcefulness
impromptu delivery
introduction
manuscript delivery
massing of detail
materials of development

materials of experience
materials of personal proof
memorized delivery
motivational appeals
narration
opinion evidence
public speech
purpose sentence
reasoning
reasoning by analogy
reasoning from cause
reasoning from example
reasoning from sign
speech plan
vividness

REVIEW QUESTIONS

1. What are the six steps involved in preparing a formal speech?
2. What does analyzing and adapting to the receivers mean? Why is it important?
3. What are materials of personal proof, of development, and of experience? Give examples of each.
4. What are the four modes of delivery? Give examples of each. When should each mode be used?

REFERENCES

Allen, R.R., and Ray E. McKerrow. *The Pragmatics of Public Communication.* Columbus, Ohio: Charles E. Merrill, 1977.

Asante, Molefi K., and Jerry K. Frye, *Contemporary Public Communication: Applications.* New York: Harper & Row, 1977.

Ehninger, Douglas, Alan H. Monroe, and Bruce Gronbeck. *Principles and Types of Speech Communication,* 8th ed. Glenview, Ill.: Scott, Foresman, 1978.

Hance, Kenneth G., David C. Ralph, and Milton J. Wiksell. *Principles of Speaking.* 3rd ed. Belmont, Cal. Wadsworth, 1975.

Hart, Roderick, Gustav Friedrich, and William D. Brooks. *Public Communication.* New York: Harper & Row, 1975.

McBurney, James H., and Ernest Wrage. *Guide to Good Speech.* 4th ed. Englewood Cliffs, N.J.: Prentice-Hall, 1975.

What to Write

Writing—and Rewriting

Grammar, Spelling, and Vocabulary

Writing to Satisfy Specific Goals

Adjusting to Audiences

Limiting the Topic

Organizing Information

Editing

Enhancing Readability

Writers as Readers

Mechanical Details

Choosing General or Specific Information

Appendix:
Concepts for Writers

After reading this appendix, you should be able to:

1. Explain the importance of writing.
2. Discuss the process involved.
3. Produce more effective written messages.

Read the following letter from Fred Smith and decide whether or not you would be interested in hiring him:

Dear Sirs,

I am writting this letter to let you know about me. I am seeking imployment as a salesmen and I wonder if you would have a opening. Your the one company i am especially interested in because of your reputation as a good company to work for and other reasons of which their are many. Frist I will give you some background about me.

I haven't never had much experience with selling before but I know I could do a good job. I dod have but one job working for barnum mens store in Pitsburg. I sold ties and sevral other mens assessories. You can write this store for a reference. Thnk you for you're consideration.

Yours truly,

Fred Smith

When this message is shown to students or to businesspersons, the majority response invariably is that the audience would not want to hire Fred. Why is the group so negative about him? Certainly, Fred has a number of things in his favor. He wants a job, and he wants to work for the company he is addressing. He has had previous experience in selling, and his employers must have thought well of him for he says he will receive a good reference from them. Why should readers be so generally unfavorable to such a person?

People don't respond well to Fred for the simple reason that he lacks essential writing skills and concepts. He would probably be a good employee if he is not asked to do much writing on his job. He may well be good at selling whatever product he is asked to sell. But he is unlikely to get the job because the recipient of his letter will judge his overall worth on the basis of how he writes.

What should we know about writing? How can we write more effectively? How can we get people to do as we wish them to as a result of our written messages? Why can't everyone write? Questions like these are debated in schools and colleges, in business, and in professions. There are, of course, no simple answers. No formula, pill, or panacea will turn nonwriters quickly into writers. There are, however, some ideas, concepts, and points of view that may help the writer along the road to being more effective. This appendix will briefly discuss some of these guidelines.

The Problem of What to Write

Suppose that someone asks you to take pen in hand and write a word. What word will you write? Chances are, you will ask yourself, "What word should I write that will convince the reader to think well of me?" and that goal will determine what word you choose.

Some people when asked to write a word write "word." They simply follow instructions. Others may choose long words; they may write "Mississippi" or "hippopotamus," or "antidisestablishment." Still others may write words that seem to be relevant to their business or to their course of study. They may write "communication" or "management" or "persuasion." In each instance the writer is trying to predict the word that will best influence the person who asked for the word to be written. Writing, then, cannot be considered independent of the writer, the reader, and the context in which the writing is to be read.

The Process of Writing—and Rewriting

The beginning writer often has a distorted concept of the process of writing. Writing for most of us is hard work. It is apt to be messy and accompanied by a lot of frustration. Much of the frustration comes from our inability to predict the reactions of our intended readers. Thus we find that as we write and rewrite we often change words, delete words, take out sentences, add new concepts.

It is instructive to examine the original manuscripts of well-known authors. They look much like everyone else's original manuscripts. They are marred with erasures, strikeovers, words between the lines, sentences in the margins, and spilled coffee.

There is no reason to expect that writing should come out right the first time. Writing has the great advantage over speech of being reworkable. We should use this advantage. We should write, read what we have written, and rewrite. We should consider one word as opposed to another. We should be grateful for the chance to reconsider and manipulate our work.

Grammar, Spelling, and Vocabulary

Beginning writers often focus too early on the wrong things. They are apt to worry at the outset about grammar, spelling, and punctuation. These areas are of course important. They do not determine clarity, however, as much as they do credibility. Recall the letter that began this appendix. You had no trouble understanding what the writer wanted. Even if you use nonstandard grammar and idiosyncratic spelling, people will probably understand what you have written. But they are unlikely to have much faith in your abilities.

There are places and times when nonstandard constructions become in effect standard. Situations will and should produce grammar. A letter to an old roommate is not the same as a letter applying for a job. The situation and the audience in the locker room are different from the situation and the audience at the president's reception. A memo to your colleague at the office will be different in form, content, and grammar from your reports to the board of directors of your company. The wise writer always asks, "What effect do I want to produce?" and writes in ways that are appropriate for the place, the time, and the people.

The best advice about the mechanics of writing is to do as well as you can and then get editorial help if you feel that your grammar, spelling, and punctuation may not be appropriate for the situation. The alternative is to read enough, study enough, and practice enough that writing appropriately will come easily to you.

To develop a writing style that is acceptable in business and the professions, it is usually necessary to go to college (although there is evidence that even attending college is no guarantee that the traditionally accepted writing skills will be learned). These skills can be developed without formal education, but they will require an equivalent outlay in time and energy.

Writing to Satisfy Specific Goals

All writers must start by defining their goals. For a college student the process may go like this: (1) I have to write at least a ten-page paper on topic X. (2) I want to write the paper, and I want to receive at least a B grade. (3) If I can learn something as I do it, that would be nice; but my overriding concern is for getting the grade and earning the credit. Or, the student's thinking may follow these lines: (1) I want to write the definitive paper on my chosen topic. (2) I don't care how long the paper becomes, and I don't care how much time and effort are involved. (3) I intend to become an authority on this topic.

There are a number of variations possible between the cynicism of the first set of goals and the idealism of the second set. But both sets are defensible and not unusual. The intended goals will produce different papers, different learning experiences, and different evaluations. The student will cast his own cost-benefit equations and make his writing decisions based on a number of variables. It is interesting to note that the first, pragmatic approach is more often adopted by undergraduates; the second, more ambitious approach by graduate students.

The consideration of reward and effort is not confined to academic settings. The monthly report to the department head, the assigned report on inventory use in the plant, the report on whether to change accounting systems throughout the company are all dependent for their length and content on the objectives of the reports.

Ultimately, we all write for personal rewards. We add up our efforts (both present and anticipated) and weigh them against our rewards (both present and anticipated). If the rewards are perceived as being less than the efforts involved, we probably won't make the effort. The reward may be money, personal satisfaction, recognition, or fame. Costs can include time, energy, and frustration.

Adjusting to Audiences

A concurrent step for writers is to decide who the audiences are. We nearly always have more than one. For a college student deciding how to write a term paper, the primary audience may be the professor while secondary audiences may be friends, parents, typists, and classmates. The businessman preparing a report has not only his supervisor as an audience but also his staff. In addition, his colleagues will know of his efforts and will be making evaluations of him based on the reception and outcome of his report.

Sometimes audiences are difficult to define and locate. This is a continual problem for preachers and parent-teacher organizations, for example. The sinners are seldom in the church to hear the sermons intended for them. The parents of the children who set fire to the school rarely attend the PTA meetings that are trying to deal with school problems.

Different audiences require different writing approaches. Suppose that you are a college graduate with a major in advertising, and you are applying for work with various agencies. What will your resumé look like? Many advertising majors will use colored paper, various type faces, cartoons or illustrations, and a writing style that might be characterized as breezy, light, and informal. In contrast, accounting majors are likely to take a traditional approach. They will use white bond paper, a conventional type face, and avoid the cartoons and the breezy style. The contrasts are due to differing assumptions about the intended audiences. These assumptions may or may not be correct, but they are always made. The advertising majors believe (rightly or wrongly) that their audience will be impressed with creativity and innovation. The accounting majors believe (rightly or wrongly) that their audience will be impressed with formality and tradition. The sensible writer will want to examine such assumptions carefully to see if they are indeed accurate.

As writers consider audiences, they must decide whether they should tell the audience what it needs to know or what it wants to be told. If the president of your company has maintained in meetings and in speeches that the future of the company lies in nuclear energy, is it better to defend solar energy and risk demotion or promote nuclear energy and get in the president's good graces? The problem is sometimes not so much writing as it is deciding.

Limiting the Topic

When we decide what we are going to write and whom we are going to address, then we must give thought to what we shall say about our topic

It would be nice if we could learn all there is to know about it. But most topics worthy of our attention are too complicated for us to learn all about them. There is always more to read, more to look up, more to research. Automobiles, for example, is a subject that one could write volumes about and still not be done. Further, there are the constraints of time, energy, and motivation. Indeed, most writers are faced with deadlines which make it impossible to continue to do more. The report must be turned in, the paper must be submitted, the book must go to the publisher.

For these reasons, writers must limit their topics. A writer must choose an aspect of his topic, and learn enough about it, so that he can influence his audience according to his goals. Cost and benefit, reward and effort, must be considered in doing the preparatory work.

Organizing Information

After the preliminary considerations have been dealt with, the writing may begin. For many writers, this is the hardest part of all. We can delay our task by saying to ourselves that we need one more trip to the library, one more interview, one more bit of research. But the point of the pencil must eventually contact the paper.

Most of us find that a previously prepared plan helps us to organize our writing. Some people call it an outline. Some people just call it a list of what to write about first, second, third, etc. There are a number of ways of ordering a written work. The following brief list may be compared with the organizational schemes provided in chapter 3 and chapter 9.

1. *Topical.* Major subtopics of equal rank or importance are treated successively. E.g., "Two major areas of study in human communication are the verbal and the nonverbal. Let us first consider the verbal domain."

2. *Chronological.* Things that occur first in time are treated first and are then followed by those things that occur second, third, etc. E.g., "The first spoken words in verbal interactions between strangers tend to be relatively fixed. They include X, Y, and Z. These are followed by A, B, and C."

3. *Spatial.* Elements are organized on the basis of physical spaces. The relationships between them are examined and treated. E.g., "Nonverbal messages occur everywhere. Some of the places that will be considered in this book are offices, restaurants, shops, and living rooms in private homes."

4. *Descending-ascending.* The most important items are placed first. These are followed by items of lesser importance. Or, the order is reversed. E.g. (descending), "To a student, the most important audience is the teacher. The teacher is followed in order by friends, parents, and classmates. We will consider each of these in turn."

5. *Problem solving.* A problem is identified and then various ways of solving the problem are discussed. E.g., "How can more interactions be created in the small-group situation? There are a number of ways that are often used by the coordinator. One of the most common is. . ."

6. *General to specific, specific to general.* The general statement is made and followed by specific examples, or vice versa. E.g. (general to specific): "American universities tend to make conformists of their students. An example of this tendency is my roommate, Fred Jones. He told me that each student in his communication class was required to write a term paper on the same topic."

Editing

Effective writers edit their work. That is, they write and then they scrutinize what they have written. A careful reading of your writing will

often reveal spelling errors, grammatical mistakes, illogical constructions, etc. The problem is one of time, reward, and effort. If you write a
paper, put it aside for a day or two, review it, edit it, and retype it, you
will almost certainly produce a better paper. The question will always be
"How much time and effort can I afford to put into this project?" The
First Law of Economics may well be called the First Law of Everything. It
is "There is no such thing as a free lunch." It simply means that an improved paper will cost the writer additional time and effort.

Enhancing Readability

Effective writers try to make reading as easy as possible for their audience. They look for short, familiar words rather than long, unfamiliar
ones. They try to write short, simple sentences rather than long, compound or complex ones.

A good case can sometimes be made for using big words and long
sentences. What is important to the writer is that he influences his reader in the intended way. Doctors, lawyers, and insurance salespersons often find that big words and long sentences best serve their purposes.
The client who really understands the insurance salesperson probably
does not need him.

If, however, it is important to the writer to have his readers understand him, the writer will do all he can to make it easy for readers to
share meanings. He will look for examples and anecdotes. He will include pictures, diagrams, and sketches where appropriate. He will try
out his written material on a sample of the intended audience. He will
apply the various readability formulas to his work to see if the difficulty
level suits the readers.

Still another way to help the reader is to provide him with signposts.
These point to what was said earlier and anticipate what is to come. Examples might be "You will recall that in chapter 2 there was a discussion
of . . ." and "This topic will be considered in more detail in section 7."

Writers as Readers

One way to become a more effective writer is to become a reader. It
probably is best to be a reader of everything from newspapers to news
magazines to literary journals to novels to history and biogra-
phy. If this is not possible, then it will help to read some works of rep-
utable authors. It is unrealistic to suppose that nonreaders can become
effective writers. Any writer needs some kind of model to guide his or
her efforts, so that certain patterns, turns of phrase, and commonly used
constructions come easily and naturally to hand.

Writers who read will increase their vocabulary, their sentence variety,
and strengthen their overall organization. They should make an effort to
notice what other writers do—how they use words, construct sentences,
and put paragraphs together.

Mechanical Details

Writers need to pay close attention to the mechanical details when it comes time to submit their work to the intended audience. It is one thing for your copy to be marred with misspellings, inserts, and crossed-out words and sentences, but it will not help your cause if the copy intended for the president or the professor or the personnel manager contains such blemishes.

Give thought to such things as color, size, and quality of paper; to typewriter quality, new ribbons, and perhaps professional typing. They will almost certainly have an effect on how your readers will evaluate your work.

Choosing General or Specific Information

Writers, particularly beginning ones, often tend to lean toward the abstract end of the abstract-specific continuum. This often leads to papers and reports that are dull and difficult to understand. (Some papers are by their nature and the expectations of both writers and readers dull. Statistical abstracts of the city, state, and nation are not intended to be lively reading.) Often it is possible to enliven a less than exciting topic by moving toward the specific and away from the abstract.

Suppose that your topic is "Orphans in the United States." One way to approach it is to discuss orphans in general, that is, to present statistics on the number of orphans, the ratios of males and females, the average annual costs to support them, the various agencies that regulate them, etc. This is a reasonable and rational way to write about the topic, and it may well be necessary given the intended goals and the expectations of the audience. It does, however, tend to result in an unexciting and pedestrian presentation.

Another approach is to deal not with orphans in general but with a particular orphan. You imagine a typical orphan, name him, describe him, follow him through a typical day, telling about his hopes and fears, his triumphs and trials. While not so formal or scientific, this approach has the advantage of allowing a reader to visualize and empathize with a real person rather than plow through an abstract set of statistics.

Again, your choice of which end of the general-specific continuum you choose will depend on your analysis of your audience, your objectives, and the context of the communication. There is, of course, nothing to prevent the writer from combining the statistical treatment and the anecdotal approach to achieve the desired effect.

CONCEPTS FOR REVIEW

choosing a topic	goals of the writer
costs of effective writing	importance of grammar and spelling
easy-to-read versus hard-to-read	importance of writing

nature of the audience	value of editing
organizing schemes	writers as readers
process of writing	

REVIEW QUESTIONS

1. Why is writing important?
2. What process is involved in effective writing?
3. How can more effective written messages be produced?

SUGGESTED READINGS

A Manual of Style. 12th ed., rev. Chicago: University of Chicago Press, 1969. Classic handbook for writers, editors, and printers. Should be on every scholarly writer's shelf.

Bernstein, Theodore M. *The Careful Writer: A Modern Guide to English Usage.* New York: Atheneum, 1965. Arranged alphabetically. Clear and complete discussions of word choice, style, spelling, etc.

Kahn, Gilbert, and Donald J. D. Mulkerne. *The Word Book.* Beverly Hills, Cal.: Glencoe Press, 1975. Indispensable for the nonconfident speller. Twenty-three thousand words spelled correctly and divided into syllables. Lightweight, small size. Every writer should have a copy.

Leslie, Louis A. *20,000 Words.* New York: McGraw-Hill, Gregg Div., 1951. Much like *The Word Book.* Take your choice.

Perrin, Porter G. *Writer's Guide and Index to English.* 3rd ed. Chicago: Scott, Foresman, 1959. A longtime favorite. Has sensible discussions of all the usual topics. Second half is an index to grammar, spelling, punctuation, etc. Well worth having on the shelf.

Strunk, William, Jr., and E. B. White. *The Elements of Style.* New York: Macmillan, 1979. Strunk's lectures updated and polished by White. Brief, wise, sensible, and readable.

Turabian, Kate L. *A Manual for Writers of Term Papers, Theses, and Dissertations.* 4th ed. Chicago: University of Chicago Press, 1973. A standard, recent manual. Paperback. Should be on the shelf of all college students.

Van Leunen, Mary-Claire. *A Handbook for Scholars.* New York: Alfred A. Knopf, 1978. New and great. Advocates abolishing bibliographic footnotes in favor of bracketed numbers and reference list. The style of the future in scholarly papers. Very readable.

Glossary

Abstraction is the selection of only certain parts of the communication process for inclusion in a model.

Achieved status is status which is derived from an individual's performance within a group.

Adaptability is the degree to which a speaker is capable of adjusting to a particular situation or audience.

Adaptation phase is the second stage of group development and is typified by the search for ideas and directions to adapt to the requirements of the group's task.

Adaptive coping is the process of successfully dealing with an information overload or underload.

Affect displays are nonverbal behaviors such as smiles or frowns used to convey emotions.

Affective effects concern changes in an individual's emotional state.

Agenda setting is the increase in perceived importance of events, ideas, or causes that results from their coverage by media sources.

Alternative options are the opportunities for a potentially trusting party to choose another desirable behavioral alternative. The existence of alternative options is necessary for the development of trust.

Appeal is the reason or justification for expecting a particular response to a persuasive message.

Argument is a claim which is supported by data and tells the listener both what to believe and why to believe it.

Artifactual codes are nonverbal codes which involve the use of inanimate objects such as clothing and furniture.

Ascribed status is status that is given to an individual by group members in recognition of some undemonstrated attribute the person is thought to possess.

Assertion is a claim made without data to support it.

Assigning priorities is a strategy for dealing with information overload. It involves ranking the tasks and completing the most important ones first.

Attitudinal consistency of a news story refers to how closely it matches a receiver's values and ideologies. News that supports an individual's point of view is more likely to be remembered.

Attraction power is the ability of one individual to influence another on the basis of the second person's attraction to the first.

Audience analysis is the process of considering aspects of the intended receivers of a message, such as demographic characteristics, that will affect their response to the message.

Audience effect is an outcome of the mass-communication process involving temporary or persisting change in a person's orientation.

Audience exposure patterns are the different ways people have of using and responding to the mass media.

Authoritarian leadership is characterized by task orientation (versus person orientation). An authoritarian leader controls the flow of communication in a group and determines the methods used to accomplish tasks.

Backing is the information which supports the warrant in the Toulmin model of argument.

Behavioral effects concern changes in the way a person acts.

Behaviorist approach (Skinner) suggests that operant conditioning rather than cognitive processes is the basis for language learning.

Bernstein, Basil, a sociolinguist, identified differences in the linguistic codes employed by middle-class and working-class families.

Biological drives are physiologically based forces which are assumed to be determinants of behavior. Hunger, thirst, and sex are biological drives.

Body is the portion of a speech in which the main arguments are developed.

Bridges are group members in an organization who have contacts with one or more other groups.

Chain network is an arrangement whereby communication flows back and forth between members of a group in a line.

Change in orientation of mass-communication receivers ranges from minor alterations of habits or moods to the creation of new states of mind.

Characteristics of group communication (Applebaum) are (1) it operates as a system, (2) it is complex, and (3) it is dynamic.

Chomsky, Noam, a cognitive theorist, proposed to distinguish between linguistic performance and linguistic competence. He also proposed a set of rules which would allow the linguist not only to describe the language, but to take the elements of the language and actually create all and only grammatically correct sentences.

Chunking is a strategy for handling information overload. It involves categorizing tasks and then dealing with tasks from individual categories at the same time.

Circle network is an arrangement whereby communication flows back and forth between adjacent members of a group in a circle.

Claim is a statement that a source wants an audience to accept or believe. When a persuasive message consists of a single argument, the claim is the same as the proposition.

Clarity is a test of evidence that measures the preciseness and objectivity of data.

Clarity is the precision with which words, phrases. and sentences describe concepts.

Closed-ended questions are questions which require direct, precise responses from an interviewee. An example is "Did you pass the last exam in COM 100?"

Coalition is the voluntary union of two or more group members for the purpose of achieving a common goal.

Code system is a collection of symbolic behaviors, either verbal or nonverbal.

Coercion power is the ability to influence an individual by the threat of force.

Cognitive effects concern changes in a person's way of thinking.

Cognitive theories of language attempt to explain the mental processes involved in translating ideas into messages. Chomsky's theory is the most well known of these.

Com-con network is an arrangement whereby each person in a group is linked to each other person.

Communication is a transactional, symbolic process which allows people to relate to and manage their environments by (1) establishing human contact, (2) exchanging information, (3) reinforcing the attitudes and behaviors of others, and (4) changing the attitudes and behaviors of others.

Communication flows refer to the regular movement of information within organizations. Three types of flows are downward, upward, and horizontal.

Communication network is the pattern of communication flow in a group.

Communication rules within an organization are the procedures for interacting or communicating and the types of content that are appropriate and expected.

Communicative analysis is the act of anticipating some of the things preceding communicative transaction which may affect its progression or outcomes.

Communicative responsibility is the act of considering some of the enduring effects which may result from a communicative transaction.

Competing messages are persuasive messages that call for opposing responses. The mass media and interpersonal environment may contain many messages that run counter to a particular persuasive appeal, thereby limiting its impact.

Complementary relationship exists when one person in a relationship assumes the dominant role while the other person assumes the submissive role.

Complex refers to the interaction of culture, situation, and individual differences and the changing influence of these factors in small-group communication.

Conclusion is the final portion of a speech; it sums up the main points or arguments, urges the receivers to believe or act according to the proposition, and signals that the presentation is completed.

Conflict avoidance is the act of evading or retreating from situations in which two involved parties are strongly at odds with each other.

Conflict management refers to a variety of techniques used by people to deal with interpersonal difficulties. The least constructive is the dissolution of the relationship; the most constructive is a resolution that is agreed to and perceived as equitable by both parties.

Connotative meaning is the meaning assigned to symbols on the basis of individual attitudes and emotions.

Content rules are communication rules in an organization which deal with what topics or issues are appropriate for discussion among certain people.

Contexts are the environments in which communication takes place.

Contingency is the likelihood of some continuing relationship between parties involved in a communicative situation. Contingency is a necessary condition for the development of trust.

Control over one's environment occurs when there is at least some correspondence between one's desired and one's obtained outcomes.

Conversion refers to changing the direction of one's orientation toward a topic. For example, going from hating Nixon to liking him.

Costs in interviewing are the outlays or losses experienced by the participants. For example, the interviewer may expend time and effort; the interviewee may lose face.

Credibility refers to a receiver's perception of a source's believability, trustworthiness, and competence. Credibility is one of the tests of evidence.

Cultural context of communication refers to the characteristics, such as language, values, and beliefs, shared by a large group of people.

Data are facts or reasons offered by a speaker or writer in support of a claim. Data is synonymous with evidence.

Deception detection is an information-gathering strategy in which one communicator (who is attempting to detect deception) takes a position on an issue and then reverses himself. If the second communicator agrees with *both* positions, his or her answers are probably not to be trusted.

Deductive pattern is a form of argument that starts with a general statement and then presents supporting data.

Democratic leadership is characterized by person orientation (versus task orientation). A democratic leader tries to include all group members' viewpoints in the problem-solving or decision-making processes.

Demographic characteristics are arbitrary groupings of people on the basis of sociological or cultural attributes such as sex, age, or nationality.

Denotative meaning is the meaning assigned to symbols on the basis of common cultural use.

Description is the act of drawing a vivid verbal picture of a scene, an event, etc. to enliven a speech.

Descriptive level of knowledge is information that is limited to the superficial, surface attributes of an individual. It permits the knower to discriminate the individual from other persons, but not to make accurate predictions about his or her behavior.

Developmental view of interpersonal communication assumes that initial communicative transactions are noninterpersonal, that is, the participants make predictions about each other's message responses according to cultural and sociological information. As the communicators begin to treat each other as individuals rather than as occupants of social roles, and as they increasingly use psychological-level analysis for making predictions, their communication becomes more interpersonal.

Deviation testing is an information-gathering strategy that involves deliberate violation of a relational norm to see how the other person reacts.

Direct evidence is proof that is immediately and directly related to a proposition.

Discussion tasks are tasks in which group members participate to resolve an issue by reaching a consensus.

Downward communication flows are the direction-giving messages that are typically sent from management to subordinates in an organization.

Dynamic refers to the continual exchange of messages and ongoing feedback that occur in small-group communication.

Ego-centered conflict is a conflict which is focused on personalities rather than on substantive issues.

Elaborated code is the language of the middle class. It uses a larger number of syntactic structures, a broader vocabulary, and has more involved explanations than the restricted code.

Elements are the identifiable parts of a code system.

Emblems are learned, highly stylized nonverbal symbols having a certain meaning within a culture; an example is the hitchhikers's thumbs-up signal.

Employment interviews enable personnel people or supervisors to evaluate job applicants and applicants to evaluate jobs.

Entertainment content is content intended to provide enjoyment, relaxation, or a means of escape to a mass-media audience.

Entertainment value refers to how enjoyable a receiver finds a subject. The more entertaining the presentation, the better it is remembered.

Environmental interference refers to external distractions such as street noises that can distort information gathered in an interview.

Environmental structuring is a strategy that seeks to elicit information from a person by manipulating the setting in which communication occurs.

Escapism/companionship are contrasting motives satisfied by entertainment content.

Evaluation of an interview is the process of assessing the degree to which the goals of the interview were met.

Exigency is an intrinsic or circumstantial necessity of a situation. When people "speak out of an exigency," they speak because something has happened that compels them to speak.

Expert power is the ability of one person to influence another because of the first person's superior knowledge or skill in an area.

Explanatory level of knowledge about a person is information which provides reasons for the individual's behaving and believing in certain ways.

Extemporaneous delivery is speaking from a set of reminder notes which have been prepared from a speech plan and using a conversational tone.

External distortion is distortion of information that occurs in an interview (1) during interaction between the interviewer and interviewee as the result of cultural conflicts, distracting mannerisms, differences in role expectations or language, etc.; or (2) due to environmental interference such as people talking, street noise, or physical discomforts.

Extrinsic rules are rules guiding a relationship that are imposed by the society or culture.

Eye when a speaker and a receiver look at each other simultaneously.

Factual evidence is data which are alleged, or can be demonstrated, to be true.

Familiarity refers to how much a receiver knows about a topic and helps determine the retention of information.

Feedback is the response to the message from the receiver to the source.

Figures of speech are the expressions such as sayings, epigrams, or metaphors that add vigor or vividness to a speech.

Forcefulness is the drive, urgency, or excitement with which a message is delivered.

Formal rules are organizational rules that have been agreed to and accepted by the majority, particularly of the managerial hierarchy.

Funnel approach is an interviewing strategy that begins with open-ended questions and moves to closed-ended questions.

Generalized trust is the typical level of trust that people manifest across persons and situations.

Goal-attainment phase is the fourth and final stage of group development. It is typified by a redirecting of the group away from conflict and back to the task of reaching an acceptable solution.

Group cohesiveness is the result of all the forces acting upon members to remain in a group.

Group norms are standardized generalizations concerning expected behavior in matters of some importance to a group.

Group pressure is the sum of the forces toward uniformity of behavior exerted by the group.

Groups that exist in organizational networks are sets of individuals who share more than half their communication contacts with one another.

Hierarchy is the ranking of individuals according to their authority.

Horizontal communication flows are the messages exchanged by co-workers in an organization.

Iconicity is the degree to which code elements and patterns resemble the things to which they refer.

Illustrators are nonverbal signs used to clarify verbal messages; pounding a lectern for emphasis is an example.

Impersonality means that the relations in an organization are characterized by role rather than person orientation. As organizations increase in size, they necessarily become more impersonal.

Impromptu delivery is speaking without any formal preparation.

Indirect evidence is proof that is only loosely linked to a proposition.

Inductive pattern is a form of argument that starts with specific data and then draws a general conclusion.

Informal rules are organizational rules which cover topics not explicitly included under the formal rule system.

Informational content is content intended to inform or educate a mass-media audience.

Information-gathering interviews are conducted for (1) news stories, reports, theses, etc.; (2) social-science research and public opinion polls; and (3) selection of job candidates or offerings.

Information-giving interviews are conducted for the purposes of orientation, counseling, persuasion, and appraisal.

Information load is the amount of information an individual is required to process.

Information processing refers to the tasks that every person engages in, on a day-to-day basis, in an attempt to deal with incoming messages.

Informative messages are messages intended to induce learning.

Innovation network carries messages about new ideas and practices in an organization.

Integration phase is the third stage of group development and is characterized by intense evaluation of possible means of achieving the group's goal, often resulting in group conflict.

Interaction zones (Hall) are the various distances people attempt to keep between themselves and others while interacting.

Interdependent refers to the characteristic ability of members of small groups to influence and be influenced by one another.

Interest value refers to how engrossing a receiver finds a subject. It is a key factor in learning.

Internal distortion is a type of information distortion that occurs because of biases within an interviewer. Bias can be a result of personal traits, experience, expectations, or selectivity of exposure, perception, or retention.

Interrogation is an information-gathering strategy which involves asking directly for the information desired.

Interview is the interaction of two people, one of whom has a distinct purpose, and both of whom will speak and listen from time to time and make moment-to-moment adaptations.

Interviewee is a person who is interviewed, i.e., the respondent. The interviewee is responsible for providing information to the interviewer, but has the right to refuse to comment or to terminate the interview.

Interviewer is a person who conducts an interview. The interviewer typically initiates the interview and defines its purpose.

Intrinsic rules are rules guiding a relationship that the participants themselves have agreed upon.

Introduction is the opening portion of a speech and is intended to (1) arouse attention, (2) maintain or improve the speaker's personal proof, and (3) direct the receivers toward what is to come in the speech.

Inverted-funnel approach is an interviewing strategy that begins with closed-ended questions and moves to open-ended questions.

Investigative interviews are interviews conducted by reporters with persons considered knowledgeable on a topic.

Isolates are individuals who have relatively few, if any, contacts with other members of an organization.

Issue-centered conflict is a conflict which is focused on a substantive matter rather than on personalities.

Job interdependency refers to the amount of linkage between tasks in an organization.

Kelman's model of communication specifies the processes communicators can use to influence others.

Kernel sentence is the simple form of a sentence and the basis on which Chomsky's rules are used to create other grammatically acceptable sentences.

Key communicators are individuals in organizations who are influential transmitters of information about innovative matters.

Kinship network consists of persons in an organization who are related by blood or marriage and who endeavor to provide benefits to one another.

Language is the set of all grammatically acceptable sentences that can be constructed from a particular set of words.

Leadership is the act of influencing group members toward a goal and guiding their interactions.

Leading questions are queries which imply that an interviewee should answer in a particular way. An example is "You think marijuana should be legalized, don't you?"

Learned motives are culturally based values which are acquired by individuals as part of the process of socialization. Examples are courage, loyalty, and competitiveness.

Learning is one of the paramount reasons for using the mass media.

Legitimate power is the ability of one person to influence another on the basis of the first person's formal position of authority in an organization.

Liaisons are individuals in organizations who link groups together but are not themselves group members.

Linguistic competence is the speaker's underlying knowledge of the language.

Linguistic performance is the actual use of language in real situations.

Linguistics is the study of language.

Loaded questions are queries which put an interviewee in a double-bind situation. An example is "Did you get absolved of the child-molesting charges?"

Logical patterns are ways of organizing material so that it can be tested against rational criteria; examples are inductive and deductive patterns.

Maintenance network carries information about social relationships and other interpersonal matters.

Maladaptive coping occurs when a person's strategy for dealing with changes in information load is detrimental to an organization.

Manuscript delivery is reading a speech to an audience from a prepared text.

Mass communication is the process of mediated communication between an institutional source and a large, diverse, dispersed audience via a mechanical device.

Mass-communication channel is a mediated channel through which messages are transmitted via some mechanical device.

Mass-communication message is the content of the media.

Mass-communication process consists of the production of a message by a source organization and transmittal of the message through a mediated channel.

Mass-communication receiver is a member of the large and diverse mass-media audience in many separate localities.

Mass-communication source is a professional communicator or commercial organization.

Massing of details is a speech-making technique that piles incident upon incident, fact upon fact, to convey a general impression.

Materiality is a test of evidence that measures how central data are to a proposition.

Materials of development are the parts of a speech that back up the rationality of claims and arguments. Materials of development may be either discovered or created by the speaker.

Materials of experience are the parts of a speech meant to attract listeners' attention, motivate them, and enable them to share vicariously in experiences or feelings.

Materials of personal proof are actions and statements that contribute to a speaker's reputation or image with an audience. Personal proof is achieved by (1) the inclusion of materials deliberately designed to increase it, and (2) the way the speaker handles the entire public speaking event.

Mediation theory (Osgood) examines observable stimuli and responses and, on that basis, tries to explain what is going on in the language user's mind.

Mediatory codes are nonverbal codes used by the media that convey meaning through devices such as lighting and camera work.

Membership groups are organizations such as social or political clubs that people join voluntarily and influence their reception of messages.

Memorized delivery is the presentation of a speech which has been committed to memory.

Metacommunication is communicating about communication.

Miller's model of communication shows the transactional nature of communication in the three critical contexts of communication.

Mirror questions are questions which call for an interviewee to indicate agreement or disagreement with a restatement of a previous response.

Model is a systematic representation which abstracts and classifies/describes potentially relevant aspects of a process.

Motivated sequence is a psychologically based pattern of organization consisting of five steps: getting attention, establishing a need, satisfying the need, visualizing the result, and identifying a course of action.

Motivation appeals seek to persuade an audience by linking a proposition to biological drives or learned motives.

Multiplier effect refers to the dissemination of information produced by training key communicators who in turn transmit the information to their groups.

Narration is the act of telling a story to convey an idea or arouse attention.

Negative evidence is indirect proof which argues that a proposition should be accepted because alternative positions are not supportable.

Networks are patterns of relations among members of an organization.

Nonverbal codes are codes which do not use words. Examples are gestures, facial expressions, and the use of proxemics and artifacts.

Obligatory norms are norms which members of a group are expected to adhere to without exception.

Obstinate audience is a name given to receivers who are resistant to persuasive appeals in the mass media.

Old-boy network consists of persons in an organization who help and identify closely with one another as a result of common backgrounds and shared work experiences.

Open-ended questions are questions which call for a broad response and allow an interviewee flexibility in answering. An example is "What do you think about the conflict in the Middle East?"

Operant conditioning is a learning process in which the organism is rewarded, or reinforced, upon making the correct response to a stimulus.

Opinion evidence is personal testimony of someone other than the speaker.

Organization is (1) a number of individuals who (2) desire to achieve a set of goals, (3) recognize that goal achievement is best attained by cooperation, (4) gather whatever materials and information are needed from the environment, (5) process materials and information, and (6) return the modified materials and information to the environment with the intent of obtaining sufficient rewards so that the goals of the various members can be met.

Organizational function of communication models helps people see how components of the communication process are ordered and related to one another.

Orientation refers to moods, knowledge, opinions, and actions of the receivers of messages carried by the mass media.

Orientation phase is the initial stage of group development, in which members attempt to adjust to one another and to the situation.

Osgood, Charles, hypothesized that observable stimuli and responses can be used to explain the mental processes involved in the use of language (mediation theory).

Overload occurs when people are required to process more information than they can handle.

Paralinguistics are nonverbal vocal behaviors such as rate, pitch, and intensity of speech.

Pattern is the arrangement of the elements of a code system according to set rules.

Performance codes are nonverbal codes which the body produces, such as facial expressions and gestures.

Permissive norms are standards of behavior that operate only sometimes in a group and are not enforced as rigidly as obligatory norms.

Persisting change is a permanent or long-term alteration of moods, knowledge, opinions, or behaviors of receivers of messages.

Personal artifacts are inanimate objects such as clothing, cosmetics, and jewelry which can be used as nonverbal communication.

Person-specific trust is the degree of trust displayed by an individual in particular situations with specific persons.

Persuasive content is content intended to change the orientation of a mass-media audience.

Phatic communication refers to ritualized, rule-governed transactions, such as greeting behaviors, that are second nature to the transactors.

Pitch refers to the highness or lowness of a voice.

Polling (surveying) is a type of information-gathering interview undertaken for the purpose of compiling a composite statement of the views or behaviors of a representative group of people.

Practical predictive functions of communication models can provide tentative predictions about the probable success of certain communicative strategies.

Predictability is a stable assumption about the way another person is likely to behave. It is a prerequisite for the development of trust.

Predictive level of knowledge about a person allows one to make accurate forecasts about the person's beliefs or behaviors.

Prior attitudes are the feelings, opinions, dispositions, etc. held by receivers of a message and affecting their response to it.

Probing questions are questions which ask an interviewee to extend, clarify, or provide an example of one of his or her answers.

Problem-solution pattern is an organizational approach to persuasive messages that details a problem and then describes how to solve it.

Problem-solving tasks evaluate the way things were done in the past. This typically involves gathering information, evaluating it, and using it to solve a problem.

Procedural rules are communication rules in an organization which deal with how one should behave in an interaction, e.g., what channels are appropriate to use.

Process implies that communication is continuous and that what occurs during a communicative transaction, as well as the outcomes that accrue from it, are influenced by many factors.

Production network carries information having to do with the work of an organization.

Production tasks are designed to create an end product such as an event, a work schedule, or a set of operating procedures.

Proposition is what a source wants a receiver to do as a result of attending to a message.

Proxemics refers to the way people position themselves in relation to other people when they talk, such as how far people stand from one another.

Pseudoconflict is a communication problem that occurs because ambiguous messages lead people to believe they are in disagreement when they are not.

Psychological context is the ways an individual is seen as unique rather than as a stereotype or role occupant.

Psychological defenses are a series of protective techniques that serve to maintain a receiver's prior attitudes and behavior patterns.

Public artifacts are public objects such as municipal buildings and monuments which can be a form of nonverbal communication.

Public speech is an orally delivered message which is prepared by a speaker, organized and adapted to suit a particular audience, and meant to persuade or inform listeners.

Purpose sentence is a clear, succinct, complete, and affirmative sentence which describes what the speaker is going to talk about or what change the speaker expects from the audience.

Qualifier is the part of the Toulmin model of argument which specifies the strength of the claim, e.g., sometimes, generally, always.

Quintamensional plan is an interviewing strategy that moves through five types of questions: (1) awareness, (2) uninfluenced attitudes, (3) specific attitudes, (4) reason why, and (5) intensity of attitude.

Rate of speech refers to the speed with which words are spoken.

Rational appeal seeks to influence an audience through the use of argument.

Real evidence is an artifact, such as a weapon, offered in support of a claim.

Reasoning is the process of inferring conclusions from evidence or from other conclusions.

Reasoning by analogy is reasoning by making a comparison between two cases that are similar in important respects and then inferring that they are similar in other respects.

Reasoning from cause is reasoning by arguing that one phenomenon (a cause) has produced another phenomenon (an effect) or that one phenomenon (an effect) is the result of another phenomenon (a cause).

Reasoning from example is reasoning wherein conclusions are inferred from specific cases or illustrations.

Reasoning from sign is reasoning wherein associations are inferred between phenomena that are not causally related.

Rebuttal is the part of the Toulmin model of argument which specifies the conditions under which the claim is not applicable.

Receiver is the recipient of a message.

Recency is a test of evidence that measures its up-to-dateness.

Reciprocity refers to the expectation that a person who uses interrogation as an information-gathering strategy should be willing to provide similar information about himself.

Regulators are nonverbal signs used to control or guide the behavior of others, such as catching a person's eye to indicate an interest in getting acquainted.

Reinforcement is the strengthening of existing attitudes.

Relativity of standards is the notion that the criteria receivers use to judge data and warrants vary from group to group or from one field of inquiry to another.

Relaxation/excitement are contrasting motives for seeking entertainment in the media.

Relevance refers to how pertinent a message is to a receiver's personal life. The more relevant the message, the better it is learned.

Relevancy is a test of evidence that measures how closely data are related to a proposition.

Research-generating function of communication models indicates that a model can suggest questions and hypotheses for future investigation.

Restricted code is the language of the working class. It uses fewer syntactic structures, has a more limited vocabulary, and is more tied to the context in which it is used than the elaborated code.

Reward power is the ability of one person to influence another based on the capacity of the first to provide something desirable to the second.

Rewards in interviewing are desirable outcomes accruing to the participants, such as monetary payments or increased self-esteem for the interviewee, or increased professional status for the interviewer.

"Risky shift" phenomenon is the tendency for groups to make somewhat riskier decisions than individuals.

Role conflict occurs when a person occupies two roles simultaneously, each of which demands different behaviors.

Roles refers both to the behaviors regularly enacted by people in a group and to the expectations of others regarding those behaviors.

Rules are agreements made by persons in a relationship which guide their interactions and topics of conversation. Rules may be determined by societal norms or may be specific to a relationship.

Selective exposure is the tendency of people to pay attention to messages that are congruent with predispositions and to ignore discrepant material.

Selective perception is the tendency of people to interpret a message in such a way that it fits in with their existing viewpoint.

Selective retention is the tendency of people to recall only those messages that are in agreement with their outlook.

Self-description is the act of communicating information about oneself, the disclosure of which involves little or no risk.

Self-disclosure is the act of communicating personally private information at some risk to the discloser.

Semantic meanings are meanings assigned to words according to cultural or individual norms.

Semantic rules are rules used in assigning meanings to words.

Shared artifacts are inanimate objects which are used by more than one person and can be a means of nonverbal communication. An example is furniture.

Situational view of interpersonal communication holds that interpersonal communication transactions can be distinguished from other transactions through a set of situational characteristics. These characteristics include a relatively small number of communicators, a high degree of physical proximity, a maximal number of sensory channels, and the availability of immediate feedback.

Skinner, B. F., a behaviorist, believed that language learning was based on operant conditioning.

SMCR model by David Berlo shows a linear, unidirectional perspective of communication: source (S) transmits messages (M) through channels (C) to receivers (R), with no feedback mechanism included in the model.

Social power is the capacity to control others through the use of rewards and punishments.

Sociolinguistics (Bernstein) is the study of the relationship between language and society.

Sociological context of communication refers to the sum of an individual's group memberships and the roles associated with those memberships.

Source is the initiator of a message.

Spatial arrangement is the way in which people are physically placed in a room where a discussion occurs.

Spatio-temporal codes are nonverbal codes involving the use of space and time in communicating; an example is the physical distance maintained between communicators.

Speech plan is the basic document from which notes are prepared for a speech. It consists of purpose sentence, introduction, body, and conclusion.

Stability of orientation is the resistance to change of ingrained patterns of thinking or acting.

Status is the importance of an individual's position in a group.

Status conferral is the increase in perceived importance of persons as a result of their coverage by media sources.

Stimulus discrimination is the act of focusing on characteristics that differentiate individual members of groups from one another.

Stimulus generalization is the act of focusing on the characteristics that members of groups have in common.

Symbol is a verbal or nonverbal device that stands for something else; e.g., words are symbols that represent things or ideas.

Symbolic suggests that communicative transactions symbolize, or stand for, something else.

Symmetrical relationship exists when neither person in a relationship assumes the dominant or the submissive role.

Syntactic meaning is the understanding gained from the way the elements of a code system are arranged into patterns.

Syntactic rules specify the ways elements of a code system can be ordered into acceptable patterns.

Systemic refers to the fact that small-group communication occurs in a system.

Tabulating is the process of grouping information obtained in an interview into chunks meaningful to the interviewer.

Tangible has to do with the material costs or rewards accruing to an interviewee as a result of an interview.

Task is the set of activities a group must complete to accomplish its goals.

Tests of evidence are the standards against which data are judged in rational systems of argument. The tests are relevancy, materiality, clarity, credibility, and recency.

Tone is the quality of a voice described by such terms as resonant, warm, harsh, nasal, or hoarse.

Toulmin model of argument is a rational model for analyzing persuasive messages, holding that all arguments have three basic components: claims, data, and warrants.

Transactional suggests that communication is relational, that the participants reciprocally affect each other's behavior.

Transitory change is a temporary change in moods, knowledge, opinions, or behaviors of receivers of messages.

Two-step flow occurs when information is transmitted through the media to receivers, who then pass it along to others.

Underload occurs when people are required to process considerably less information than they can handle.

Upward communication flows are the reports, replies, etc. that the lower levels of an organization send to the upper levels.

Utility of a model is the extent to which a model enhances theoretical and practical understanding of the communication process.

Verbal codes are codes utilizing sets of words to transmit messages.

Verbal evidence is any statement offered in support of a claim.

Vividness is the degree to which the language employed in a speech helps the listener to experience the images presented.

Warrant is a general statement which links the data with the claim in a persuasive message. Warrants may be implicit or explicit.

Wheel network is an arrangement whereby communication flows back and forth between one central member of a group and all other members.

Whorf-Sapir hypothesis posits that (1) without language we cannot think; (2) language influences perception; and (3) language influences thinking patterns. This hypothesis is concerned with the relationship of culture and language.

Index

Abstraction, 30
Achieved status, 154
Acknowledgment introduction, 271
Adaptability, 276
Adaptation phase of group development, 148
Adaptive coping, 173
Advertising, 209–215
  influence of, 213–215
Affect displays, 63
Affective effects of mass media, 203–205, 208, 214
Agenda setting, 208
Allen, V. L., 24
Alternative options, trust and, 129
Altruism, appeals to, 265–266
Analogy, reasoning by, 262
Anthropological view of language behavior, 54–55, 58
Appeal conclusion, 271
Appeals. See Motivational appeals; Rational appeals
Applebaum, R. L., 144
Appraisal interview, 232
Arguments
  chain, 90
  organization of, into messages, 92–95
    deductive patterns, 92–93
    inductive patterns, 94–95
  Toulmin model of. See Toulmin model of argument
  using multiple data, 89–90
Artifactual codes, 63–64
Asch, S. E., 160
Ascribed status, 154

Assembly line, 173
Assertion, 81
Atkin, Charles, 206, 214, 220
Attitudes
  of others
    changing, 19–20
    reinforcing, 18–19
  prior, 11
Attitudinal consistency, 207
Attraction power, 157, 158
Atwood, L. Erwin, 208
Audience
  obstinate, 210
  in public speaking. See Receivers—in public speaking
  writer's adjustment to, 291
Audience analysis, 88
Audience effects, dimensions of, 202–205
  methods for studying, 204–205
  typology of, 203–204
    linking media stimuli to, 205
Audience-exposure patterns, 199–202
Authoritarian leader, 159–160
Authority network, 183, 185–186

Backing, 90, 91, 94
Bandura, Albert, 217
Batons, 62
Bauer, Raymond, 210
Beavin, J. H., 7–8, 12
Behavioral effects of mass media, 203–205, 209, 215
Behaviorist approach to language learning, 49–50

Berger, Charles R., 113, 119, 120, 123, 127
Berlo, David K., 8, 30–32
  SMCR model of, 31–32
Bernstein, Basil, 56–58
Biological drives, 96, 98
Body of speech, 269–271
Booth, Alan, 206
Bridges, 186–188
Brockriede, W., 92
Burgoon, M., 18

Cable television, 201
Calabrese, Rick, 113, 123, 124
Cattell, R. B., 143
Cause, reasoning from, 263
Chain argument, 90
Chain network, 151–152
Change
  of attitudes and behaviors of others, 19–20
  in orientation, mass media and, 202–203
Channel, mass-communication, 198
Chomsky, Noam, 47–49, 52–53
Chronological organization, 293
Chu, Godwin, 208
Chunking, 173, 176
Circle network, 151
Circumstantial evidence, 83, 89
Claim, 80–82, 94
Clarity
  of evidence, 85–86
  in public speaking, 276
Clark, Herbert, 54
Class, language use and social, 56–58
Clique, high-school, 142–144
Closed-ended questions, 241, 242, 245
Coalition formation, 149
Code systems, 42–67
  meanings and, 42–45
  nonverbal. See Nonverbal codes
  verbal. See Verbal codes
Coercion power, 158
Cognition, verbal codes and, 53–54

Cognitive effects of mass media, 203–205, 214
Cognitive theories of language learning, 49, 52, 53
Coherence, language and, 46
Cohesiveness, group, 153–154
Com-con network, 151, 152
Communication
  defining characteristics of, 8–20
    process, 8–11
    relation to and management of environment, 14–20
    symbolic, 13–14
    transactional, 11–13
  effective, 6–7
  models of, 30–36
    functions, 31–34
  view of all activity as, 7–8
Communication flows (information flows), 173–175, 180–183
  two-step, 206
Communication networks, 151–152
  organizational. See Organizational communication—networks
Communication rules, organizational, 176–180
  formal and informal, 179–180
  procedural and content, 178–179
Communicative analysis, 10
Communicative contexts (contexts of communication), 20–29, 103–224
  cultural, 20–24, 35
    socio-, 54–58
  psychological, 26–29, 35, 36
  sociological, 24–26, 35
  See also Interpersonal communication; Mass media; Organizational communication; Small groups
Communicative responsibility, 10
Companionship, mass media as, 215
Competence of source of evidence, 86
Competing messages, 210–211
Complementary relationship, 12
Complexity, 9–11
  of small-group communication, 144

Comstock, George, 220
Conclusion of public speech, 271
Conditioning, 49–51
Conflict, 132–137
  management of, 133–137
  avoidance vs., 132–133
  role, 157
Connotative meaning, 44, 51
Consistency, attitudinal, 207
Contact, establishment of human, 15–16
Content rules, 28
  organizational, 178–180
Context-bound meaning, 56
Contexts of communication. *See* Communicative contexts
Contingency, trust and, 128
Control
  environmental, 15, 17, 26, 33 (*See also* Environment—relation to and management of)
  in organizations, 171
  small groups and, 144, 145, 155, 157, 158
Control function of language, 56, 57
Conversion, 213
Coordination, organizational communication and, 171
Coping, 173
Coser, L. A., 132
Costs of interview, 235–237
Counseling interviews, 232
Credibility, 11, 84, 86–87
  of news source, 207
  of public speaker, 254, 259, 260
Critical detachment, 79
Criticism, ability to accept, 191–192
Cross-cultural communication, 21–22
Culbert, S. A., 125
Cultural context, 20–24, 35
  socio-, 54–58
Cultural information, prediction based on, 113, 115, 116, 124
Cultural rules, 23–24, 28, 29, 117
Culture
  group membership and, 146
  language and, 54–56, 58

organization as, 171, 188–192
  women and, 191–192
Cushman, D. P., 155

Dance, F. E. X., 30
Danielson, Wayne, 206
Darwin, Charles, 58
Data. *See* Evidence
Davidson, Emily, 220
Deception (deceit), 124–126
Deception detection, 127
Deductive patterns, 93, 95
Deductive speech plan, 269–271, 283–284
Defenses, psychological, 210–212
Delivery of public speech, 267–268, 272–279
  extemporaneous, 273–275
  impromptu, 272–273
  manuscript, 273
  memorized, 273
  suggestions for improvement of, 275–278
    nonverbal delivery, 277–278
    vocal delivery, 276–277
Democratic leader, 159, 160
Demographic characteristics, 88
Denotative meaning, 44
Descending-ascending organizational scheme, 293
Description, 265
Descriptive level of knowledge, 119, 122
Detachment, critical, 79
Deutschmann, Paul, 206
Development, materials of, 260–264
Developmental view of interpersonal communication, 113–124
  changes in levels of knowing, 119–122
  changes in prediction-making data, 114–117
  changes in rules governing relationships, 117–119
  implications of, 122–123
Deviation testing, 127

Direct evidence, 82–83
Direct introduction, 271
Discussion tasks, 161
Distance, appropriate social, 22, 23, 66
Distortion of information, 232–234, 246–248
Downward communication flows, 180–181
Dress, 59, 64
Dynamism of small-group communication, 144

Editing, 293–294
Ego-centered conflict, 136, 137
Ehninger, D., 92
Ekman, Paul, 61
Elaborated code, 56–58
Elements, 42–43, 45
Emblems, 61
Employment interviews, 231, 237–240, 243–244, 247–248
Entertainment content of media messages, impact of, 205, 215–221
  learning and, 217–221
  reasons for appeal, 215–217
Entertainment value, 207
Environment
  perception and, 12
  relation to and management of (environmental control), 14–20, 32, 33
    changing attitudes and behaviors of others, 19–20
    establishing human contact, 15–16
    information exchange, 16–18
    reinforcing attitudes and behaviors of others, 18–19
Environmental interference, 234
Environmental structuring, 127
Epstein, Edward, 207
Escapism, mass media and, 215, 217
Evidence (data), 79
  direct, 82–83
  factual, 261
  indirect or circumstantial, 83, 89

multiple, 89–90, 263
negative, 83
opinion, 261
public speaking and, 261–262
real, 84
tests of, 84–87
in Toulmin model, 80–88
verbal, 83–84
Example, reasoning from, 263
Excitement, mass media and, 215, 217
Exigency, speaking out of, 257
Experience, materials of, 260, 264–268
Expert power, 158
Explanatory level of knowledge, 120–124
Extemporaneous delivery, 273–275
External distortion, 233, 234
Extrinsic rules, 113
Eye contact, 278

Facial expressions, 63
  public speaking and, 278
Factual evidence, 261
Familiarity with news topic, 207
Farace, Richard V., 170, 172, 180
Fear appeals, 266
Figures of speech, 265
Fisher, Marilyn, 220
Forcefulness in public speaking, 276
Formal network, 183, 185–186
Formal rules, 179–180
French, J. R. P., Jr., 157
Friesen, Wallace, 61
Funnel approach, 241, 242

Galloway, John, 206
Gallup, George, 239–240, 242
General to specific organizational scheme, 293
Generalized trust, 129
Generative-transformational grammar, 48
Gilbert, S. J., 125, 126
Goal attainment, small group and, 148
Goffman, Erving, 46

Gouldner, A. W., 124
Goyer, Robert S., 230
Grammar, 289–290
Greenberg, Bradley, 206, 215, 219, 220
Group cohesiveness, 153–154
Group development, phases of, 147–149
Group norms, 143, 155–156
Group pressure, 160
Groups
 membership, 88–89
 in organizational communication networks, 186
 small. *See* Small groups

Hall, Edward T., 21–22, 66
Halliday, Michael, 53
Hance, Kenneth G., 262
Harari, H., 143
Harrison, R. P., 59, 61, 64
Hayakawa, S. I., 46
Heald, Gary, 214
Hennig, Margaret, 191
Hierarchy, 168, 170, 181, 183
Horizontal communication flows, 181–183
"Human interest" news, 207
Hyman, Herbert, 206

Iconicity, 60
Ideology, 21
Illustration-quotation conclusion, 271
Illustration-quotation introduction, 271
Illustrators, 61–63
Image
 language and, 46
 mass media and, 207–208
Imaginative function of language, 56, 57
Impersonal communication, 113, 114
Impersonality in organizations, 169
Impromptu delivery, 272–273
Indirect evidence, 83, 89
Inductive patterns, 92–95

Inductive speech plan, 270
Influence, Kelman's processes of social, 33, 34
Informal rules, 179–180
Information, distortion of, 232–234, 246–248
Information exchange, 16–18
 language and, 45
Information flows (communication flows), 173–175, 180–183
 position in, 172–173
 two-step, 206
Information-gathering interview, 237
Information-gathering strategies, 123–128
Information-giving interviews, 232
Information load, 172–173, 175
 analysis of, 175–176
Information overload, 172, 173, 175
Information processing, 171–176
 information-load analysis, 175–176
 job interdependency, 173–175
 position in information flow, 172–173
 time pressure, 175
Information underload, 172, 173, 175
Informational content of media messages, effects of, 205–209
 hard and soft news, 206–208
 indirect, 208–209
 priority, 208
Informative messages, construction of, 72–76
 principles of, 73–75
 space patterns for, 75–76
 time patterns for, 75–76
"In-house" language system, 178–179
Innovation network, 184–188
Instructional function of language, 56, 57
Intangible rewards and costs of interview, 235
Integration phase of group development, 148
Interaction zones, Hall's concept of, 66
Interdependency
 job, 173–175
 in small groups, 143–146

Interest value, 207
Internal distortion, 233, 234
Interpersonal communication,
     103–104, 108–109
  conflict in, 132–137
  developmental view of. *See* Develop-
     mental view of interpersonal
     communication
  information-gathering strategies
     and, 123–128
  situational view of, 108–112
  trust and, 128–132
Interpersonal communication rela-
     tionships, 116
Interpersonal context of language, 56,
     57
Interrogation, 123–125
Interview (interviewing), 225, 226,
     230–248
  definition of, 230–231
  distortion of information and,
     232–234, 246–248
  information-gathering, 237
  information-giving, 232
  managing, 234–237
  purposes of, 231–232
  steps in, 237–248
     adapting to style of interviewee,
        244–246
     arrangement, 243–244
     closing, 246
     determining general objective,
        237
     determining specific information
        needed, 238–239
     evaluation, 246–247
     opening, 244
     preparing questions, 240–243
     selecting interviewee, 239–240
     selecting interviewer, 243
     tabulating information, 247–248
  team, 243
Interviewee, 231
  adapting to style of, 244–246
  costs and rewards to, 236, 237,
     246
  selection of, 239–240

Interviewer, 231
  costs and rewards to, 235–236
  selection of, 243
Intrinsic rules, 113
Introduction to public speech,
     271–272
Inverted funnel approach, 241–242
Investigative interviews, 237, 247
Isolates, 174–175, 186–188, 191
Issue-centered conflict, 136

Jackson, D. D., 7–8, 12
Jardim, Anne, 191
Job interdependency, 173–175
Job interview (employment inter-
     view), 231, 237–240, 243–244,
     247–248
Johnson, Bonnie McDaniel, 172, 177

Kelley, H. H., 121, 134
Kelman, Herbert C., 30
  social influence model of, 33, 34
Kernel sentence, 48, 52
Key communicators, 188
Kinship network, 183
Klapper, Joseph, 210
Knapp, Mark L., 13, 59–60
Knowledge, changes in levels of,
     119–122

Language, 13, 42
  definition of, 45
  functions of, 45–47
  "in-house," 178–179
  inside, 192
  learning, 49–53
  sociocultural context and, 54–58
  thought and, 52, 55
  See also Code systems; Linguistics
Lazarsfeld, Paul, 208
Leaders (leadership), 168
  in small groups, 159–160
Leading questions, 240
Learned motives, 96, 98

Learning
  language, 49–53
  mass media and, 203, 206–207, 214, 216–222
Legitimate power, 158
Leibert, Robert, 220
LeMasters, E. E., 110–111
Lenneberg, Eric, 52–53
Liaisons, 186–188
Lilly, J. C., 13
Limitation of topic
  in public speaking, 257–259
  in writing, 291–292
Linear view of communication, 12, 20, 32
Linguistic competence, 47–48, 52
Linguistic performance, 47
Linguistics, 47–48
  socio-, 56
Lippmann, Walter, 207
Loaded questions, 240
Logical patterns, 92–95, 100
  deductive, 93
  inductive, 94–95

Mabry, Edward, 147
McCombs, Maxwell, 208
McDavid, J. W., 143
MacLean, M., Jr., 30
Magazines, 199–200
Maintenance network, 184, 185
Maladaptive coping, 173
Manuscript delivery, 273
Mass media (mass-media communication; mass communication), 19, 24, 104–105, 109
  audience-exposure patterns, 199–202
  future, 201–202
  definition of, 197
  effects of, 196, 202–222
    dimensions of, 202–205
    entertainment content, 215–222
    indirect side, 205
    informational content, 205–209
    linking media stimuli to effects typology, 205

methods for studying, 204–205
  persuasive content, 209–215
  typology, 203–205
  process of, 197–199
Massing of detail, 265
Materiality of evidence, 85
Materials of development, 260–264
Materials of experience, 260, 264–268
Materials of personal proof, 259–261
Meaning, 264
  code systems and, 42–45
    verbal, 53, 54
  connotative, 44, 51
  context-bound, 56
  denotative, 44
  semantic, 43–44
  syntactic, 43
Media. See Mass media
Mediation theories of language learning, 49, 51–53
Mediatory codes, 64
Mehrabian, A., 13
Membership groups, 88–89
  See also Small groups
Memorized delivery, 273
Merton, Robert, 208
Message, mass-communication, 198
Message construction, 72–102
  informative messages. See persuasive messages
Metacommunication, 12
Miller, Gerald R., 15, 17, 18, 23, 28, 30
  on interpersonal communication, 110, 113–116, 125, 131, 133
  speech communication model of, 32–33
Miller, M. Mark, 221
Mills, J. M., 143
Mirror questions, 245
Mixed-level relationships, 116
Mob behavior, 160
Models
  of communication process, 30–36
    functions of, 31–34
    definition of, 30–31
Monge, Peter R., 170, 172, 180

Monroe, Alan H., 99
Motivated sequence, 99
Motivational appeals, 96–100
  definition of, 77
  motivated sequence, 99
  problem-solution pattern, 100
  in public speaking, 265–266
Motivational bases of trust, 132
Motives
  biological, 96, 98
  learned, 96, 98
Multiple data
  argument using, 89–90
  reasoning from, 263
Multiplier effect, 188

Narration, 265
"Native speaker" method, 47
Nayman, Oguz, 206
Neale, John, 220
Negative evidence, 83
Networks, communication, 151–152
  organizational. See Organizational
    communication—networks
News, 205–209
  hard and soft, 206–208
Newspapers, 199, 201, 206, 208, 213
Nonverbal codes (nonverbal code sys-
    tems), 13, 14, 42, 45, 58–67
  artifactual, 63–64
  interaction of verbal code systems
    and, 59–61
  mediatory, 64
  performance, 61–63
  spatio-temporal, 65–66
Nonverbal communication, 58
  cultural variations in, 21–22
Nonverbal delivery in public speaking,
    277–278
Nonverbal status trappings, 25–26
Norms, group, 143, 155–156

Objectivity, 78–79
Obligatory norms, 155, 156
Obstinate audience, 210
Old-boy network, 183–184, 190

Open-ended questions, 241, 245
Operant conditioning, 49–50
Opinion evidence, 261
Organizational communication, 104,
    109, 168–193
  communication flows, 180–183
  communication rules, 176–180
    formal and informal, 179–180
    procedural and content, 178–179
  functions of, 170–171
  information processing. See
    Information processing
  networks, 183–188
    analysis, 185–188
    formal, 183
    kinship, 183
    old-boy, 183–184
    special communication purposes,
      184–185
Organizational function of models,
    31–32, 35–36
Organizations
  as culture, 188–192
    women and, 191–192
  definition of, 170
  early, 168–169
Orientation, mass media and
  change in, 202–204
  stability of, 212–213
Orientation interviews, 232
Orientation phase of group develop-
    ment, 147–148
Osgood, Charles, 49–52
Outline, 293
Overload, information, 172, 173, 175

Paralinguistics, 14, 61
Patterns, 43, 45
  logical, 92–95, 100
Pearce, W. Barnett, 128–130, 155
Perception
  environment and, 12
  language and, 54–55
  selective, 211, 212
Performance codes, 61–63
Permissive norms, 155–156
Persisting change in orientation, mass

media and, 203, 204
Person-specific trust, 129
Personal artifacts, 64
Personal proof, materials of, 259–261
Persuasive content of media messages, impact of, 205, 209–215
  advertising, 213–215
  factors limiting, 210–213
Persuasive interviews, 232
Persuasive messages, construction of, 72–73, 75–100
  motivational appeals. *See* Motivational appeals
  rational appeals. *See* Rational appeals
Persuasive public speech, 257, 259, 262, 269
Peters, R. S., 113
Phatic communication, 23
Plax, T. G., 159
Pluralistic societies, 21
Pointers, 62
Political advertising, televised, 214–215
Polling, 231, 237, 246
Powell, F. A., 27
Power
  information and, 17
  social, 157–159
Practical predictive function of models, 33, 36
Predictability
  organizational rule system and, 177–178
  trust and, 128–129
Prediction-making data, changes in, 114–117
Predictive function of models, practical, 33, 36
Predictive level of knowledge, 120–122
Premack, D., 13
Preservation, appeals to, 265
Pressure
  group, 160
  time, 175
Presummary, 74
Pride, appeals to, 265

Prior attitudes, 11
Probing questions, 244
Problem-solution pattern, 100
Problem solving, information exchange and, 17–18
Problem-solving organizational scheme, 293
Problem-solving tasks, 161
Procedural rules, 28, 178, 179
Process, communication as, 8–11, 111
Production network, 184
Production tasks, 161
Proposition, 76–77, 257, 259
Prosocial behavior, televised, 219, 220
Proxemics, 14
Pseudoconflict, 135, 136
Psychological context, 26–29, 35, 36
Psychological defenses, persuasive impact of mass media and, 210–212
Psychological information, prediction based on, 115–117
Public artifacts, 64
Public speaking, 225, 226, 252–284
  analysis of and adaptation to receivers, 252–256
  choice and adaptation of subject and purpose, 256–259
  composition of purpose sentence, 257–259
  limitation of subject, 257–259
  delivery. *See* Delivery of public speech
  development of content of speech, 259–268
    materials of development, 260–264
    materials of experience, 260, 264–268
    materials of personal proof, 259–261
  evaluation of speech, 279
    form, 280–283
  notes for, 274, 275
  structuring the speech, 268–272
    body, 269–271
    conclusion, 271
    introduction, 271–272
    purpose sentence, 268

Public speech, 252
Public-opinion polling, 231, 237, 246
Purpose sentence, 268, 271
  composition of, 257–259

Qualifier, 90, 91, 94
Quintamensional plan, 242

Radio, 199, 201, 214
Rational appeals, 77–95, 98, 101
  definition of, 77
  organization of arguments into messages, 92–95
    deductive patterns, 92–93
    inductive patterns, 94–95
  Toulmin model. *See* Toulmin model of argument
Rationality, 78–80, 101
Raven, B., 157
Readability, enhancement of, 294
Reading, writing and, 294
Real evidence, 84
Reasoning, 262–264
  by analogy, 262
  from cause, 263
  from example or multiple data, 263
  from sign, 264
Rebuttal, 90, 91, 94
Receivers, 12
  in mass communication, 197–199
  in public speaking
    analysis of and adaptation to, 252–256
    arresting and holding attention of, 266–268
  See also entries starting with Audience
Recency of evidence, 87
Reciprocity, 124, 125, 127
  of roles, 156–157
Redding, W. Charles, 230
Reeves, Byron, 221
Regulative function of language, 56, 57
Regulators, 63
Reinforcement
  of attitudes and behaviors of others, 18–19

mass media and, 213
Relationship, 11
  complementary, 12
  symmetrical, 12
Relaxation, mass media and, 215, 217
Relevance
  of evidence, 85
  of news, 207
Reluctant testimony, 84
Research, social-science, 231, 237, 239, 246, 247
Research-generating function of models, 32–33, 36
Responsibility, communicative, 10
Restatement questions, 245
Restricted code, 56–58
Reward appeals, 266
Reward power, 157–158
Rewards of interview, 235–237
Richetto, Gary M., 230
Rickey, John T., 230
"Risky shift" phenomenon, 160
Rituals, 146
Robinson, John, 206
Rokeach, M., 27
Role conflict, 157
Roles, 24–26
  language and, 46
  sex, mass media and, 219–222
  in small groups, 143, 156–157
Roper Organization, 206
Rosenfield, L. B., 159
Rules
  cultural, 23–24, 28, 29, 117
  definition of, 23
  governing relationships, changes in, 117–119, 123
  organizational, 176–180
    communication, 178–180
  psychological, 28–29
  sociological, 25, 28–29, 113, 117
Russell, Hamish M., 170, 172, 180

Sapir, Edward, 55
Sarbin, T. R., 24
Seating arrangements, 150–151
Secrets, 130–131

Selective exposure, 211, 212
Selective perception, 211, 212
Selective retention, 211–212
Self-concept
  conflict and, 136
  small groups and, 104, 146
Self-description, 125, 126
Self-disclosure, 125–127, 130
Self-preservation, appeals to, 265
Semantic meanings, 43–44
Semantic rules, 43
Sermat, V., 124
Sex, appeals to, 266
Sex-role learning, mass media and, 219–221
Shannon, C., 30
Shared artifacts, 64
Shaver, K. G., 121
Shaw, Donald, 208
Shaw, Marvin E., 143, 150–153, 158–161
Sheatsley, Paul, 206
Shyness, 16
Sign, reasoning from, 264
Simons, H. W., 132
Situational view of interpersonal communication, 108–112
Skinner, B. F., 49–50, 52
Small groups (small-group communication), 104, 142–165
  definition of, 142–145
  formation of, 145–149
    coalition formation, 149
    phases of development, 147–149
    reasons for membership, 145–146
  operation of, 149–153
    communication networks, 151–152
    satisfaction, 152–153
    spatial arrangements, 150
  recommendations for organizing and participating in, 162–163
  social environment of, 153–160
    cohesiveness, 153–154
    group pressure, 160
    leadership, 159–160
    norms, 155–156
    roles, 156–157

    social power, 157–159
    status, 154–155
  task environment of, 161–162
SMCR model, 31–32
Smith, M., 143
Smyth, M., 124
Social class, language use and, 56–58
Social distance, 22, 23, 66
Social exchange model, 235
Social influence, Kelman's processes of, 33, 34
Social learning theory, mass media and, 217–219, 221–222
Social power, 157–159
Socialization of new members of organization, 189–190
Social-science research, interviewing for, 231, 237, 239, 246, 247
Sociocultural context, verbal codes and, 54–58
Sociolinguistics, 56
Sociological context, 24–26, 35
Sociological information, prediction based on, 113, 115, 116, 124
Sociological rules, 25, 28–29, 113, 117
Source, 12
  in mass communication, 197
Space patterns, informative messages and, 75–76
Spatial, 62
Spatial arrangements of small groups, 150
Spatial organizational scheme, 293
Spatio-temporal codes, 65–66
Speaking, public. See Public speaking
Specific to general organizational scheme, 293
Speech, public, 252
Speech evaluation form, 279–283
Speech plan, 268–272, 274–275
  deductive, 269–271, 283–284
  inductive, 270
Spelling, 289, 290
Stability of orientation, mass media and, 210, 212–213
Standards, 79
  of evidence, 84

relativity of, 88–89
See also Norms
Statistical evidence, 86
Status, 25–26
  in small groups, 154–155, 158
Status conferral, 208
Steinberg, M., 15, 17, 28
  on interpersonal communication, 113, 115, 116, 125, 131, 133
Stimulus discrimination, 27, 28
Stimulus generalization, 27–28
Structural rule, 28
Summary, 74
Summary conclusion, 271
Surveying, 237
Symbolic nature of communication, 13–14
Symbolization, 42
Symmetrical relationship, 12
Syntactic meaning, 43
Syntactic rules, 43
Systemic dimension of small-group communication, 144

Tangible rewards and costs of interview, 235
Tasks, small groups and, 161–162
Television, 64, 199, 205, 206, 213
  cable, 201
  learning and, 217–220
  political advertising on, 214
  two-way, 201–202
  violence on, 204, 218–220
Testimony, 84
Thesis (proposition), 76–77, 257, 259
Thibaut, J. W., 134
Thought
  language and, 52, 55
  logical patterns of, 92–95, 100
  rational, 78–80, 101
Time, 65–66
Time patterns, informative messages and, 75–76
Time pressure, 175
Topical organizational scheme, 293
Toulmin, Stephen, 80, 81

Toulmin model of argument, 80–94
  claim in, 80–82, 94
  complex arguments and, 89–92
  data in, 80–88
  relativity of standards and, 88–89
  warrant in, 80, 81, 87–89, 94
Transactionality of communication, 11–13
Transitory change in orientation, mass media and, 203, 204, 206
Trust, 108–109
  generalized, 129
  person-specific, 129
  role of, 128–132
Trustworthiness of source of evidence, 86–87
Turner, R., 24
Two-step flow of information, 206

Underload, information, 172, 173, 175
Upward communication flows, 181–182
Utility of model, 31, 34

Vanocur, Sander, 248
Verbal codes (verbal code systems), 13, 42, 43, 45–58
  cognition and, 53–54
  elaborated, 56–58
  interaction of nonverbal code systems and, 59–61
  learning, 49–53
  restricted, 56–58
  sociocultural context and, 54–58
Verbal evidence, 83–84
Verbal status distinctions, 26
Violence on television, 204, 218–220
Vividness in public speaking, 276
Vocabulary, 289–290

Walters, Barbara, 244
Warrant, 80, 81, 87–89, 94

Watzlawick, P., 7–8, 12
Weaver, W., 30
Weiss, Walter, 210
Westley, B. H., 30
Wheel network, 151, 152
Whitlow, Sylvia, 208
Whorf, Benjamin Lee, 55
Whorf-Sapir hypothesis, 55

Women
    culture of organizations and, 191–192
    television portrayal of, 219–221
Writing, 288–295

Zima, Joseph P., 230
Zimbardo, Philip, 16